SEX AND DEATH IN VICTORIAN LITERATURE

Sex and Death in
Victorian Literature

Edited by
Regina Barreca

Indiana University Press
Bloomington and Indianapolis

Manufactured in Great Britain

Library of Congress Cataloging-in-Publication Data

Sex and death in Victorian literature/edited by Regina Barreca.
p.   cm.
Includes index.
ISBN 0–253–31015–6
1. English literature—19th century—History and criticism.
2. Death in literature.   3. Sex in literature.   I. Barreca, Regina.
PR468.D42S4   1990
820.9'354—dc20

1 2 3 4 5   93 92 91 90 89   89–11020

Contents

Notes on the Contributors

Regina Barreca is author of *Punch Lines: Comedy and Subversion in Women's Writing*. She is editor of *Last Laughs: Perspectives on Women and Comedy* and editor of the critical journal *LIT*. She is an Assistant Professor at the University of Connecticut, Storrs.

Elisabeth Bronfen is Assistant Professor of English Literature at the University of Munich. She is the author of a book on literary space in the work of Dorothy M. Richardson and is currently writing a book on the representations of feminine death.

Mary Ann Caws is Distinguished Professor of Comparative Literature, French and English at the Graduate School of City University of New York. Among her many books on poetics and contemporary writing are *The Eye in the Text: Essays on Perception, Mannerist to Modern, Reading Frames in Modern Fiction*, and most recently, *The Art of Interference: Stressed Reading in Visual and Verbal Texts*.

Regenia Gagnier, author of *Idylls of the Marketplace: Oscar Wilde and the Victorian Public*, is completing a study of subjectivity, value and the uses of literacy in the lifewriting of Victorian working-class, public and boarding school, and canonical literary subjects. She is Assistant Professor of English at Stanford University.

Gerhard Joseph is Professor of English at Lehman College and the Graduate School of the City University of New York. He is author of *Tennysonian Love: The Strange Diagonal* and various articles on nineteenth-century and medieval subjects. He is currently working on another book, *Tennyson and Silence*.

James Kincaid is the author of books on Dickens, Tennyson, Trollope, and of several editions. He is now Aerol Arnold Professor at the University of Southern California. He is completing a study on Victorian pedophilia.

Carol Hanbery MacKay, Associate Professor of English at the University of Texas, is author of *Soliloquy in Nineteenth-Century Fiction* and editor of *Dramatic Dickens*. She has written several articles on Ann Thackeray Ritchie as well as the critical introduction to *The Two Thackerays*. Her major work in progress is a study of Victorian novelists as thwarted dramatists.

Sylvia Manning is author of *Dickens as Satirist* and *Images of the City: London in Eighteenth and Nineteenth-Century British Literature*. She has written on Dickens, Tennyson, Thackeray, and other Victorian authors. She is a Professor of English and Vice-Provost of the University of Southern California.

Hilary Schor is Assistant Professor of English at the University of Southern California. The author of several reviews and articles on Victorian literature, she has completed a book on Elizabeth Gaskell, and is at work on a study of female narrative in the novels of Charles Dickens.

Robert Steiner, Associate Professor of English and Comparative Literature at the University of Colorado at Boulder, is the author of five novels, most recently *Dread* and *Matinee*. He is currently at work on a comparative study of *Finnegan's Wake* and the paintings of Jackson Pollock.

Garrett Stewart is Professor of English and Film at the University of California, Santa Barbara. He is author of *Dickens and the Trials of the Imagination* and *Death Sentences: Styles of Dying in British Fiction*, as well as of numerous articles on fiction and film narrative.

Robert Tracy is Professor of English at the University of California at Berkeley where he specialises in Victorian and Irish literature. He is author of *Trollope's Later Novels* and has translated Osip Mandelstan's early poems in *Stone*. He is at work on further translations from Mandelstan, and on a study of nineteenth-century Irish writers.

Robert Zweig has completed a full-length study of Dante and the Victorians. He has written on both Italian and English literature. He is an Assistant Professor at Borough of Manhattan College.

1

Introduction: Coming and Going in Victorian Literature

Regina Barreca

Sex is worth dying for. It is in this [strictly historical] sense that sex is indeed imbued with the death instinct. When a long while ago the West discovered love, it bestowed on it a value high enough to make death acceptable . . . sex claims this equivalence, the highest of all.[1]

> And a voice said in mastery, while I
> strove —
> 'Guess now who holds thee?' — 'Death,'
> I said. But, there,
> The silver answer rang — 'Not Death, but
> Love.'[2]

Sex and death provide an important matrix of artistic possibilities for the Victorian writer; these apparently irreconcilable forces combine, occasionally explicitly but more often implicitly, to produce an ineradicable alignment of sexuality and mortality in nineteenth-century poetry and fiction.

What are the significant points of convergence? The idea of sin frames both. Balancing mortality with sexuality sets up a dialectic for the interplay between fear and desire as the perpetual human condition. Fear of eternal damnation was placed beside desire for the 'eternity in a moment' of orgasm. Herbert Marcuse has claimed, in *Eros and Civilization*, that 'timelessness is the ideal of pleasure', parallel to the timelessness of death. Similarly, the loss of self during orgasm apparently mirrored the loss of self in death. Sex and death both indicated the limits of human control and were therefore to be feared.

1

Additional points of connection between sex and death include the fact that both are basically physical actions, more scientifically defined by the functions of the body than the spirit. Either the heart races or it stops altogether. The need to indicate sexual activity without being able to name it caused the repressed sexuality in a text to be reflected in speech patterns and rhetorical structures. Clearly, repressed sexuality and a fervid interest in mortality are not the exclusive property of Victorian literature. Yet, as a number of critics from Foucault to Gay, from Steven Marcus to Elaine Showalter have indicated, the twinning of sex and death provided the novels and the poetry of the period with a sort of counter-balanced framework within which fertile narrative strategies operated. The essays in this volume will carry the sex/death dialectic even further and will place the complex interweaving of desire and fear – love and death – at the centre of their wide-ranging arguments.

> She had the sort of knowledge which links love not only with clarity, but also with violence and death – because death seems to be the truth of love, just as love is the truth of death.[3]

The pleasures of death, in contrast to the pleasures of sex, have long been the focus for all forms of Victorian literature, from the intricate fugues of Tennyson's 'In Memoriam' to the stunningly obvious melodrama of the nineteenth-century stage. In his study of death and dying in the novel, Garrett Stewart comments that '[s]ome characters must die in any period of novel writing. As everyone allows, characters die more often, more slowly and more vocally in the Victorian age than ever before or since' (Stewart, 1984). Death scenes, ranging from Sikes' murder of Nancy (which, according to Philip Collins, certainly inflamed Dickens' passions to a dangerous extent during his public readings of the scene) to Maggie Tulliver's fatal union at the end of *The Mill on the Floss*, from Thackeray's report of George Osborn's death in an embedded clause to Pompilia's closing scenes in Browning's *The Ring and the Book*, could be relied upon to produce an ultimately satisfying conclusion to the narration. Satisfaction, in fact, is what a Victorian death scene can be counted on to provide: either the satisfaction of our righteous indignation or the satisfaction of other-worldly recompense for an otherwise destitute and unthinkable existence. In contrast, of course, implications of sexuality in a scene could signal an ultimate refusal to offer any sexual resolution, despite the sexual tensions plotted out. Death scenes could offer full play for language and enlarge the possibilities for emotion and indulgence. Such passages are certainly more convincing and moving than their erotic counterparts. Wedding nights, unless they involve murder or abandonment, are rarely described.

How does marriage fit into this set of literary structures? Marriage is to heaven as sex is to death: marriage seems to be the route to heaven and sex seems the route to death. The popular concept of nineteenth-century sex within marriage was, according to Foucault, 'acknowledged in social space as well as at the heart of every household, but it was . . . utilitarian and fertile', represented by 'the parent's bedroom'.[4] Both happy marriage and heaven, however, are ideal states of little interest to the reader who has rarely met with verifiable instances of either. Even within the family, Foucault suggests, there existed the possibility for 'a network of pleasures and powers linked together at multiple points'.[5] Victorian literature for the most part veils any sexual relation inside the domestic union and so readers must judge from the evidence of taboo sexual behaviour provided by adulterous, or at the very least adventurous, figures. And, based on such evidence, we must conclude that the mortality rate for immorality is exceedingly high.

Not that the portrayal of sex was wholly absent from Victorian literature, of course. It did require what we now perceive as a sacrifice of verisimilitude for a writer such as Dickens to portray a character of passionate desire, like Bradley Headstone in *Our Mutual Friend*, without overtly acknowledging his sexuality. Without being able to explore, except metaphorically, the sexual nature of characters, writers fell upon the highly wrought and deeply upholstered symbolism so often associated with Victorian literature.

An inability to explore sex without concurrently exploring morality is the hallmark of Victorian literature. Death was regarded, even by proclaimed agnostics, as a sort of passage rather than a final snapping shut of life. Against a belief in heaven, few deaths could sustain horror – thus the horror of Stoker's permanent non-death in *Dracula*. His tale managed to touch our deepest dread of mortality without raising the question of whether there could ever be horror in death considering that we inhabit a 'redeemed' world. Stoker grants us permission to have access to our own fears without sacrificing a shred of belief in our own ultimate salvation so that we can free our repressed emotion without accusing ourselves of doubt. Stoker's vampire is, of course, one of many such figures indicating the fusion of desire and fear.

> [Mona Lisa is] older than the rocks among which she sits; like the vampire, she has been dead many times and learned the secrets of the grave.[6]

> 'Let her go! Her thirst she slakes
> Where the bloody conduit runs,
> Then her sweetest meal she makes
> On the first-born of her sons.'

> 'Tell me tales of thy first love —
> April hopes, the fools of chance —
> Till the graves begin to move,
> And the dead begin to dance.'[7]

There have been a number of discussions dealing with the Victorians' widely accepted equation of sexual activity with a shortened lifespan. Men's sexual release was regarded as a kind of 'expenditure' that depleted his physical strength as well as his moral resolve, bringing him closer to death with every orgasm. Sexually active women also seem to die young in Victorian works, but that is more often because they are struck down rather than gradually depleted (if anything, such women seem to feed off of sexuality). There persisted in the equation of 'sex with women equals loss of vitality' the notion that women draw energy from men. This may be regarded by some as an elaborate reaction-formation to the fact that women of the day did, in many cases, give up their lives to the service of men. It was men who took vitality from women, it can be argued – women who should have feared the vampire-like feeding of husbands and children.

Fear of death, punishment for sin, and the sapping of physical strength control much of the action in Victorian novels and narrative poems. Fear forces the characters to translate sexual desire into more acceptable forms, among them ambition and anger. Sexual desire, therefore, might appear in a number of guises. The desire for sex with the Other might emerge as the desire for the death of the Other. 'Possession of the beloved object', writes Bataille in *Eroticism*, 'does not imply death, but the idea of death is linked with the urge to possess.' Bataille continues: 'If the lover cannot possess the beloved he will sometimes think of killing her; often he would rather kill her than lose her.'[8]

> That moment she was mine, mine, fair,
> Perfectly pure and good; I found
> A thing to do, and all her hair
> In one long yellow string I wound
> Three times her little throat around,
> And strangled her.[9]

> O Lilith, whom shed scent
> And soft-shed kisses and soft sleep shall
> snare?
> Lo! as that youth's eyes burned at thine, so
> went
> The spell through him, and left his
> straight
> neck bent
> And round his heart one strangling golden
> hair.[10]

The erotics of the death-bed scene have been discussed by a number of critics. Terminal illness provides one of the very few occasions by which we enter the bedrooms of Victorian households. The lushness of these scenes, with the curtains drawn against the light, the highly charged emotions of the spectators (not to mention the participant), the mystery of the moment of death: all these echo the sexual act through their inability to be absorbed, finally, into the domestic. 'Man is an animal who stands abashed in front of death or sexual union,' claims Bataille.

For one thing, characters in Victorian literature certainly cannot speak about either sex or death while going through such experiences; rational discourse is literally unthinkable. Both accounts must be altered, discussed symbolically, metaphorically, in somehow camouflaged terms. Without the romantic eulogising of sentimental clichés, sex and death are clinical experiences, full of anatomy. The play between the two *topoi* undercuts the apparently paradoxical relationship between an act of generation and an act of closure. The intersections between the two bring to light 'the erotic component in the death instinct and the fatal component in the sex instinct'.[11]

Heav'n but the Vision of fulfilled Desire,
And Hell the Shadow from a Soul on fire,
Cast out on the Darkness into which Ourselves,
So late emerged from, shall so soon expire.[12]

Interesting to note that the very concepts of 'coming' and 'going' indicate a passage from place to place or state to state, arriving at or departing from a particular fixed point. Perhaps, too, the Victorian obsession with control and order is at work in tying together sex and death in this manner. What points of arrival and departure are at stake? Death was clean, linked to order. The tidying-up described after the death of, for example, Enoch Arden with his exemplary funeral, indicates the privileged poison of ritual and rite. Sex, however, breaks the rules, both social and moral, and indicates far more than death ever could the inherent possibility of the abyss existing outside social and ideological constructs. Death exemplifies the passing from one orderly realm to another; sex exemplifies the passing out of the range of order altogether. To draw once again from Bataille's *Eroticism*: 'Eroticism always entails a breaking down of the established patterns . . . of the regulated social order basic to our discontinuous mode of existence as defined and separate individuals.'[13]

Sex and death are ecstatic experiences, literally 'out of the body' experiences. During both, the character is separated from the conventions of the everyday. It is as if one were outside looking in; all boundaries are permeable. New territory is mapped – one proceeds into the darkness with little hope of explanation or utterance. It is worth noting, however, that terms such as 'passion', 'consummation', and 'ecstasy' serve efficiently as bridges between the two categories of meaning, connecting sex and death through a shared and yet particular language. These bridge words are themselves not categorically defined. They are not metaphoric in that they do not cross from one more appropriate category to another, thereby not involving the idea of the 'mistake' of metaphor. Rather, they become equally applicable to the erotic and to the deadly.

Victorian death scenes fastened on to the earliest attributes of passion, contextualising passion as the suffering of pain, the passion of Christ and the early martyrs. Death involved high passion, and permitted an abandonment to feeling. Affliction, not affection, was the Victorian construct of passion. The passions of desire were shifted on to the passions of death through a metaphysical and metaphorical sleight of hand. Approaching death, a character could be described in detailed physical terms, could achieve a heightened bodily, even sensual, awareness, experience an ecstatic, profound and epiphanic transformation which, under other more favourable circumstances, would certainly appear orgasmic in nature.

> Death alone – or, at least, the ruin of the isolated individual in search of happiness in time – introduces that break without which nothing reaches the state of ecstasy.[14]

> > She thought of Jeanie in her grave
> > who should have been a bride
> > But who for joys brides hope to have
> > fell sick and died.[15]

This book is a collection of essays written by distinguished critics in the fields of literary criticism and Victorian studies. The essays, whether focused on the reading of texts in the traditional Victorian canon or dealing with more liminal works, such as Stoker's *Dracula*, indicate the range and depth of various critical approaches, reflecting current thought in feminist, deconstructive and political theory. The essays presented here must be prefaced by the conventional disclaimer that they do not attempt to give a unified reading of a period neatly bound by the dates of Victoria's reign. They instead represent nearly as wide a selection of textual interpretations as is possible to present in a single volume. Robert Tracy's account of Count Dracula's eternal seductions, James Kincaid's account of Tess's mortal wounding, Gerhard Joseph's chronicle of the development of Tennyson's sword in all its forms, Sylvia Manning's discussion of the relationship between the expression of desire and the desire for stasis in Tennyson, Mary Ann Caw's radical examination of Ruskin, Garrett Stewart's exploration of the pairing of eros and thanatos in George Eliot's fiction: these essays, among others, all exemplify the eclecticism of twentieth-century critical approaches to the most important works of nineteenth-century literature. Some of the essays in this collection attempt to 'undo' quite a bit of preceding critical wisdom. All offer insight into the central concerns of the period. The dialectic of sex and death, these critics finally claim, must be viewed as one of the most influential patterns in Victorian poetry and prose. '[W]e suddenly come up against death, the end par excellence. Death is the origin and the essence of life', writes Todorov. Bataille concludes that 'Poetry leads to the same place as all forms of eroticism – to the blending and fusion of separate objects. It leads to eternity, it leads us to death, and through death to continuity.'[16]

> 'Pain melted in tears, and was pleasure;
> Death tingled with blood, and was life.[17]

Notes

1. Michel Foucault, *The History of Sexuality* (New York: Vintage Books, 1980) p. 156.
2. Elizabeth Barrett Browning, 'Sonnets from the Portuguese,' *The Poetical Works of Elizabeth Barrett Browning*, Cambridge Edition (Boston: Houghton Mifflin, 1974) p. 215.
3. Georges Bataille, 'Emily Bronte', *Literature and Evil* (New York: Marion Bayars, 1985) p. 16.
4. Foucault, p. 3.
5. Foucault, p. 46.
6. Walter Pater, *The Renaissance: Studies in Art and Poetry. The Norton Anthology of English Literature*, Vol. 2, 4th edn (New York: W. W. Norton, 1979) p. 1579.
7. Alfred Tennyson, 'The Vision of Sin', *A Collection of Poems by Alfred Tennyson*, edited by Christopher Ricks (Garden City, New York: Doubleday, 1972) pp. 230–1.
8. Georges Bataille, *Eroticism: Death and Sensuality*, translated by Mary Dalwood (San Francisco: City Lights Books, 1986) p. 20.
9. Robert Browning, 'Porphyrias Lover', *Pocket Volume of Selections from the Poetical Works of Robert Browning* (London: Smith, Elder, 1890) p. 131.
10. Dante Gabriel Rossetti, 'The House of Life', *The Collected Works of Dante Gabriel Rossetti*, edited by William Rossetti (London: Ellis & Elvey, 1897) p. 216.
11. Herbert Marcuse, *Eros and Civilization* (Boston: Beacon Press, 1974) p. 51.
12. Edward Fitzgerald, 'The Rubaiyat of Omar Khayyam', *Fitzgerald, Selected Works*, edited by Joanna Richardson (Cambridge, Massachusetts: Harvard University Press, 1963) p. 261.
13. Bataille, *Eroticism*, p. 18.
14. Bataille, 'Emily Bronte', p. 26.
15. Christina Rossetti, 'The Goblin Market', *The Complete Poems of Christina Rossetti*, Vol. 1, edited by R. W. Crump (Baton Rouge, Louisiana: Louisiana State University Press, 1979) p. 19.
16. Bataille, *Eroticism*, p. 25.
17. Algernon C. Swinburne, 'Dolores', *Poems and Ballads: Atlanta in Calydon*, edited by Morse Peckham (New York: Babbs Merrill, 1970) p. 146.

2

'You did not come': Absence, Death and Eroticism in *Tess*

James Kincaid

She would have laid down her life for 'ee. I could do no more.[1]

'Somebody might have come along that way who would have asked him his trouble, and might have cheered him. . . . But nobody did come, because nobody does; and under the crushing recognition of his gigantic error Jude continued to wish himself out of the world.'[2] This is Hardy at the bone: the ache, the simple longing for help, for a kinder scheme of things. The *somebody* who might, but does not, happen by with a coherent explanation of, variously, Greek grammar, the universe, human love, or women, is Hardy's central character. Explanations, compassion, contact of some sort, even a hug or a touch of the hand, ought to be there. But they are not: 'nobody did come, because nobody does'. Hardy's fiction runs on this motor, on the propulsive hope for that which, very definitely, will not be, an image which cannot be realised. This absent ghost is called into being in the minds of decent, moving characters who flounder and are squashed like bugs who have squirmed to get out of the muck and thereby called upon themselves the attention of wanton boys, careless forces that strew pain around, particularly upon the good, without reason and without end. These recurrent tragedies or absurdist destructions move always on the edge of absence; without the impalpable image of what is not and cannot be there, nothing would be possible.[3] Without this never-present *somebody*, Hardy could ask, with Trollope, 'Where would be my novel?'[4]

As it is, *somebody* does not show up, right on cue, and all is well. Not being there, *somebody* is much more energising than any presence could be. *Somebody* becomes an image that can be decked out in any form whatever and, just as important, used for the exercise of nearly any feeling, erotic ones certainly not excluded. The speaker (narrator or character) in Hardy typically assumes a passive role, feels cheated, abandoned by the non-appearance of *somebody*. In fact, that broken appointment allows for an enormous range of activity, beginning with the effective killing of *somebody* and continuing with a manipulation of the corpse so as to provide an outlet for all manner of stagings and emotional eruptions. Like a skilled homicidal mortician with necrophiliac tastes, then, the characters, narrators, and readers can cavort themselves in ways a real live presence would certainly resist. This play of turning absence into malleable images is so often eroticised in Hardy that I would like to focus on that process, particularly on the sadistic form that such eroticism usually takes. I will discuss the poem 'A Broken Appointment' and, at greater length, *Tess of the d'Urbervilles*.

I

The poem first:

> You did not come.
> And marching Time drew on, and wore me numb —
> Yet less for loss of your dear presence there,
> Than that I found lacking in your make
> That high compassion which can overbear
> Reluctance for pure lovingkindness' sake
> Grieved I, when, as the hope-hour stroked its sum,
> You did not come.
>
> You love not me,
> And love alone can lend you loyalty;
> —I know and knew it. But, unto the store
> Of human deeds divine in all but name,
> Was it not worth a little hour or more
> To add yet this: Once you, a woman, came
> To sooth a time-torn man; even though it be
> You love not me?

Certainly this woman did us a great favour by staying away; we can scarcely imagine Hardy writing an interesting poem on the subject had she come. And that is because she does the speaker of the poem a great favour too. He can, thereby, set the poem nicely in memory, that great theatre for endlessly-revisable, self-satisfying drama. He can also transform her absence into an uncomplaining cadaver that will oblige him by taking any form, by accepting any imposition of motive or character.

The poem draws all its self-pitying power from that which was not (because it never is) to be: a joyous and fulfilling meeting with his lover – or what he thought was his lover – at the hope-hour – or what he thought was the hope-hour. By her not showing up, Hardy can create, first, a blunt image of faithless bitchiness and a shadow image of beautiful constancy. The reiterated 'You did not come' of the first stanza carries a shadow, 'You might have come', and the 'You love me not' of the second stanza suggests 'You might have loved me'. More important, it suggests 'You still might love me'. The hectoring, self-satisfied argument of the first stanza runs: what really grieves me is that I found you something of a malignancy, incapable even of common sympathy or compassion. This argument contains within its apparent protective name-calling an alternative strain of wooing, talk of 'your dear presence' and of the sweet possibility of 'lovingkindness'. This is an odd form of courtship, perhaps, though probably not so uncommon. It masks with its lip-quivering acceptance of finality and utter desolation – 'you did not come'; 'you love not me' – secret undercurrents that seek to use the negative as a grounds for the positive, the finality as a new beginning. The second stanza, after all, turns to a kind of pleading – couldn't you have done at least this? – and projects for his audience an image of a woman coming to soothe a time-torn man, a fulfilment, a possibility that moves the poem out of the past and into the future. The argument thus runs: you have proved yourself utterly beneath contempt; that is closed and settled – on the other hand, I will hold out to you the possibility that it is not all closed and settled, that you still have a chance to reclaim yourself and, not incidentally, me as well.

Benumbed or crushed sexual desire is thus undermined by rising sexual expectation. But to read the poem in this way, to foreground a psychology of grief and hope, is, perhaps, to miss all the fun. Another way to receive the poem is as an expression of sexual anger, an exercise in sadistic revelry. Why does the poem, first of all, keep going on past its many endings? 'You did not come' in the first line seems conclusive enough; it represents, after all, the extent of his knowledge on the subject. The poem threatens to stop after these four words. Further, 'I know and knew it' (l.11) would seem absolutely to close off the inquiry into *why* she did not come: she does not love him; that being so, there is no particular reason why she should come. The poem really works, however, on the extending 'Yet' (l.3) and 'But' (l.11), which function not to qualify but to ignore the conclusions, to keep things proceeding to the real business of the poem: the creation of images and the projection of a psychology of anger. He hopes not that she will come some other time or learn after all to love him; he hopes to give pain. One notes that the poem is absolutely certain about its addressee and the postal service: there is no doubt that 'you, a woman' (as he has formulated her) will get this poem/letter and feel the full force of these manufactured images. Alternative possibilities for absence – that she may have been thrown by her horse, struck senseless by a falling timber, or eaten by wild beasts – do not enter his mind. Such things do not cohere with the images he is having so much fun with.

And not very attractive images they are. In the first stanza he creates her as one lacking in her 'make' (her essence and that of her parents too; a genteel equivalent of 'Yo mama!') 'that high compassion' which would allow her to get past mere 'reluctance'. How he trivialises the resistance attributed to her, so much so that 'high compassion' can be shrunk to simple 'lovingkindness' in this catalogue of what she does not have. Sounds like she's the type who would kick kittens. She is missing from him, in other words, because she is missing a good deal inside. He, on the other hand, has oodles of character, unselfishly lamenting not his own loss but the discovery of her (presumably genetic) character defects. Self-pity, that is, barely masks or cooperates with the delight in furious name-calling, a kind of letter-to-the-editor luxury he allows himself more openly in the second stanza, where he changes the image of himself from one of sturdy, if wounded rectitude to one of enfeebled time-torn pitiableness in order to extend, with variations, the attack on her. She is so self-consumed, he says, she cannot spare even that 'little hour or more'. Now why this particular hour ('or more', depending on how things might have developed, one supposes) is 'little' might seem unclear, but Hardy's 'little hour' is certainly kin to popular conceptions of 'little Nell' or 'little Eva': packed with sobs. This stanza is also packed with fury. Since she chooses not, or is not fitted, to add to divine deeds, she is, one might presume, something like Satanic. No poem could more plainly manufacture an image, tell it to go to hell, and then send it there.

That all this is plainly erotically charged and is an exercise in sadism, I will not claim, though I think such a claim is reasonable enough. I do, however, think it is clear that the 'loss of your dear presence there' is precisely the agency that releases the rage, that in turn creates the obsessive images, and that pours such fantastic energy out over those images. That such energies are at least often erotically focused is obvious, I think, in many of the poems and in all of the novels, but nowhere more relentlessly than in *Tess*.

II

What disappears most emphatically in *Tess* is Tess – and long before she is objectified as the black flag that marks her obliteration. She struggles throughout the novel to bring herself into palpable being, and fails tragically. Tess's being, most especially her body, disappears into form; put another way, her being is never more than the formulations of others and of herself. Others objectify her by separating her into parts, only to submit these parts to a curious blurring process and then to eroticise this blur as a wonderfully malleable or chameleon image. Tess takes on any shape for those she meets, but it is a conveniently empty shape, ready to be filled in and then longed for. In an indistinct, blurred form, she fits perfectly into erotic fantasies, especially fantasies where sexual feeling and sexual pleasure are not only unlocated, spread all over the body, but somehow totally unindividualised, making no distinctions between the participants, flowing from one to the other.

For the Victorians, this absorbing, non-genital sexual drama is enacted most notably in the discourse of sex and pain, in erotic beating and spanking fantasies (pornography, if you must), where the sexual sensation is said to be undifferentiated, both or all parties sharing the same generalised and intense erotic feeling. The process, in summary, looks like this: a person is first figured by being emptied of anything that would disrupt the image; the image is then constituted so as to suit the other's purpose, and in *Tess*, or for the character Tess, that purpose is the promoting of the erotic satisfactions of pain (satisfactions I will from this point, with some uneasiness, call sadism). Others perform this vanishing act on Tess so resolutely that they kill her, finding, it seems, the ideal sadistic object in a corpse they can dress up and manipulate at will.

These 'others' we have been defaming seem pretty awful: homicidal, perverted creeps. Who are they? Alec, most obviously, but also Angel, and also Hardy's narrator, and also the reader. The most disgusting insistence of this novel, of this study of how we formulate others, is that we all formulate in the same way, and perhaps for the same ends. We are all of us Alecs, Angels, Hardys; we all wish to create images by distancing, even or especially if that distancing means annihilating. We are all sadists, producing images or cadavers to induce sexually titillating pain.[5]

That is an overstatement, the reader will be saying. Hardy might sardonically agree with you, but the qualifications offered by *Tess* are not at all the comforting ones we will be rushing in to find or to make. There is, first of all, a suggestion that this procedure of image-drawing by absenting in order to eroticise sadistically may be confined to men. Women seem to possess a different and more complete ability to merge and absorb into one another and into nature, a merging that is not narrowly eroticised. Still, though this is arguably so in the novel and though women do not so obviously inflict the pain, the blending they manage is mostly through participation in pain, a participation they do little to resist. Witness the four young women at Talbothay's. Their parts in this sadistic drama were written for them, of course, but they seem sadly unwilling not to go by the script. The other qualification on the reader-as-sadist claim does even less to protect us from the insult. The manoeuvres of sadism seem so common in and through *Tess* that the notion of 'perversion' as a peculiar and bizarre practice safely removed from the 'normal' is erased. Formulating images in order to torture seems the normal way of doing business. If we find Tess's career both terrifying and attractive, tragic and titillating, then we are doing no more than dutifully playing the part of the implied reader. We are not abnormal, perhaps, but the inclusive idea of normality is an unwelcome one.

It may be worth a short interruption to suggest briefly that Hardy here is reflecting a common nineteenth-century attitude toward sexuality, an openness of inquiry we repressed moderns find so shocking we treat it as non-existent. More exactly, we ludicrously turn the tables, using the metaphor of 'repression' to invent a Victorian narrowness to contrast with our own self-endowed liberation, a liberation that ironically roots itself in an hysterical insistence on normal attitudes and behaviour, characteristic of just about no one, and a labelling of everything else, that is, the variety characteristic of just about everyone, as an aberration. By knowing more, we allow ourselves to understand considerably less about sexuality than did the Victorians. We are obsessed with the subject, but we have no curiosity and certainly no daring. With Hardy it was different – and with many of his contemporaries.

Not long before Freud, Havelock Ellis, in his monumental *Studies in the Psychology of Sex*, approached the general issue of pain, sex and love in a manner that, according to one's point of view, appears either more capacious or more loony than Freud's. Ellis is extremely interested in pain and its connection to courtship rituals and sexuality in all species, humans included. He does *not* see, much less assume, any necessary linkage between pain and cruelty, provocatively entitling his very long section on the subject, 'Love and Pain'.[6] Pain and the erotic seem to him often allied and he sees nothing abnormal in that alliance.[7] He even investigates dispassionately what is to us the creepiest of subjects, erotic child-beating. On the topic, he says, 'There is nothing necessarily cruel, repulsive, or monstrous in the idea or the reality of a whipping' (p. 129). Further, 'the general sexual association of whipping in the minds of children, and frequently of their elders, is by no means rare and scarcely abnormal' (p. 137). Whipping, he adds, not only provides pleasurable sexual stimulation but has a general tonic effect on the body and nerves. He admits that it arouses anger but, most significantly, says that anger is here a fundamental part of the courtship ritual, not a cruel desire to dominate. Ellis notes that children love to play at spanking and says they do so, in a term we would use now, unneurotically. He agrees that pain is essential in erotic whipping but argues that it is always felt and given as love. Thus, in sum, sadism is certainly compatible with a high degree of tender-heartedness and is generally reciprocal.

Astonishing stuff, this – and probably repulsive too. It should not be necessary to say, but it is, that Ellis is not advocating sadism, nor is Hardy, nor am I. It does seem to me, though, that we should be a little more hesitant to throw up neurotic protections, claiming either that *Tess* is a portrait of neurotics or that this reading of *Tess* is neurotic. Whether neurotic or not, that reading has, so far, only been outlined. I would like now to fill in some of these blank images myself, illustrating the creation of absence, the imposition of forms on Tess, and the sadistic sexualising of these forms. I will deal first with the general process of distancing and image formation and then, separately, with the novel's two leading sadists, Alec and Angel.

III

The creation of absence is intimately connected to a habit of distancing experience by means of generalisation, large moral explanations, abstractions – in short, by 'the habit of taking long views' (Chapter I) which the narrator marks sarcastically as characteristic of the age. This habit, he says, flattens 'emotions to a monotonous average'; it also makes so remote the physical, the particular that it acts to empty them of significance, to obliterate them. The novel opens with such a procedure. Parson Tringham wantonly drops the catastrophic suggestion – it is taken as fact but has no authority other than this comment – on the wobbling haggler Jack Durbeyfield that he is 'Sir John', member of a great and honoured line, denied a title only because knighthood is not hereditary. What motivates the Parson to such mischief we cannot tell, but he knows, looking at the puffed-up, half-moronic drunk before him, that it is indeed mischief. Or he knows it briefly. He wipes away the knowledge, and Sir John as well, with a handy formula: 'Our impulses are too strong for our judgment sometimes.' There's taking the long view for you! Surprisingly, the narrator habitually takes a long view too, often literally: 'It is a vale [Blackmoor] whose acquaintance is best made by viewing it from the summits of the hills that surround it', the details of the 'recesses' being apt 'to engender dissatisfaction' (Chapter II). He makes acquaintance – and keeps acquaintance – with characters often in the same way, not only distancing them (and us) with maddening equivocation but treating them as 'forms', 'shapes', 'images'.

   Tess is introduced as something of a blur: 'She was a fine and handsome girl – not handsomer than some others, possibly – but her mobile peony mouth and large innocent eyes added eloquence to colour and shape' (Chapter II). Even those features we look at – that peony mouth and those large eyes – are strangely dissociated, unintegrated, and are, further, quickly dissolved into the murk, made contributory to 'colour and shape', whatever they are. 'Possibly' there is no difference at all between Tess and the white crowd, apart from her accidental red ribbon, a kind of pathetic insistence on particularity that prefigures the black flag that finally contains her. Angel looks down on her from the hill and sees her as a 'white shape', ominously 'so soft in her thin white gown' (Chapter II), and her own family sees her as the same blank 'white shape' (Chapter VII) as she leaves for the d'Urberville farm. Tess cannot escape these hazy forms: even puberty comes on her only as 'a luxuriance of aspect' (Chapter V).

Tess tries to form a being for herself out of the coalescence of 'her flexuous and stealthy figure' with that time of day when it is neither light nor dark, but that formation, the narrator bluntly tells us, 'was a sorry and mistaken creation of Tess's fancy' (Chapter XIII). But this sorry invention is the only defence against a terrifying possibility that she has no integral being at all. She fears herself that she is simply a part of an unindividualised historical pattern and that if she reads she will discover 'in some old book somebody just like me, and . . . that I shall only act her part' (Chapter XIX). To others, she is only a generic image, 'a fine and picturesque country girl and no more' (Chapter II), 'only a passing thought' (Chapter XIV), 'but a transient impression, half forgotten' (Chapter V). There is little wonder that she repeats after all the historical pattern she had feared, the one so common to women, turning to men and sexual relations to establish a being she can find nowhere else. The men, tragically, are the last ones who want being; they, like the narrator and like us, are only too satisfied with a 'white shape'.

IV

Poor Alec Stoke-d'Urberville is made to bear the load of our desperate wish to dissociate ourselves from these sadistic-murdering dynamics. He is set up, as all readers have noted with relief, as a sort of moustache-twirling stage villain, presumably without conscience but with a surplus of animal drives. He is, presumably, all genitals and no heart, and can thus focus and drain off our resentment and fear. Tess and most readers position him as a contrast, a black contrast to Angel's whiteness (and her own), to the narrator's grim compassion, and to the reader's stalwart decency. We code Alec as a monster. After all, he likes flash clothes, fast horses, money, and pretty girls. He not only likes pretty girls; he likes to scare them and sleep with them. How unnatural! How unlike us!

Clearly, I am claiming that the series of signals we solidify as

'Alec' function as a loaded and deceptive rhetorical ploy, inviting us to create comforting distance where there is none. It is true that we can see Alec as something of an animated sadism machine; but he differs, if at all, from customary operations only by being somewhat crude, obvious in his devices. He functions on the surface and threatens to give the game away. We are so clearly bombarded in front with his unsubtle mode of operating that we really should be expecting some sneak attack from the rear.

Alec is frightening to us partly because he and the force he represents seem so impersonal. He puts Tess on his sexual rack simply because she has wandered by; any other 'crumby' girl would do as well. He has no other way of proceeding but by the instruction manual of sadism: absence and pain. The narrator suggests that he performs his erotic torturing arts even on his blind old mother, who loves her son 'resentfully', is 'bitterly fond' (Chapter IX). We are unlikely to notice much the narrator's comment that such ghastly perversion is not so perverse after all but really rather common: 'Mrs. d'Urberville was not the first mother compelled to love her son resentfully. . . .'

With Tess, his moves are obvious. He announces as much with his first words, '"Well, my Beauty, what can I do for you?"' (Chapter V). Tess exists for him, from the beginning, as an abstrac- tion, as a 'Beauty', that is, as an image with vague form but no substance. She is, further, *his* Beauty, that he can do for, with, or to, as he likes. This image of Beauty becomes more specific for him only in reference to her 'luxuriance of aspect' (Chapter V) (her breasts?) and her social class: '"You are mighty sensitive for a cottage girl!"' (Chapter VIII). The unwarranted snobbishness is less offensive to us than the depersonalising typecasting. But variations on this same term, 'cottage girl', are used by Angel and by the narrator. They read the term a little differently: the narrator personalises it a little; Angel purifies it idyllically; Alec debases it. But it is a term they are reading, not Tess (whatever we take 'Tess' to mean), and it is a purely literary term, adaptable to different genres: the narrator reads it in reference to psychological realism, Angel the pastoral idyll, Alec naturalism. But all are dealing with images. Tess is expelled so that the image may prevail.

The image Alec produces can then be terrified and hurt, eroticised and controlled. His driving a horse that he says nearly killed him and that he nearly killed in return is an obvious instance. He can both pain and master Tess in the same way, and he does: 'her large eyes star[ed] at him like those of a wild animal' (Chapter VIII), says the narrator. The narrator seems to be caught up in Alec's procedures, offering to him and to us the perfect simile; for what does one do to a wild animal? Tame it, of course, which is what Alec goes on to do, stamping her with 'the kiss of mastery' (Chapter VIII) and forcing from her the admission, '"See how you've mastered me!"' (Chapter XII). This mastery involves investing her with the proper feelings, not adoration but anger – I hate and detest you! (Chapter VIII) – an anger, as Ellis says, basic to sadism and precisely, as the narrator says (Chapter XI), what Alec wants.

Her 'confused surrender awhile' (Chapter XII) follows from all this as a matter of course. It is not that she is stunned by the rape so much as that Alec has successfully sent her packing and can do what he will with the image he has formulated. She is simply caught in the relentless working out of the sadistic plotting. The scene of her rape is presented so entirely in the way of absences that a term like 'rape' signals only our need to fill up the emptiness with some substance, to imagine somehow that there are two *people* involved. There are, in fact, only forms; at least Tess is only a form. Whatever we picture as happening, at any rate, is prefigured by the remarkable country dancing scene and the grotesque blending: the whirling and falling figures, the cloud of dust, the odd light, the 'twitching entanglement of arms and legs'; 'of the rushing couples there could barely be discerned more than the high lights – the indistinctness shaping them to satyrs clasping nymphs' (Chapter X). It is a marvellous stroke to make the active shaping agency here 'indistinctness' itself. Unwillingly, we are free to suppose, Tess adds to the sadistic foreplay, pettishly offering both resistance and compliance, an indecisiveness Alec is free to read as compliance masked by the show of resistance, a sadist's dream: 'she drew a quick pettish breath of objection, writhing uneasily on her seat, looked far ahead, and murmured, "I don't know – I wish – how can I say yes or no when –"' (Chapter XI).

What is raped or seduced, then, is 'a pale nebulousness at his feet, which represented the white muslin figure' (Chapter XI). Note that the expulsion of Tess is doubled in force here: she is replaced by the familiar white figure, which in turn is vaporised into an even more adaptable 'pale nebulousness', a distant representation of a representation. It is, we note, the narrator who is doing this 'figuring' and 'nebulousnessing', though perhaps he is representing, though still cooperatively, Alec's perception. When we leave Alec as he

stoops over Tess and join the narrator, however, we do not see
much change. The narrator describes whatever it is that is going on
as enacted 'upon this beautiful feminine tissue, sensitive as gossamer, and practically blank as snow'. All this about tissue, gossamer,
and convenient blankness should be familiar to us by now. It is the
voice of the sadist.

Alec's later career invites us further to compartmentalise and
channel our protective outrage, to regard these sadistic currents as
little ugly rivulets and not the main channel. He stirs within Tess
only the feeblest of attempts to assert a being, a presence. When she
offers the sad but conventional explanation, '"I didn't understand
your meaning until it was too late"', Alec retorts, '"That's what
every woman says"'. This awakens what the narrator calls her
'latent spirit', but the best that latent spirit can do is, Did it never
strike you that what every woman says some women may feel?
(Chapter XIII). Tess can manage only to qualify the generalisation,
not to specify herself. She is still indistinguishable from 'some
women', scarcely more individualised than 'a cottage girl' or 'a
white shape'. Alec thus has an easy time reappropriating her later
on in his devices of sexual play, now refined to including pain for
both parties. He has discovered the pleasures of 'having a good slap
at yourself' (Chapter XLV) and initiates Tess into those delights.
When she whales him with her mace-like glove and bloodies him
up, she invites him to '"punish me! . . . whip me, crush me"'
(Chapter XLVII). Perhaps the tables have turned in such a way that
Tess is able to absent Alec now, reducing him to 'a spot', a figure
of blood. But the mechanisms are the same, and that is hardly
cheering.

V

Angel, we hope, is a different matter. Despicable as we may find
him, we want to locate or invent a difference. So does Tess, and she
has every apparent justification for doing so. She is lured into the
valley that contains Crick's dairy and Angel partly on the basis of its
difference from Blackmoor: 'The secret of Blackmoor was best discovered from the heights around; to read aright the valley before her
it was necessary to descend into its midst' (Chapter XVI). This spot
seems to disdain the terrifying abstractions, the murdering distances, and to promise discrimination, particularity, being. Tess

tries to assert that difference immediately, reading on her first view of Angel a 'something . . . differing' beneath his ordinary dairyman's attire. She reads the attire as mere camouflage for distinctiveness, trying to do unto others what certainly has not been done unto her. Through the vale and through Angel, she tries to individualise and to escape the literal nothingness forced on her by earlier sadistic patternings. But Angel is not the ticket away from that Inferno. He is, in fact, only a form himself, 'not altogether a distinct figure', containing a 'something nebulous' in and about him (Chapter XVIII). Tess, ironically, is beginning to fill him up just as Alec filled her, and she soon, accordingly, finds herself creating erotic sensations mixed inextricably with pain.

Angel sits at an open window strumming on his harp, as Tess wanders in a garden outside (Chapter XIX). Of course it is, as the narrator insists, the commonplace window of an ordinary dairyman's house; Angel's harp and his musical abilities are frankly 'poor'; the garden is a most prelapsarian Eden, slushing over with cuckoo-spittle, mashed snails, slug-slime, and infested with ripping thistles. But Tess slogs her way through Nature's vomit, responsive only to 'a stark quality like that of nudity' in the air and the lousy music, which hypnotises her, makes her 'undulate' and get all aflame in her cheeks. One wonders what she would have done had Angel received the benefit of a few lessons. She eroticises a void, what is really 'a typical summer evening' and a not-too-bright and certainly untalented performer. She is playing Alec's game, the only one she knows. Angel spots her, finally and fatally, or rather spots 'her light summer gown'. There is that white form again, and the two are off and running.

Angel, it turns out, is a much more versatile imagiser than is Alec. He too can see her during their courtship as a 'milkmaid' or 'daughter of the soil', ominous generic types he will return to later; but he can do better, turning 'the merest stray phenomenon' into 'a rosy warming apparition' (Chapter XX). Tess and Angel together are so formless they are 'impregnated by their surroundings' (Chapter XXIV), Tess being internalised over and over to a portrait, a 'cameo' (Chapter XXIV), appearing 'ghostly', with 'a sort of phosphorescence' in the 'luminous gloom' (Chapter XX). Sounds like Alec in the Chase all over again, doesn't it? This will-o-the-wisp phosphorescent gloom not only aids in eroticising them for one another; it is the substance of the *them*. 'It was then', the narrator tells us, at this strange, insubstantial time, 'that she impressed him most deeply.

She was no longer the milkmaid, but a visionary essence of woman –
a whole sex condensed into one typical form. He called her Artemis,
Demeter, and other fanciful names' (Chapter XX). These fanciful
names represent a fanciful being. Tess's physical being is present to
him only as a model for mental reproductions: he studies 'the curve
of those lips' so intently only so that 'he could reproduce them
mentally with ease' (Chapter XXIV). This imaginative construction
of 'essence of woman' becomes so fixed that it takes a great jolt to
alter it even slightly. When he learns of Tess's presumably distinguished ancestry, he simply does some touching up, expresses
pleasure that the new image will be more presentable to his parents,
and speaks quite in the old style of 'the well-read woman that I mean
to make you'. Victor Frankenstein had nothing on Angel.

But what do we make of this construction *we* devise and call Angel
Clare? Hardy's narrator explains him often, but the terms of those
explanations – 'I will not say'; 'It might have been that' – give and
then take away, in fact seem to take away much more than they give.
They leave him blanker than ever. The explanations that seem solid
are not only multiplied but fly all over the map, in circles and in
opposite directions. Critics often try to invest with peculiar authority
the statement that Angel is 'more spiritual than animal', 'less
Byronic than Shelleyan' (Chapter XXX), as if these comparatives and
sliding more-this-than-thats could be pinned down and as if the
problem were purely hormonal. And we are tempted to rush in with
what is surely the least interesting explanation available: that Angel
has too little of what Alec has too much of in the way of . . uh . . er . .
sexual needs. What do we make of the scene where he lugs the other
girls across the water and then returns to nuzzle and fondle Tess, all
sighs and hot breath? What about the claim that Tess and her face
especially are something more than simply lovable: 'there was
nothing ethereal about it; all was real vitality, real warmth, real
incarnation' (Chapter XXIV)? It is all, we are told, very *real*. 'It was
for herself he loved Tess' (Chapter XXVI), the narrator blandly
explains. For *herself*? Against this we have the statements that his
love 'inclined to the ethereal' (Chapter XXX), was rooted 'ideally
and fancifully' (Chapter XXXII). Even Tess suspects he is in love
with an image: '"O my love, my love, why do I love you so!" she
whispered there alone; "for she you love is not my real self, but one
in my image"' (Chapter XXXIII).

One might hush this hubbub a little by arguing that Angel is in
love, and passionately, with the very real image he has created, an

image, the narrator suggests, which constitutes the only reality anyhow. I am less interested here, though, in making claims about a single coherent pattern than in arguing for a perception of Angel as a part of a pattern of sadistic manoeuvring. He is not figured as passionless or sexless; he is drawn to his image of Tess 'by every heave of his pulses' (Chapter XXV). It is just that these pulse-heaves lead him to evacuate Tess and to figure a coalescence of eroticism and pain. Into the emptiness he has formed he intrudes himself, like Alec, as a master. Tess 'caught his manner and habits, his speech and phrases, his likings and his aversions' (Chapter XXXII) and becomes focused on but one point, a full cooperation in the sadistic programme: 'Her one desire, so long resisted, to make herself his, to call him her lord, her own – then, if necessary, to die – had at last lifted her up from her plodding reflective pathway' (Chapter XXXIII).

The reference to death makes explicit what she will, in fact, find it 'necessary' to do. All along at Talbothay's, Angel, no less than would Alec, sweeps through the female population as a smiling, ubiquitous sadist. Not only Tess but all the dairy girls find him 'ecstasizing them to a killing joy'; they live in his presence with a 'torturing ecstasy' (Chapter XXIII). The narrator, seeking to make explicit the sado-masochistic proceedings, even reaches for direct allusions to, of all people, Swinburne: 'pleasure girdled about with pain' (Chapter XXV). Tess herself sees her life at this time as a kind of lariat, 'twisted of two strands, positive pleasure and positive pain' (Chapter XXVIII).

All this pleasure and all the pain are directed toward an Angel who is absent, inaccessible, and can therefore be filled with qualities that will arouse this twining, this mixture of sexuality and pain. In this sense, the sadism is imaginative, imagistic – however effective. But there is nothing imaginary about the pain Tess feels on her honeymoon, where she jolts Angel's image of her roughly, shatters it, and discovers the real pain during the time when he must cast about for a new mental compartment for her. His erotic energies, for once, are directed outward in one of the most ghastly scenes of sadistic acrobatics I know of. Angel's considerable eroticism is now no longer contained or controlled; if he were somehow biologically deficient, Tess would not have such a terrible time of it. After her confession, Angel exposes his obsession with sex – or with Tess's sexual past as a narrative he can really play and replay in his own mind, really a form of pornographic fixation. This fiction compels sexual energy, a compulsion D. H. Lawrence, describing what he took to be a modern malady, described as 'sex in the head'. Such sadistic novel-writing is so focused in the honeymoon sequence, that I would like to dwell on it.

The episode, beginning with the end of Tess's tearless, unflinching narrative of her time with Alec, features an immediate unfocusing of perspective, acting, finally, to blend our vision with what turns out to be Angel's: 'But the complexion even of external things seemed to suffer transmutation as her announcement progressed' (Chapter XXXV). Who is seeing this apparent change, the impish fire and the grinning fender? Why does it occur? What does it amount to? On the last point the narrator is bluntly clear: 'Nothing had changed since the moments when he had been kissing her; or rather, nothing in the substance of things. But the essence of things had changed.' To whom? Why to Angel, of course – and to us. What is this essence? Is it really the same as the 'complexion' of 'things'? Surely these *things* and Tess too are the same – or so we would like to think. But the complexion of things, the perception of things – of the fender and of Tess – has changed, and the perception of that complexion, that internal imaging, is, sadly, all the essence that she has. These images are made essences, for the reader and for Angel; and we are pounded to participate with him as he proceeds to unleash his anger on images he can shift at will. Apparently freed now from any sadistic inhibitions, he writes a series of versatile pornographic scenes for his own – and our – pleasure.

Angel first does virtually nothing, stirring the fire in what the narrator describes as an 'irrelevant act'. Such irrelevant delay forces Tess to wait in grinding suspense, but that tension is only a prelude. He turns on her a blankness, 'the most inadequate, commonplace voice' she had heard from him, as he tries to hold on to the old image he had posed: '"Am I to believe this? . . . My wife, *my* Tess – nothing in you warrants such a supposition as that?"' Nothing, that is, in his old image can immediately find a place for a Tess who has an independent existence, a past, particularly a sexual past, an existence outside of '*my* Tess'.

His befuddlement is amazingly short-lived. After going through a very brief period of denial – imagining Tess is out of her mind and the like – he finds the formula he needs. Tess, in her agony, makes her most poignant and, one would suppose, most irresistible appeal: '"In the name of our love, forgive me!" she whispered with a dry mouth. "I have forgiven you for the same."' Her logic seems unbreakable here; further, it seems unlikely a man like Angel Clare would deny anyone at least the words of forgiveness. But if he forgives Tess, the game is up, and the last thing he wants is to end things so quickly. So he evades, disallows the question: '"O Tess, forgiveness does not apply to the case! You were one person; now you are another."' The problem in the forgive-me plea is not, clearly, 'forgive' but 'me'. Her *me* exists for Angel only as a construction now shattered, so he proceeds to replace his former construction of an innocent maid with a new one, the corrupted woman, the deceiver, and he can write a new script, safe in the narrative formula he has created. It is a narrative Tess cannot penetrate with reason or with love; she can only suffer.

Angel launches immediately into his sadistic operation with 'horrible laughter – as unnatural and ghastly as a laugh in hell'. He gets just the effect he is after; Tess's response could have been copied verbatim from one of the many Victorian flagellation novels: '"Don't – don't! It kills me quite, that!" she shrieked. "O have mercy upon me – have mercy!"' '"I thought Angel," she says, "that you loved me – me, my very self! If it be I you do love, O how can it be that you look and speak so?"' Whether Tess is any less an imagist in her construction of Angel is uncertain, but this plea for a love of her very self is hopeless: '"I repeat, the woman I have been loving is not you."' She sees that he regards her now merely as a 'species of impostor; a guilty woman in the guise of an innocent one'. The terms, guilt and innocence, are less horrifying than the terrible abstraction into roles, generalised 'species'. She responds with 'terror . . . upon her white face', her constricted mouth forming itself into 'a round little hole'. This is the sort of thing he wants, and he works this image transformation until she finally bursts into tears.

The narrator at this point offers some startlingly clear commentary: 'Clare was relieved at this change, for the effect on her of what had happened was beginning to be a trouble to him'. He had, apparently, been approaching a 'trouble', a kind of shut-off point in sadism, an end to pleasure when the pain in the subject is too great or too obvious. Seeing Tess get some relief in 'self-sympathetic tears', he overcomes his 'trouble' and is freed to press on. His cold neutrality is among his strongest weapons for causing pain. When Tess asks, for instance, whether she is too wicked to allow them to live together, Clare answers, '"I have not been able to think what we can do."' But he is capable of direct attack: when Tess offers to lie down and die for him, he whips out, '"You are very good. But it strikes me that there is a want of harmony between your present mood of

self-sacrifice and your past mood of self-preservation.''' Tess recognises the anger well enough, and maintains a silence that
prolongs the scene. Later, when he switches centres in the drama
and forgives Tess or says he does, Tess asks if he can love her, 'to
which question he did not answer'. Such devices have the effect, of
course, of prolonging the suffering and prolonging his pleasure.
That pleasure is most titillated, as always, by absence, conducive
both to pain and to image-making: '"Tess, . . I cannot stay – in this
room – just now. I will walk out a little way."' So that we will miss
nothing in this sexual drama, the narrator points out that 'cruelty
was mighty in Clare now', quotes Swinburne on sadism again ('And
the veil of thine head shall be grief, and the crown shall be pain'),
and marks the relationship of sadism to absence: 'What a weak thing
her presence must have become to him!' He leaves to pump up a
sexual feeling that finds presence an irritating distraction.

Tess has surprising insight into what is going on in Angel's mind,
but when she threatens to make an entry into his narrative, he
retreats to his old, maddening and terrifyingly self-enclosed
formula. Tess says, '"It is in your own mind what you are angry at,
Angel; it is not in me. O, it is not in me, and I am not that deceitful
woman you think me!"' "Hm – well," Angel says, '"Not deceitful,
my wife; but not the same."' She can only force him to make small
adjustments in his mental fiction; she cannot transform it – nor can
she find a real role in it. Like absence, Angel's sadistic fiction-
making robs her of any essence outside it. One of the reasons these
scenes are so nightmarish is that Tess's repeated insistence that she
is what she has always been, more fundamentally that she *is*, that
she exists, is an insistence on a different plot, one we could be
anxious to complete in our own minds. But we find ourselves, like
Tess, stymied by and, what is worse, caught up in Angel's more
authoritative plot.

He keeps the plot going the next day (Chapter XXXVI) by re-
hearsing the whole thing – '"Tess! Say it is not true!"' – and by
demanding more details:

'"Is he living?" Angel then asked.
"The baby died."
"But the man?"
"He is alive."
 . . .
"Is he in England?"'

"Yes."'''

The brutal way in which he ignores the news of the baby's death, rushing onward without a pause to the man, exposes, I think, his obsessive sexual interest and his desire not so much to gain information as to hurt.

He then explains to Tess his 'position', which is one he says 'any man' would hold: '"I thought – any man would have thought – that by giving up all ambition to win a wife with social standing, with fortune, with knowledge of the world, I should secure rustic innocence as surely as I should secure pink cheeks; but – However, I am no man to reproach you, and I will not."' He reproaches her bitterly and then deflects criticism for having done so. The horror of all this is not merely that it is no position at all, that it is a self-pitying pose designed to lacerate her; it is that Tess is sucked into the whole thing: 'Tess felt his position so entirely that the remainder had not been needed.' He then, once again, is free to proceed: '"O Tess – you are too, too – childish – unformed – crude, I suppose! I don't know what you are."' He is right about the last, at least, but he has been able to cause 'a quick shame mixed with misery' to come upon her. This leads her to suggesting what is simply the logical outcome for this sadistic programme:

'"What were you thinking of doing?" he inquired.

"Of putting an end to myself."

"When?"

She writhed under this inquisitorial manner of his. "Last night," she answered.

"Where?"

"Under your mistletoe."

"My good—! How?" he asked sternly.'

Note Angel's grisly and quick interest in the narrative details – When? Where? How? – and the absence of condemnation or discouragement of the impulse. When he does get around to that, it is only to deliver another whiplash: '"Wicked! The idea was unworthy of you beyond description."' The awkwardness here may suggest that the idea simply has not yet entered his image ('description') of her, interesting as it is. Perhaps suicide is not quite the fillip he wants in his snuff movie; murder would be better, a murder he enacts with her and the handy tombs in dumb show (Chapter XXXVII). It is only with a corpse that he can be tender: '"My poor, poor Tess – my dearest, darling Tess! So sweet, so good, so true!''' Perhaps necrophilia is indeed the inevitable end of sadism.

Still, though Tess has been reduced to feeling that she is 'so utterly worthless', heroically, she will not give up. She again returns to an appeal that has considerable logical and emotional strength: '''I told you I thought I was not respectable enough long ago – and on that account I didn't want to marry you, only – only you urged me!'' She broke into sobs, and turned her back to him. It would almost have won round any man but Angel Clare.' Angel now has passed into a state where there is no mechanism of control. His sexual fiction is so powerfully fixed that it can carry him through all that time in Brazil.

In a novel filled with and based on absence, Angel's putting an ocean between them is crucial. As Clare says, '''I think of people more kindly when I am away from them''' (Chapter XXXVI). He also, clearly, thinks of them more erotically: while in Brazil, 'he almost talked to her in his anger, as if she had been in the room. And then her cooing voice, plaintive in expostulation, disturbed the darkness, the velvet touch of her lips passed over his brow, and he could distinguish in the air the warmth of her breath' (Chapter XXXIX). Angel can make passionate love to a corpse or a mental image, even feel her warm breath, perhaps the same 'warm breath' Alec feels when he seduces Tess. Angel has not somehow been magically sexualised in Brazil; he is sexualised as he always has been, still controlled by 'what Tess was not' (Chapter XXXIX), by a vacancy he can fill.

We are, I suppose, free to suppose that Angel comes back with a new 'make' and new erotic needs, but we have to do some pretty energetic inner constructions of our own to fill up his blank in that transformational way. We are told only that he has acquired some rather cynical and disjointed philosophic views and that he was 'arrested' now less by 'beauty' than by 'pathos' (Chapter XLIX). Sounds pretty dangerously like the old Angel, one might think. His memory is most stirred, after all, by Izz Huett's pathetic honesty: 'The words of Izz Huett, never quite stilled in his memory, came back to him . . . . Tess would lay down her life for him, and she herself could do no more' (Chapter XLIX). That image of Tess dead as a doornail proves to be irresistible.

Tess, we might say, re-enters the old scene, murdering Alec and appearing to Angel again as the same old white shape, a 'figure' (Chapter LVII). Angel leads her to Stonehenge, where, with Tess saying, '''I shall not live for you to despise me!''' (Chapter LVIII), he can complete his sadistic exercise, reformulating her as sacrificial victim and a black flag – more images. The use of Liz-Lu, an even more perfect blank than Tess, may seem to us less a sign of rejuvenation than of ghastly reiteration.[8] Tess offers her to Angel as a pure implement: '"If you would train and teach her, Angel, and bring her up for your own self! . . . She has all the best of me without the bad of me; and if she were to become yours . . ."' (Chapter LVIII). Liz-Lu appears in the second half of the novel also as a 'figure' (Chapter XLIX) and at the end ascends a hill with Angel to gaze on Tess's execution from the summit. We are all used by now to these distant prospects and what happens to 'figures' who join them. They go off hand-in-hand with the world presumably all before them, but we are likely to suspect it is but a narrow, torture-wracked world Angel can create.

So we come to the end of a novel figuring a world of flitting phenomena, changing forms. The attempt to fix or imagine solidity depends on distancing or absenting the corporeal so as to make room for images. Eroticising these images, then, is a free and unrestricted operation; one can easily turn an absence into a corpse, and sexuality might as well become sadism. Images, after all, are one's own possession and can be whipped or rubbed out at will.

Awful stuff, isn't it, but Angel is never presented as especially perverse. He is just a 'well-meaning young man, a sample product of the last five-and-twenty years' (Chapter XXXIX). The comforts of the idea of abnormality are pointedly denied us. Even the narrator seems always to turn an erotic Tess into a bleeding Tess: 'A bit of her naked arm is visible between the buff leather of the gauntlet and the sleeve of her gown; and as the day wears on its feminine smoothness becomes scarified by the stubble, and bleeds' (Chapter XIV). One is reminded of Roland Barthes' orgiastic 'gaps', worked on some by de Sade. Worse, this narrator tells us with casual indifference that we all seem to be involved in this: 'Clare had been harsh towards her; there is no doubt of it. Men are too often harsh with women they love or have loved; women with men' (Chapter XLIX). Each man kills the thing he loves – and loves to do it. *Tess* becomes, thus, a titillating snuff movie we run in our own minds. The novel offers us the terrifying suggestion and demonstration that our own lives are nothing more than this criminal movie in the head, made over in the flesh.

It is perhaps too strong to say that the novel suggests that happy sexuality can exist only in fictions, constructs of what is not there, inner pornographic narratives or fables. Still, the power of these negations is dreadful, as if absences were writing the novel in defiance of presence. At one point, Tess complains to her mother, '''Why didn't you tell me there was danger in menfolks? Why didn't you warn me? Ladies know how to fend hands against because they read novels that tell them of these tricks; but I never had the chance of learning in that way''' (Chapter XII). One might suppose that this is offered as a kind of justification for the novel in front of us, a hope that the work will be effectively cautionary, providing the chance for learning. But we know from the same novel that narratives are never read or constructed in such a straightforward way. There are always counter-narratives, negations that overwhelm opportunity and freedom. In Hardy, one never learns, even from novels.

Notes

1. Thomas Hardy, *Tess of the d'Urbervilles: A Pure Woman Faithfully Presented*, 2nd edn, edited by Scott Elledge (New York: Norton, 1979) Chapter XI. This edition will be the source of further citations, noted in the text by chapter number.

2. Thomas Hardy, *Jude the Obscure*, edited by Norman Page (New York: Norton, 1978) Part I, Chapter IV.

3. See an earlier discussion of mine, 'Hardy's Absences', in Dale Kramer (ed.) *Critical Approaches to the Fiction of Thomas Hardy* (London: Macmillan, 1979) pp. 202–14. That discussion, concerned with *Jude* and *A Pair of Blue Eyes*, now seems to me, unhappily, divorced from concerns of sexuality and secretly married to some formalist assumptions. See also J. Hillis Miller, *Thomas Hardy: Distance and Desire* (Cambridge, Massachusetts: Harvard University Press, 1970), a splendid book which, however, does not, despite its title, coincide with the model or argument here.

4. See Anthony Trollope, *Barchester Towers* (Oxford: The World's Classics, 1980) Chapter XXX: 'But then where would have been my novel?'

5. I realise that I am humanising and solidifying these characters, but that is for convenience only. What we call 'Alec', 'Tess', or 'Angel' should be regarded not as real people but as vehicles for setting up intricate and various structures of sexual expression and responsiveness. But it is certainly less clumsy to speak of 'Alec', 'Tess', and 'Angel' than of coded vehicles.

6. Havelock Ellis, *Studies in the Psychology of Sex*, Vol. I, Part Two (New York: Random House, 1936) pp. 66–188. Further references to the same work are cited in the text.

7. Pain in conjunction with sexuality seems to him abnormal only if it

substitutes for intercourse; it is common and normal if pain leads to intercourse.

8.   Miller (*Distance and Desire*, p. 155) also suggests that this ending can be read as the beginning of a new cycle of the same thing.

3

Loving You All Ways: Vamps, Vampires, Necrophiles and Necrofilles in Nineteenth-Century Fiction

Robert Tracy

Van Helsing went about his work systematically. Holding his candle so that he could read the coffin plates, and so holding it that the sperm dropped in white patches which congealed as they touched the metal, he made assurance of Lucy's coffin. Another search in his bag, and he took out a turnscrew. (Stoker, *Dracula*, p. 197)

I am sure [Bram Stoker] was unaware of the sexuality inherent in *Dracula*. (Farson, *The Man Who Wrote Dracula*)

A close analysis will show that the only emotions which in the long run harm are those arising from sex impulses, and when we have realised this we have put a finger on the actual point of danger. (Stoker, 'The Censorship of Fiction', *The Nineteenth Century and After*, September 1908)

If sex and death are constants, so is a tendency to equate them. Hades ('Αΐδης), the Greek god of death, is literally the god of that which is unseen. His name is etymologically closely related to aidoia (αιδοîα), Homer's word for the private or unseen parts. It is Hades who comes to lead Alcestis away from her husband into the underworld in Euripides' play, perhaps the first important literary use of the motif of sex as death, and therefore a prototype for the treatment of the Undead or Vampire figure in *Dracula* and other nineteenth-century tales of horror. But the motif is much earlier than Euripides. It is already clearly present in the myth of Hades and Persephone – as Stoker may have half-realised when he sent Dracula to England and Lucy Westenra on board a vessel named *Demeter*.

The successful courtship of a beautiful young woman is the most popular of fictional plots. The death of a beautiful young woman, Poe tells us, is the most powerful poetic theme. Though these elements are often combined in literature, and extremely common in nineteenth-century literature, their combined use by Stoker and other writers of vampire fiction is direct, unguarded, and – to put it crudely – crude. Because these writers use the motif in an unsophisticated way, we can recognise it clearly, and can then recognise its more subtle manifestations in the work of the period's major writers.

The treatment of the motif by both skilled and unskilled writers also suggests the nature of certain nineteenth-century anxieties and obsessions. If the eighteenth-century Gothic novel is about psychological terror, the vampire novel is about physical, and specifically sexual, fear. The shift from ghosts to vampires indicates a re-ordering of the categories of fear. A ghost can only frighten or warn. It is bodiless, and therefore incapable of causing physical harm – though, as Horatio shrewdly suggests, it might frighten a victim into harming himself. But the vampire has a body, and therefore represents at once a physical, a supernatural or spiritual, and a sexual menace.[1]

Most of the vampires we meet in nineteenth-century fiction are strong and agile. They are more than a match for their opponents in a physical struggle. When General Spielsdorf recognises Carmilla as the vampire who destroyed his daughter, and swings at her with an axe, her 'tiny grasp . . . closed like a vice of steel' on his wrist and stays his blow (Le Fanu, *Carmilla*, pp. 332, 339); Dracula 'has the strength of many in his hand' (Stoker, *Dracula*, p. 239). These attributes emphasise the vampire's physicality and perverse vitality – a carter describes Dracula as '"the strongest chap I ever struck, an' him a old feller, with a white moustache, one that thin you would think he couldn't throw a shadder"' (ibid., p. 263).

Though they do physically harm their victims, and often bring about their deaths, the vampires also threaten their victims' souls. The victim who dies will become another vampire. '". . . To fail here is not mere life or death,'" Professor Van Helsing warns his band of crusaders. "'It is that we become . . . foul things of the night like him . . . To us for ever are the gates of heaven shut . . . We go on for all time . . . an arrow in the side of Him who died for man'" (ibid., p. 237).

This double threat, at once physical and spiritual, is in practice presented as essentially sexual. Carmilla's clearly sexual advances to Laura, her chosen victim, are at once a manifestation of and a metaphor for the threat she represents. It is an 'artful courtship' (Le Fanu, *Carmilla*, p. 337) which creates in Laura 'a strange tumultuous excitement that was pleasurable . . . mingled with a vague sense of fear and disgust'. Laura even fantasises that Carmilla is a boy who has entered the house in disguise to woo her.

> Sometimes . . . my strange and beautiful companion would take my hand and hold it with a fond pressure, renewed again and again; blushing softly, gazing in my face with languid and burning eyes, and breathing so fast that her dress rose and fell with the tumultuous respiration. It was like the ardour of a lover; it embarrassed me; it was hateful and yet overpowering; and with gloating eyes she drew me to her, and her hot lips travelled along my cheek in kisses; and she would whisper, almost in sobs, 'You are mine, you *shall* be mine, and you and I are one for ever.' (ibid., pp. 292–3)

Dracula's penetration of Lucy's and later Mina's throat signals the essentially sexual way that he comes to possess them, and the effects on both women stress their loss of chastity. Once violated, they become, like prostitutes, 'foul things of the night' (Stoker, *Dracula*, p. 237). Confronted by night in the graveyard, Lucy as vampire is

> Lucy Westenra, but yet how changed. The sweetness was turned to adamantine, heartless cruelty, and the purity to voluptuous wantonness . . . Lucy's eyes in form and colour; but Lucy's eyes unclean and full of hell-fire, instead of the pure, gentle orbs we knew. At that moment the remnant of my love passed into hate and loathing; had she then to be killed, I could have done it with savage delight. As she looked, her eyes blazed with unholy light, and the face became wreathed with a voluptuous smile. Oh, God, how it made me shudder to see it! . . she advanced to [Arthur]

with outstretched arms and a wanton smile . . . and with a
languourous, voluptuous grace, said:—

'Come to me, Arthur . . . My arms are hungry for you. Come,
and we can rest together. Come, my husband, come!' (ibid.,
p. 211)

Mina, assaulted in her bedroom beside her sleeping husband,
describes herself as 'Unclean' (ibid., p. 284), and when Van Helsing
touches her with a consecrated Host the touch burns a 'mark of
shame' upon her forehead (ibid., p. 296). Dracula's assault on Mina
is the only one specifically described. It involves both penetration,
as he bites her throat and sucks her blood, and a kind of impreg-
nation: he opens a vein in his breast and forces her to drink some of
his blood, to make her '"flesh of my flesh; blood of my blood; kin of
my kin"' (ibid, pp. 287–8). Dracula is able to taunt his pursuers with
a stinging truth: '"Your girls that you all love are mine already"'
(ibid., p. 306).

The vampire's combination of death and sexual activity brings
one of the nineteenth century's major public preoccupations –
death, the dead, funerals, tombs – together with its major private
and secret preoccupation, sex and sexuality. One could be talked
about and celebrated incessantly; the other could not be talked
about at all, except by thus combining it with death and so dis-
guising it. The vampire story supplies a metaphoric vocabulary to
represent certain obsessions and anxieties not otherwise admissible
into literature – in Le Fanu's terms, 'a strange tumultuous excitement that was pleasurable . . . mingled with a vague sense of fear
and disgust' (Le Fanu, *Carmilla*, p. 292). The nineteenth century
reader perhaps relished its very lack of subtlety, which allowed a
closer approach to forbidden topics. As the vampire emerges from
beneath his or her lying tombstone, with its promise of quiescence –
and the misleading inscriptions on tombstones are specifically
challenged in *Dracula* (pp. 66–7) – so does sexuality emerge from
beneath the supernatural terrors which are the ostensible business
of vampire fictions.[2]

Though young women are the favourite victims of supernatural
threats in Gothic fiction, it is usually their property rather than their
chastity that is at issue. Monk Lewis introduces the explicit sexual
threat – in most of its subsequent permutations – in *The Monk* (1796),
and relates it to permanent damnation: Ambrosio is sexually attracted to a handsome young fellow monk, Rosario, who is a woman

in disguise, but actually a demon sent to tempt Ambrosio to destruction. It re-emerges in the first important vampire novel in English, John Polidori's *The Vampyre* (1819). Polidori establishes the basic elements of vampire fiction for British writers: his vampire is aristocratic, nocturnal, ingenious, and ruthless. The theory of vampires is rooted in Eastern Europe, where some of the action takes place. Lord Ruthven, the vampire, preys on young women, 'forced every year, by feeding upon the life of a lovely female to prolong his existence for the ensuing months' (Polidori, *Vampyre*, p. 271). But he is also a sexual threat:

> the possession of irresistible powers of seduction, rendered his licentious habits more dangerous to society. It had been discovered, that his contempt for the adulteress had not originated in hatred of her character; but that he had required, to enhance his gratification, that his victim, the partner of his guilt, should be hurled from the pinnacle of unsullied virtue, down to the lowest abyss of infamy and degradation: in fine, that all those females whom he had sought, apparently on account of their virtue, had, since his departure, thrown even the mask aside, and had not scrupled to expose the whole deformity of their vices to the public gaze. (ibid., p. 269)

Though Sheridan Le Fanu's 'Strange Event in the Life of Schalken the Painter' (1839) is not literally a vampire story, it is about the undead and about marriage with the dead, and is also important as a predecessor to Le Fanu's *Carmilla*. The story anticipates, and deftly provides, that 'loophole for a natural explanation' of apparently supernatural events which M. R. James recommended to the aspiring writer of supernatural tales, but also follows his advice that 'the loophole be so narrow as not to be quite practicable' (James, *Ghosts*, p. vi). Did Schalken's jealousy make him see Rose Velderkaust's suitor as demonic and sepulchral rather than merely elderly? Did the mysterious suitor enter Schalken's studio unobtrusively, or did the painter evoke him by cursing his picture and its subject, the temptation of St Anthony? Was Rose suffering some kind of breakdown when, after her marriage to the sinister Vanderhausen, she arrived home half-naked and hysterical, or was she pursued by the Undead? Did Schalken only dream that he saw her years later in an 'old-fashioned Dutch' bedroom (Le Fanu, 'Schalken', p. 46) which turns out to be the burial crypt of a Rotterdam church?

Le Fanu's description of the 'repulsive' (ibid., p. 40) Vanderhausen shows him to be, like Dracula, an animated corpse, and hints at his sexuality:

> the entire character of the face was sensual, malignant, and even satanic . . . There was something indescribably odd, even horrible, about all his motions . . . it was as if the limbs were guided and directed by a spirit unused to the management of bodily machinery . . . During the stay, his eyelids did not once close, or, indeed, move in the slightest degree; and farther, there was a deathlike stillness in his whole person, owing to the absence of the heaving motion of the chest, caused by th process of respiration. (ibid., pp. 38–9)[3]

Nevertheless, Rose's uncle insists that she marry Vanderhausen. When she flees and returns home in terror, she repeats over and over the phrase, '"the dead and the living cannot be one: God has forbidden it"' (ibid., pp. 42–3). Her uncle and Schalken fail to protect her from the demon; when they leave her alone for a moment, the door of the bedroom slams shut, they hear her shriek, and find her gone, leaving no trace.

But Rose reappears, or seems to, some years later, in a church at Rotterdam where Schalken has gone to await his father's funeral. He falls asleep – the loophole – and is awakened by a woman robed and veiled in white, who leads him into the crypt, then lifts her lamp to reveal herself as Rose: 'There was nothing horrible, or even sad, in the countenance. On the contrary, it wore the same arch smile which used to enchant the artist.' She leads him to a bedroom, and to a curtained bed, 'frequently turn[ing] towards him with the same arch smile', then draws the curtain to show 'the livid and demoniac form of Vanderhausen'. Schalken faints, to be discovered next morning by the church attendants 'in a cell . . . which had not been disturbed for a long time . . . he had fallen beside a large coffin, which was supported upon small pillars' (ibid., p. 46).

The story is introduced by a description of Schalken's painting commemorating this adventure, which shows Rose in the crypt, her face illuminated by the lamp; 'her features wear such an arch smile, as well becomes a pretty woman when practising some prankish roguery' (ibid., p. 29). There is also 'the dim red light of an expiring fire' and a shadowy man – Vanderhausen? Schalken himself? – about to draw his sword. The white robes, at once bridal and ceremental, the expiring fire, and the sword all hint at the sexual implications of the scene. Le Fanu's reiterated emphasis on Rose's arch smile, and her ironic enticement of Schalken to the bed she shares with her Undead husband, suggest that, like the women at Dracula's castle, and Lucy Westenra, she has become sexually accomplished and provocative after a marriage which initiates her at once into sex and into death.

Le Fanu often returns to this theme of marriage with the Undead, notably in 'A Chapter in the History of a Tyrone Family' (1839), often seen as a source for *Jane Eyre*; in 'Ultor de Lacy' (1861), where the bride of the Undead, when later glimpsed, wears a 'slanting, cunning smile' (Le Fanu, *Best Ghost Stories*, p. 464) and in 'Laura Silver Bell' (1872). It is obliquely present in 'The Child That Went with the Fairies' (1870), which explicitly draws on the Irish folklore familiar to Le Fanu and Bram Stoker, both born and educated in Ireland, and in doing so partially explains why these writers should have been drawn to the Undead theme. The Irish fairies, or *sidhe* are not the airy creatures of Shakespeare but the dead, the people of the mounds (*sidhe* is the genitive form of *sí*, which means mound), that is, the dead buried in the many ancient burial mounds which are common in Ireland. In many legends the *sidhe* entice away young men or women to join them underground, to marry into a lengthy or permanent life in death. For Le Fanu and Stoker, both members of the Protestant Anglo-Irish ruling class of nineteenth-century Ireland, these legends were at once local folklore and metaphors for their class's anxieties about the unhyphenated Irish, who were emerging from centuries of suppression to demand political and economic power. The Anglo-Irish feared intermarriage with the Irish, which would lead to racial degeneration, and the loss of power which would inevitably follow letting the Irish gain ownership of land. These anxieties underlie such works as *Carmilla* and *Dracula*.

The most conspicuous work of vampire fiction between *The Vampyre* and Le Fanu's *Carmilla* is *Varney the Vampire, or, The Feast of Blood* by either James Malcolm Rymer or Thomas Peckett Prest, published serially in the early 1840s and in collected form in 1847. Like Ruthven, Carmilla, and Dracula, Varney is an aristocrat. He establishes the convention that young women are most likely to attract vampires when in deshabille and apparently tucked up safely in their beds at night. We first encounter Flora Bannerworth in her antique bed 'hung with heavy silk and damask furnishing; nodding feathers are at its corners – covered with dust are they, and they lend a funereal aspect to the room' (Prest, *Varney*, Vol. 1, p. 2). Her 'neck and bosom that would have formed a study for the rarest sculptor that ever Providence gave genius to, were half disclosed . . . one shoulder is entirely visible.' The rare opportunity to read descriptions of young women in a state of near undress seems to have been an attractive feature of vampire fiction. The original illustrator of *Carmilla* shows Laura asleep, her breasts highlighted and very prominent, her nightdress so thin that breast and nipple are plainly visible – and Carmilla apparently reaching to seize and fondle a breast, while Laura's father is rushing in, his naked sword at the ready. When Van Helsing begins to open Lucy's coffin, it seems 'to be as much an affront to the dead as it would have been to have stripped off her clothing in her sleep whilst living' (Stoker, *Dracula*, p. 197). The comment, by equating the two acts, makes the opening of the coffin a sexual assault, as does Margaret Trelawny's objection to the unswathing of Queen Tera's mummy in Stoker's *The Jewel of Seven Stars* (1903) – another tale of the Undead: '''All you men. . .! And in the glare of light!''' (Stoker, *Jewel*, p. 239). When the mummy is unswathed, and 'lay completely nude before us', the male narrator feels 'a rush of shame . . . It was not right that we should be there, gazing with irreverent eyes on such unclad beauty: It was indecent . . . And yet the white wonder of that beautiful form was something to dream of' (ibid., p. 245).

Does any nineteenth-century British or American writer *not* dealing with vampires and the Undead ever describe a woman in this sensual and provocative way? How did it become an acceptable convention of vampire fiction? Perhaps partly because the writers and their readers sensed that mythic nexus of sex and death, prurience and terror, which underlies all such fictions. But we can also speculate that the supernatural or ghostly aspect seemed to sanitise the strongly sensual content. Though sexual themes are almost blatantly present, they are somehow veiled by the fact that, after all, Dracula is not really a sexually active male but something else, something partly unreal as well as Undead; Carmilla and Lucy act like sexually active and aggressive women, but they too are ultimately unreal, and therefore descriptions of their activities are implicitly licensed.

Varney the Vampire also establishes several other conventions of the vampire genre. Though Flora Bannerworth eventually escapes, Varney attempts other victims in the course of this almost unreadable novel's 220 chapters. One of them, Clara Crofton, does become a vampire, to be exhumed and penetrated with what is to become the obligatory stake:

> The blacksmith shuddered as he held the stake in an attitude to pierce the body . . . at length . . . he thrust it with tremendous force through the body and the back of the coffin.
>
> The eyes of the corpse opened wide – the hands were clenched, and a shrill, piercing shriek came from the lips – a shriek that was answered by as many as there were persons present . . . (Prest, *Varney*, Vol. 2, p. 843)

Varney seems to introduce the notion that vampires' victims become vampires themselves into British vampire lore, and, like Dracula later, craves to '"make humanity a slave to me"' (Prest, *Varney*, Vol. 1, pp. 71 and 154). He also unexpectedly reveals a conscience, a tendency to remorse and hints of a potentially better self – he eventually destroys himself – which foreshadows that 'look of peace' (Stoker, *Dracula*, p. 377) that passes over the faces of Dracula and his female vampires when they are destroyed and so released.

Though these fictions clearly equate sex and death, and establish the conventions of vampire fiction which Le Fanu and Stoker are to use most successfully, they do not prepare us for a remarkable shift that takes place with *Carmilla* (1871–2) and thereafter persists in vampire stories and related stories of the Undead. Lord Ruthven and Sir Francis Varney were straightforwardly heterosexual, cold in pursuit of beautiful and passive young women. *Carmilla* turns the sleeping beauties of earlier fictions into sexually aggressive women, who sometimes pursue men but also clearly display homoerotic tendencies, and therefore resonate at an even deeper level of sexual anxiety than the male predators of Polidori and Rymer/Prest. Even in *Dracula*, despite the apparent preponderance of heterosexual rape, this homoerotic aspect is predominant, and it is also central to Stoker's subsequent use of the vampire and related themes.

We have already observed Carmilla's eager seduction of Laura, a daytime activity which is supplemented by nocturnal invasions of Laura's bedroom to suck her blood. Carmilla's other recorded victims – a peasant girl and General Spielsdorf's daughter – are also female. As the story ends – it has been written by Laura for the casebook of Doctor Hesselius, who reappears as Stoker's Van Helsing – Laura is still half infatuated with Carmilla:

. . . to this hour the image of Carmilla returns to memory with ambiguous alternations – sometimes the playful, languid, beautiful girl; sometimes the writhing fiend I saw in the ruined church; and often from a reverie I have started, fancying I heard the light step of Carmilla at the drawingroom door. (Le Fanu, *Carmilla*, p. 339)

The catalogue of themes that Maurice Richardson found in *Dracula* – 'a kind of incestuous, necrophilous, oral-anal-sadistic all-in wrestling match' (Richardson, p. 427) – is by no means exhaustive. Richardson emphasised the Oedipus complex, while other critics have focused on incest (Twitchell), feminine sexuality (Griffin, Roth), fascism (Wasson), or homosexuality (Craft). Daniel Farson, Stoker's grand-nephew and biographer doubts 'if Bram realised the homosexual implications of Whitman's concept of idyllic boy-love' (Farson, p. 22). Stoker admired Whitman, but urged him to excise certain passages from *Leaves of Grass* in order to reach a wider public (Ludlam, p. 74), which certainly implies that he understood the book very well. 'I doubt if he recognised the lesbianism in *Carmilla* . . .', Farson adds, 'and I am sure he was unaware of the sexuality inherent in *Dracula*' (Farson, p. 22). This is highly unlikely. Stoker was a man of the world moving in London literary and theatrical circles at a time when prostitution was highly visible, the sexual and personal rights and needs of women were a matter of debate – Lucy and Mina in *Dracula* tease one another about the emancipated 'New Woman' (pp. 88–9) – and London was rocked by the trial of Oscar Wilde (1895), and the earlier Cleveland Street Scandal (1889), which featured a homosexual brothel catering to the aristocracy. Stoker could not have been unaware that he had larded *Dracula* with virtually every form of unacceptable sex and evaded censure at a time when Zola's English publisher was imprisoned for indecency and Havelock Ellis's clinical studies of sexual behaviour were banned.

Stoker acknowledged his debt to *Carmilla* with an act of homage intended to serve as the first chapter of *Dracula*, but removed at his publisher's advice, presumably because it anticipated too much of what was to come. The reader of *Dracula* first meets Jonathan Harker at Budapest, on 3 May, on his way to Dracula's castle. But Stoker originally intended us to meet him a little earlier, near Munich on May Eve – Walpurgisnacht, when evil spirits are abroad. Harker foolishly visits an abandoned village and eventually finds himself at the tomb of 'Countess Dolingen of Gratz in Styria' (Stoker, *Dracula's Guest*, p. 9), a suicide and presumably a vampire. Dracula himself, in the form of a grey wolf and a well-timed telegram, has to rescue him. The Countess's address and nature strongly associate her with Carmilla, who is also from near Gratz in Styria.

This early glimpse of Carmilla's avatar is the first note of female predominance in *Dracula*. All the vampires in the book are women except for Dracula, and even he has a feminine ending to his name (Dracul or Drakul would be the nominative form; Dracula, 'of the dragon', is genitive). Though he is the antagonist, he is rarely present in the text, from which he is displaced first by the three sister vampires at the castle, then by Lucy as she first mimics the vampire by receiving constant blood transfusions which are specifically described as sexual acts, until she becomes an aggressively sexual vampire herself. '"Young miss is bad, very bad"', Van Helsing exclaims during her illness. '"She wants blood, and blood she must have or die"' (Stoker, *Dracula*, p. 121). When Seward gives her blood, Van Helsing warns him that any knowledge of the act would frighten her fiancé 'and enjealous him, too' (ibid., p. 128). After Lucy's funeral, Van Helsing is moved to grim and uncontrollable laughter when he remembers how Arthur – Lucy's fiancé – had declared '"that the transfusion of his blood to her veins had made her truly his bride . . . If so that, then what about the others?"' (ibid., p. 176). Van Helsing knows that 'the blood of four strong men' (ibid., p. 151) has entered Lucy. '"Then this so sweet maid is a polyandrist"', he points out, '"and me, with my poor wife dead to me, but alive by Church's law, though no wits, all gone – even I, who am faithful husband to this now-no-wife, am bigamist"' (ibid., p. 176).

When we first meet Lucy she is excitedly telling Mina – by letter – about her admirers, and her preference for Arthur Holmwood: '"I wish I were with you, dear, sitting by the fire undressing, as we used to sit; and I would try to tell you what I feel"' (ibid., p. 55). A mere page later she has received '"THREE proposals in one day!"' (ibid., p. 56): from Dr Seward, who '"kept playing with a lancet in a way that made me nearly scream"' and so foreshadows Dracula's penetration of Lucy and her numerous transfusions; from Quincey Morris, '"I couldn't help feeling a sort of exultation that he was number two in one day"'; and finally from Arthur. '"Why can't they let a girl marry three men, or as many as want her, and save all this trouble?"' she asks (ibid., p. 59). In the course of the story, Lucy 'marries' not three men but five: her three suitors, Van Helsing, and Dracula himself. She leaves each of them limp and exhausted, except for Dracula, who exhausts her. Until she dies, and afterwards as a vampire, Lucy is insatiable, her vampire state a kind of nymphomania. '''I have an appetite like a cormorant, am full of life, and sleep well''' (ibid., p. 106), she writes Mina, after a month of Dracula's attentions.

The Lucy/Dracula liaison keeps the plot tidy by limiting the cast: the friendship of Lucy and Mina is a way of connecting Jonathan Harker's adventures in Transylvania and Dracula's activities in England. But Lucy has certain traits which presumably attract Dracula from afar, as a female insect in heat can signal males over a wide area. At Whitby, where she first meets him, her favourite promenade is the graveyard, her favourite seat above a suicide's grave. She has a history of walking in her sleep, and that is how she first visits the vampire, passing through the nocturnal streets in her nightgown as later she is to walk abroad at night in her shroud; her first nocturnal tryst with Dracula makes Mina anxious about Lucy's 'reputation' (ibid., p. 92). After death she becomes, quite literally, a nocturnal streetwalker. If she plays with the idea of marrying three men, Dracula has three women already, the trio of female vampires he has left behind. Dracula clearly recognises and arouses in her a sexuality which is not so much latent as repressed. When that sexuality reveals its insatiability, her first four 'husbands' combine to penetrate her in a collective effort with the phallic stake. Beside her coffin, Van Helsing delicately suggests that Arthur, as her fiancé, should have the privilege of driving in the stake, and hands it to him with a hammer:

Then he struck with all his might.
The Thing in the coffin writhed; and a hideous, blood-curdling screech came from the opened red lips. The body shook and quivered and twisted in wild contortions; the sharp white teeth clamped together till the lips were cut and the mouth was smeared with a crimson foam. But Arthur never faltered. He looked like a figure of Thor as his untrembling arm rose and fell, driving deeper and deeper the mercy-bearing stake, whilst the blood from the pierced heart welled and spurted up around it. His face was set, and high duty seemed to shine through it. (ibid., p. 216)

Though Arthur drives the stake, it is Van Helsing, the self-described bigamist, who is the active force in quelling Lucy's insatiable lust. He is in a sense Dracula's alter ego, the leader of the crusaders opposing the vampire and the only one who fully understands the vampire nature. In his own way, he is as ruthless as Dracula. And, with Dracula and Mina Harker, he is part of an emotional triangle which transcends the book's marital loyalties. He, rather than Jonathan Harker, is Dracula's rival for Mina, after she replaces Lucy as female protagonist about half way through the novel. He frequently praises her – '''Ah, that wonderful Madame Mina! She has man's brain – a brain that a man should have were he much gifted – and woman's heart''' (ibid., p. 234) – and is determined to win her back after Dracula has violated her and made her 'Unclean'. Together they organise the attack on Dracula, Van Helsing supplying the supernatural weapons and information, Mina organising the various diaries, letters and newspaper clippings which track Dracula's activities and therefore become a danger to him – as he realises when he follows his rape of Mina by attempting to destroy those records. '''. . . He made rare hay''' of Dr Sewards study, Arthur reports. '''All the manuscript had been burned, and the blue flames were flickering amongst the white ashes; the cylinders of your phonograph too were thrown on the fire, and the wax had helped the flames''' (ibid., p. 285; Dr Seward dictates his diary into an early phonograph, which uses wax cylinders rather than discs). While Van Helsing controls the pursuit, Mina controls the narrative, which makes her in a sense a representative of Stoker himself within the novel.

Dracula is able to enter Mina's mind once he has seduced her. But her role as his 'wife' also means that she can enter his consciousness and report his movements in a limited way. Van Helsing establishes a regular ritual of hypnotising her, a more subtle form of penetration than Dracula's. Her body and soul become the arena of a struggle between the Professor and the vampire until Dracula is destroyed, and his mark vanishes from Mina's brow.[4]

Stoker, who was of Dutch ancestry, made Van Helsing Dutch. He gave him his own name, Abraham (ibid., p. 112). He also gave him his own red hair (ibid., p. 182; for Stoker's 'reddish hair', see Farson, p. 232). Van Helsing is an idealised self-portrait and perhaps there is a personal agenda that partly shapes the events and attitudes of the story. We know that Van Helsing is trapped in a marriage that is only nominal, '''my poor wife dead to me''' (Stoker, *Dracula*, p. 176).

Farson indicates that Stoker was in a similar position, quoting Stoker's granddaughter's belief that Stoker's wife 'refused to have sex with Bram' (Farson, p. 214) after the birth of their only child in 1879. He also tells us that Stoker died of tertiary syphilis, contracted 'possibly as early as the year of *Dracula*, 1897' (ibid., p. 234) presumably from prostitutes after Florence Stoker ceased to permit sexual intercourse.

Stoker partly portrays himself as Mina, who has organised the story into a coherent narrative: 'it is due to her energy and brains and foresight that the whole story is put together in such a way that every point tells' (Stoker, *Dracula*, pp. 247–8). Her 'Unclean' mark is his disease. And he also portrays himself as the night-prowling vampire, the prostitutes he encountered as the 'carnal and unspiritual' (ibid., p. 214) voluptuous vampire women, creatures of the night. They are at once tempting and abhorrent, as they are to Jonathan Harker when he encounters them in the castle:

> In the moonlight opposite me were three young women, ladies by their dress and manner . . . All three had brilliant white teeth, that shone like pearls against the ruby of their voluptuous lips. There was something about them that made me uneasy, some longing and at the same time some deadly fear. I felt in my heart a wicked, burning desire that they would kiss me with those red lips . . . The fair girl advanced and bent over me till I could feel the movement of her breath upon me. Sweet it was in one sense, honey-sweet, and sent the same tingling through the nerves as her voice, but with a bitter underlying the sweet, a bitter offensiveness, as one smells in blood . . . The fair girl went on her knees and bent over me, fairly gloating. There was a deliberate voluptuousness which was both thrilling and repulsive . . . the skin of my throat began to tingle . . . I closed my eyes in a languorous ecstasy and waited – waited with beating heart. (ibid., pp. 37–8)

But if Stoker is also, and more obviously, Van Helsing, he portrays himself as the leader of a group who successfully destroy such women, re-enacting, with a mixture of moral outrage and prurience, the 1888 murders of Whitechapel prostitutes attributed to Jack the Ripper. The staking of Lucy and the other vampire women are at once fantasies of total sexual power and of sexual revenge. The vampires, spreading 'corruption' and 'infection' are a version of the diseased prostitutes presumably responsible for Stoker's illness, which he knew would destroy him. In describing them, Stoker at once delights in their voluptuous and uninhibited sexuality, their 'ribald coquetry' (ibid., p. 39) and revenges himself upon them by destroying them.

Stoker's attitudes may be based on personal experience and resentment, but they perhaps also echo or at least portray the anxieties of his male contemporaries faced with the 'New Woman' and her demand for social and sexual privileges which had been traditionally reserved for men. These anxieties, however, are but the surface agitation which indicate deeper and more turbulent currents in Stoker's novel. To the lesbian themes of *Carmilla*, he adds a gallery of sexual ambiguities connected with the duality of sex and death. These are marked in *Dracula* and are clearly present in other supernatural fictions of the period which resemble *Dracula* in the treatment of women's sexuality and in combining that theme with the myth of the sexually active Undead: H. Rider Haggard's *She* (1887), Arthur Machen's *The Great God Pan* (1890), the short stories 'Amour Dure' and 'Oke of Okehurst, or, the Phantom Lover' by 'Vernon Lee' (Viola Paget), which appear in her *Hauntings* (1890), Henry James's *The Turn of the Screw* (1898), and three later Stoker novels, *The Jewel of Seven Stars* (1903), *The Lady of the Shroud* (1909), and *The Lair of the White Worm* (1911). Taken together, these fictions enable us to explore the fascination with sexually aggressive women and the sexual ambiguities available in miscegenation between the living and the Undead for the supernatural writers of the period.

The relationship between Mina and Lucy only hints at a potentially lesbian current running between them. They are mutually affectionate, and Mina struggles to keep Lucy from the vampire when he first attacks, though she does not understand what threatens Lucy. Her abandonment of Lucy to attend and then marry Jonathan Harker leaves Lucy more vulnerable and contributes to the latter's death. After Lucy's death, Mina in a sense becomes Lucy. Lucy's suitors all transfer their loyalties to her. She becomes, as Dracula reminds her, '"their best beloved one"' as well as '"flesh of my flesh; blood of my blood; kin of my kin"' (Stoker, *Dracula*, p. 288). The child she eventually bears is named for Lucy's three suitors, Jonathan Harker, and Van Helsing. If Lucy has five husbands, and Dracula five wives, Mina has six husbands, the five crusaders and Dracula. Her son is born a year after the defeat of Dracula, on 'the same day as that on which Quincey Morris died', Harker tells us (ibid., p. 378) – but he does not add that the boy is also born on the anniversary of Dracula's final death. Mina's displacement of Lucy points to the affinity between them, and is a kind of possession. Later, near Dracula's castle, the three women vampires materialise to smile at Mina and speak to her in the seductive tones they used on Jonathan, 'those so sweet tingling tones that Jonathan said were of the intolerable sweetness of the water-glasses: — "Come, sister. Come to us. Come! Come!"' (ibid., p. 367).

Though *She* – Haggard always italicises the pronoun – is clearly a New Woman, ruling over a matriarchy where women choose their husbands, and plans to overthrow Queen Victoria to seize political power in England (Haggard, *She*, pp. 192–3), she is sexually ambiguous only in her apparent self-sufficiency. *She* is not a vampire, but she is Undead or at least undying until her dramatic end. *She* is sexually aggressive, and necrophiliac. She lives in a tomb and sleeps beside the embalmed corpse of her long dead lover. Her clothes are gauzy and transparent, and she removes them entirely to bathe 'naked in the naked fire . . . I would give half my remaining time upon this earth thus to see her once again' (ibid., p. 220).

Her successors are more ambiguous. Machen's Helen Vaughan/ Mrs Herbert/Mrs Beaumont has been engendered by the god of lust during a mysterious and blasphemous experiment. She is apparently steeped in all 'nameless infamies' (Machen, *Tales*, Vol. 1, p. 58) before her final enforced dissolution, when a witness sees her 'form waver from sex to sex, dividing itself from itself, and then again reunited. Then I saw the body descend to the beasts whence it ascended. . .' (ibid., p. 65). Vernon Lee's Medea da Carpi is another of the Undead, able to seduce and destroy a young Polish scholar three centuries after her own death. To love Medea – allegedly 'worse than her namesake of Colchis' (Summers, p. 271) – is to die. She contrives the deaths of five lovers before her own execution and, appropriately enough, manifests herself to her nineteenth-century victim in the long abandoned church of San Giovanni Decollato – 'the decapitated, or as they call him here, decollated John the Baptist' (ibid., p. 278). The church contains 'a picture of the daughter of Herodias dancing, upon the altar' (ibid., p. 281); if all these writers draw upon Geraldine ('Christabel'), Lamia, and Ligeia for their fatal and undying women, Vernon Lee probably also owes something to Gustave Moreau's 'Salomé Dancing' (1876) and to Flaubert's 'Herodias' (1877). Medea's latest conquest describes himself as:

wedded to history, to the Past, to women like Lucrezia Borgia . . .
or that Medea da Carpi, for the present . . . Were it only possible
to meet a woman of that extreme distinction of beauty, of that
terribleness of nature, even if only potential, I do believe I could
love her, even to the Day of Judgment . . . The possession of a
woman like Medea is a happiness too great for a mortal man; it
would turn his head . . . no man must survive long who conceives
himself to have a right over her; it is a kind of sacrilege. And only
death, the willingness to pay for such happiness by death, can at
all make a man worthy of being her lover; he must be willing to
love and suffer and die. This is the meaning of her device –
'Amour Dure – Dure Amour'. The love of Medea da Carpi cannot
fade, but the lover can die; it is a constant and a cruel love. (ibid.,
pp. 268, 270)

Once Medea has used him as the instrument of her supernatural
revenge across time, she kills him, as the vampire kills. He too will
become a pale loiterer at the scene of his brief and fatal infatuation,
and so pass into a kind of half-life. Medea herself disdains all men.

Medea is a kind of vampire and sexually self-sufficient. Vernon
Lee treats the protagonist of 'Oke of Okehurst' more ambiguously.
Alice Oke resembles and is possessed by her seventeenth-century
ancestress and namesake, who encouraged a lover, then helped her
husband to murder him. The modern Alice disdains her husband
and apparently avoids sexual intercourse with him. Before the
house stands 'a huge oak, short, hollow, with wreathing, blasted,
black branches, upon which only a handful of leaves shook'
(Summers, p. 292). The condition of the oak, and the oak/Oke pun,
hints at castration, as does the decollation element in 'Amour Dure'.
We are not surprised that Dracula is eventually decapitated – Stoker
avoids the perhaps redundant phallic stake in quelling him – but the
decapitation of Lucy, which ends her sexuality, is another hint at her
sexual ambiguity.

The earlier Alice Oke shot her lover as he and her husband
attacked each other with their swords. When she did so, she was
dressed as a man and asserted control over a masculine encounter in
a transparently masculine way. The two Alices seem to inhabit some
private realm from which men are excluded, and eventually the
modern Alice appears in her ancestress's masculine dress. Her
jealous husband finally shoots her, to reclaim his own sense of
masculine control.

As the only woman writer in this group, Vernon Lee is of particular interest. Unlike her male contemporaries, and certain predecessors of her own sex – Mrs Henry Wood, Mary Elizabeth Braddon – she is less vindictive toward her sexually aggressive women. Apart from leaving a Jamesian loophole – in both stories, the male protagonist may be hallucinating – she hints that these women are essentially a law unto themselves and must be recognised as such. They are destroyed by men who fear them and cannot understand them.

Henry James was always well aware of his lesser contemporaries and their activities, and his much more subtle treatment of sexual aggression and sexual ambiguities in *The Turn of the Screw* retains and yet transcends tensions already present in *Carmilla* and *Dracula*. The governess's description of a posthumous and intense relationship between Peter Quint and Miles, Miss Jessel and Flora, invites, or at least permits, us to see those relationships as vampiric and homoerotic; Dracula, after all, is a child molester, and so is Lucy. If the screw be turned by describing *two* haunted children and *two* ghosts, it is turned again by introducing a haunted governess, whose own sexual anxieties are fed by her romantic excitement about her employer and her infatuation with both children. We can resolve the long debate about the supernatural or hallucinatory nature of what the governess sees if we believe the children and Mrs Grose when they deny that they have seen the ghosts. The governess alone sees them, for they have come only to her. They are a response to her sexual eagerness, Quint as a vampiric or demon lover, Miss Jessel as at once a rival and a warning of what the consequences of yielding to Quint will be. There is something unsavoury about the governess's excitement over the children, Miles especially, and that excitement summons the ghosts, who presumably achieved or attempted sexual relationships with the children, just as Lucy Westenra's wish for three husbands summons Dracula. It is not the governess's veracity that is at issue, it is her voracity.

Stoker's repeated use of marriage with the Undead in three novels subsequent to *Dracula* indicates the hold that the theme had upon him. In each novel the vampire figure is a woman and, in two of these novels, she preys upon women. They are Lucy's daughters, not Dracula's. Queen Tera, in *The Jewel of the Seven Stars*, has rebelled against a masculine priesthood in Eleventh Dynasty Egypt. They have tried to deny her the right to rule, and to protect herself she has become an adept in 'real magic – "black" magic; not the magic of the temples, which . . . was of the harmless or "white" order' (Stoker, *Jewel*, p. 140). The paintings in her tomb emphasise

> the fact that she, though a Queen, claimed all the privileges of kingship and masculinity. In one place she was pictured in man's dress . . . In the following picture she was in female dress, but still wearing the Crowns of Upper and Lower Egypt, while the discarded male raiment lay at her feet. (ibid., p. 140)

She also spent a month alive in the tomb, 'swathed and coffined and left as dead', perhaps a dress rehearsal, for she is still not exactly dead. She is entombed with certain magic instruments and formulae by which she will bring about her own resurrection in the distant future, when the power of the priests – who have cursed her throughout eternity – is ended. Carmilla and Lucy Westenra have been dispatched into real death from which they cannot return by men combined into a self-ordained priesthood; Queen Tera will avoid such officiousness. In creating the situation, Stoker suggests that he did understand some of the issues recent feminist critics have raised about the staking of Lucy.

But if Tera has evaded final death, she is also apparently unwilling to undergo premature resurrection, or to come back to life under male auspices. She wreaks a terrible revenge over the centuries on several invaders of her tomb, who disturb her arrangements. When the archaeologist Trelawny transfers her mummy and tomb to England, he assembles, like Van Helsing, a gang of four men to be present in her tomb, unwrap her mummy until she is naked, and then utilise her equipment and rituals to resurrect her. He wishes to use the Queen: she will instruct him in the lore of the ancients. Trelawny's mixture of science and superstition and his learning make him a version of Van Helsing. His associates, like Van Helsing's, include a doctor and a lawyer, and the doctor's name – Winchester – recalls Quincey Morris's predilection for Winchester rifles.

When *The Jewel of the Seven Stars* was republished in 1912, Stoker's publishers asked him to change the ending 'to provide a happier denouement' (Ludlam, p. 128). He did so, and subsequent reprints have usually used that altered text, in which the experiment fails, reducing the Queen to a little heap of dust; Trelawny and his colleagues are briefly overcome by mysterious fumes, but soon recover, and the novel ends happily with the narrator's marriage to Trelawny's daughter, Margaret.

Only the narrator survives in the original (1903) version, but the
Queen has obviously come alive as planned, and made her escape,
destroying those males who took it upon themselves to rouse her
and dared to look upon her naked. In both versions, she has long
since taken possession of Margaret, who is her double, wears her
jewellery, and was born on the day Trelawny first entered the
Queen's tomb. The 1912 version hints that the Queen is somehow
fused with Margaret and has abandoned her old imperiousness and
hatred of men for love and domesticity in nineteenth-century
England, but in the earlier version, Margaret too is destroyed; the
Queen has entered her for a time in order to oversee certain
arrangements, then kills her when she has no further use for her.
Though the Queen disdains men, she has been buried with a
marriage robe, presumably a hint at intended posthumous sexual
activity; the possession of Margaret implies that this will be ruthlessly homoerotic.

In *Dracula*, Jonathan Harker and Van Helsing successfully resist
the allure of the beautiful women vampires, though they are strongly
attracted. The hero of *The Lady of the Shroud* yields. '. . . If we find out
that Mina must be a vampire in the end', Jonathan Harker writes in
his diary, 'then she shall not go into that unknown and terrible land
alone.' He too will become a vampire. 'I suppose it is thus that in old
times one vampire meant many; just as their hideous bodies could
only rest in sacred earth, so the holiest love was the recruiting
sergeant for their ghastly ranks' (Stoker, *Dracula*, p. 297). When
Rupert Sent Leger meets the Lady in Eastern Europe, he falls in love
with her despite – perhaps partly because of – her macabre dress,
cold touch, and nocturnal habits; much is made of the freedom with
which she moves about and visits him, activities hardly possible for
a conventional Edwardian young lady. Though he sees her by day
asleep in her glass-topped coffin, and his second-sighted aunt tells
him she has seen in vision his marriage with a woman in the garb of
the dead, he decides in hell's despite to go through a marriage
ceremony with her at midnight in an empty church. We are literally
in Dracula territory: Rupert meets the Lady in the Balkan castle he
has inherited, and her title – *voivodina* – is the feminine form of
Dracula's local title, voivode (ibid., p. 240). Rupert is also a trained
psychic researcher, well aware of vampires and their habits. That
the Lady is not really dead but masquerading as a vampire for not
very convincing political reasons, is beside the point, as is most of
the absurd plot. When Rupert marries her, he is pretty sure she is a

vampire, but he eagerly goes through with the ceremony, stirred deeply by her beauty, habits, and informal dress and behaviour. He enters into the bond that the crusaders of *Dracula* abhor.

If the destruction of Lucy represents Stoker's fury at the prostitutes who had infected him, and perhaps simultaneously at the unavailable wife for whom they substituted, Sent Leger's marriage with an apparent vampire hints at an acceptance of ambiguous ladies of the night. But with *The Lair of the White Worm*, Stoker again becomes the outraged male determined to exterminate aggressive and ambiguous feminine sexuality. The novel is at times nearly incoherent (both *The Lady of the Shroud* and *The Lair of the White Worm* are also severely and misleadingly truncated in modern reprints). But for all its incoherence, it is clearly about women who threaten both by their sexuality and by their ambiguity. Lady Arabella is possessed by, and so embodies, the Great White Worm, which is at once masculine and feminine: a phallus that dwells deep inside a hole. She has become the Worm's more socially acceptable manifestation after being bitten by a snake in a grove near her ancestral home. Now snakes flee from her, but she fears the snake-killing mongoose. She carries, and uses, a revolver. Her home is at Diana's Grove, a spot named by the Romans who recognised it as sacred to an ancient local power they connect with Diana – a goddess of moonlight, chaste but aggressive, who neither wants nor needs men. Carmilla, *She*, Medea da Carpi, Machen's Vaughan/Beaumont, Lucy Westenra and the three vampire women at Dracula's castle, and the Lady of the Shroud are all frequently ill met by moonlight. Lady Arabella, as Worm, has lived for centuries, like the vampire. She wears the now predictable white garments, at once ceremental and bridal, provocative and repellent:

> She was certainly good to look at in herself, and her dress alone was sufficient to attract attention. She was clad in some kind of soft white stuff, which clung close to her form, showing to the full every movement of her sinuous figure. She was tall and exceedingly thin. Her eyes appeared to be weak, for she wore large spectacles which seemed to be of green glass. Certainly in the centre they had the effect of making her naturally piercing eyes of a vivid green. She wore a close-fitting cap of some fine fur of dazzling white. Coiled round her white throat was a large necklace of emeralds, whose profusion of colour quite outshone the green of her spectacles – even when the sun shone on them. Her

voice was very peculiar, very low and sweet, and so soft that the dominant note was of sibilation. Her hands, too, were peculiar – long, flexible, white, with a strange movement as of waving gently to and fro. (Stoker, *Lair* (1911) pp. 31–2)

Arabella tears a mongoose apart with her bare hands, hurls a voodoo practitioner into the hole, kills a young woman by exerting psychic energy, and tries to capture a male victim.[5]

The awkwardness and incoherence of *The Lair of the White Worm* give away the novel's central sexual anxieties: not only fear of sexually aggressive women, and perhaps of all women, but especially fear of a woman who aggressively seeks and uses men, and who also represents a sexual threat to other women. Stoker's hero – who is suggestively named Adam – destroys Arabella and her Worm by lowering dynamite into her hole in enormous quantities. A fortuitous lightning bolt does the rest. The hole erupts with foul substances, as Stoker tells us in a passage that draws on all his considerable resources of bad taste:

At short irregular intervals the hell-broth in the hole seemed as if boiling up. It rose and fell again and turned over, showing in fresh form much of the nauseous detail which had been visible earlier. The worse parts were the great masses of the flesh of the monstrous Worm, in all its red and sickening aspect. Such fragments had been bad enough before, but now they were infinitely worse . . . the whole mass seemed to have become all at once corrupt! The whole surface of the fragments, once alive, was covered with insects, worms, and vermin of all kinds. The sight was horrible enough, but, with the awful smell added, was simply unbearable. The Worm's hole appeared to breathe forth death in its most repulsive forms. (ibid., p. 190)

This may record Stoker's final revulsion against women as the proximate source of the disease which he knew was killing him. His Adam destroys at once Eve and the Serpent, who are seen as one, a notion that sends a lurid glare back over Stoker's own earlier vampire fiction and the other vampire fictions of the period, with their Undead, insatiable, sexually aggressive female protagonists.

Not all these fictions present literal vampires, undying drinkers of blood, but they do employ women who live beyond the natural allotment of time and use their extreme longevity to pursue sexual conquests, as the presumably related meanings of vamp and vampire indicate. Furthermore, these Undead women reveal sexual ambiguities that make them doubly threatening. While their sexual aggressiveness toward male-victims violates the conventions of the period, that heterosexual aggressiveness is frequently combined with hints of lesbian tendencies, which the age found even more profoundly unsettling. Because the Undead is already ambiguous in her very mode of existence, and sex with the Undead is ambiguously real, the Undead invites and sustains further sexual ambiguities. Through Lucy, Dracula enters into a kind of homosexual encounter with her four human 'husbands': he takes from her the seminal blood they have given her. 'Even we four who gave our strength to Miss Lucy, it also is all to him' (Stoker, *Dracula*, p. 203), Van Helsing remarks bleakly. '"You shall be avenged in turn,"' Dracula tells Mina as he penetrates her, then forces her to drink his (but also her?) blood, '"for not one of them but shall minister to your needs"' (ibid., p. 288). Later he taunts the crusaders: '"Your girls that you all love are mine already; and through them you and others shall yet be mine – my creatures, to do my bidding and to be my jackals when I want to feed"' (ibid., p. 306).

Lucy represents a threat that is at once heterosexual and doubly homoerotic. She becomes a projection of all possible male anxieties – she and her sisters at the castle are even brutal towards children, and instead of nursing them, drain their blood. For Lucy and her ilk reflect male anxieties about men as well as anxieties about women. They are variants of that popular nineteenth-century figure, the *Doppelgänger*, or Double. The protagonists in stories about Doubles – Gogol's 'The Nose', Dostoevsky's 'The Double', Stevenson's 'Dr Jekyll and Mr Hyde' – create alternate versions of themselves who are more aggressive in every way, but are especially aggressive sexually. Their recreation of themselves as alternative male figures emphasises their inability to relate to women. So does Wilde's analogous *The Picture of Dorian Gray* (1890), though Wilde includes a not very convincing heterosexual seduction among Dorian's otherwise usually nameless sins.

The Undead women of nineteenth-century vampire fiction are Doubles who are doubly monstrous because they combine masculine sexual aggression with feminine forms. They embody a sexual threat that is at once disguised and enhanced by the supernatural threat they ostensibly represent. They threaten the body and its integrity rather than the soul. And at a deeper level they threaten the writer's – and perhaps the reader's – own sexual identity, by suggesting that women can be like men, and simultaneously suggesting that these women are primarily attracted to their own sex.

Notes

1. Freud's disciple, Ernest Jones, discusses the sexual aspects of the vampire legend at length in *On the Nightmare* (1931), though he does not discuss vampire fictions. '. . . The latent content of the belief yields plain indications of most kinds of sexual perversions,' Jones declares, 'and . . . the belief assumes various forms according as this or that perversion is more prominent' (Jones, *Nightmare*, p. 98). Citing mostly German sources, Jones points out that 'Vampires always visit relatives first, particularly their married partners . . . Widows can become pregnant as the result of such visits' (ibid., p. 102). He relates this to 'sexual guilt . . . an unconscious guiltiness . . . this unconscious guiltiness owes its origin to infantile incestuous wishes' (ibid., pp. 102–3). 'The belief is, in fact, only an elaboration of that in the Incubus, and the essential elements of both are the same – repressed desires and hatreds derived from early incest conflicts . . . hate and guilt play a far larger part in the Vampire than in the Incubus belief' (ibid., p. 130). Jones notes Freud's theory 'that morbid dread always signifies repressed sexual wishes' (ibid., p. 106), and lists legends of bloodsucking night monsters from all over the world, connecting them both with cannibalism and the 'Incubat–Succubat, two facts which alone reveal the sexual origin of the belief' (ibid., p. 116). 'The explanation of these phantasies is surely not hard,' he concludes. 'A nightly visit from a beautiful or frightful being, who first exhausts the sleeper with passionate embraces and then withdraws from him a vital fluid: all this can point only to a natural and common process, namely to nocturnal emissions accompanied with dreams of a more or less erotic nature. In the unconscious mind blood is commonly an equivalent for semen . . . in the Vampire superstition . . . the simple idea of the vital fluid being withdrawn through an exhausting love embrace is complicated by more perverse forms of sexuality, as well as by the admixture of sadism and hate' (ibid., pp. 119–20).
2. Stephen Dedalus, who must have read *Dracula*, repeatedly emphasises the sexuality of the vampire. 'Behold the handmaid of the moon,' he thinks, as he watches a woman he believes to be a prostitute. 'In sleep the wet sign calls her hour, bids her rise. Bridebed, childbed, bed of death, ghostcandled. *Omnis caro ad te veniet.* He comes, pale vampire, through storm his eyes, his bat sails bloodying the sea, mouth to her mouth's kiss' (Joyce, *Ulysses*, p. 40). Stephen is clearly recalling the *Demeter*/Whitby episode in *Dracula*. He turns his recollection into a poem:

On swift sail flaming
From storm and south
He comes, pale vampire,
Mouth to my mouth
(ibid., p. 109)

Later Stephen describes various unnatural modes of conception, in-cluding 'by potency of vampires mouth to mouth' (ibid., p. 319). In Bella Cohen's brothel, he parodies the broken English of a tout for a Paris peep-show, where one can 'see vampire man debauch nun very fresh young with *dessous troublants*' (ibid., p. 465). When Stephen's dead mother appears in the brothel, he addresses her as 'Lemur' (ibid., p. 473), that is, lamia.

3. The text printed in *Best Ghost Stories* is the text as Le Fanu revised it for *Ghost Stories and Tales of Mystery* (1851). When Vanderhausen first appeared, in the pages of the *Dublin University Magazine*, vol. 13 (May 1839), his 'mouth was writhed considerably to one side, where it opened in order to give egress to two long, discoloured fangs, which projected from the upper jaw, far below the lower lip' (*DUM*, p. 586). Though his face was 'malignant, even satanic', it did not become sensual until 1851. The other passages quoted are substantially the same in both versions. The 1839 text is reprinted in Le Fanu's *The Purcell Papers*. This was a posthumous publication, compiled from early issues of the *DUM*.

4. Van Helsing lectures at Amsterdam, where he has trained Dr Seward in new methods of treating the insane. Seward describes him as 'philosopher . . . metaphysician . . . one of the most advanced scientists of his day' (Stoker, *Dracula*, p. 112). Van Helsing himself reveres Jean Martin Charcot (1825–93): '"the great Charcot – alas that he is no more!"' (ibid., p. 191). Charcot, who worked at the Salpêtrière – which had evolved from a women's prison to a women's mental hospital – used hypnosis as a treatment for hysteria. Van Helsing also uses hypnosis, as a way of tracking Dracula through Mina's con-sciousness, but also as a kind of treatment after she has been raped by the vampire. Her physical symptom, the 'Unclean' mark on her forehead, recalls those physical symptoms of psychic origin – paralysis, loss of sensation – which troubled Charcot's patients. Freud studied with Charcot (1885–6), and translated his *Leçons du Mardi de la Salpêtrière* (1888, revised 1892) into German (1892–4). Later, Freud described Charcot as one of the three early mentors whose apparently unconsidered remarks revealed to him the sexual origins of neuroses (Freud, *History*, pp. 13–14). These remarks all had to do with sexually unsatisfied women. In view of the controversy surrounding Freud's decision that the many sexual molestations in childhood described by his early patients were fantasies, it is interesting to note that Laura is genuinely 'molested' while still a child by Carmilla, Lucy and Mina are really raped by the vampire, and the children attacked by Lucy are, despite the skepticism of the *Westminster Gazette* (Stoker, *Dracula*, pp. 177–8), telling the truth. For Freud's decision, see Janet Malcolm, *In the Freud Archives* (New York:

Knopf, 1984) and Jeffrey Moussaieff Masson, *Assault on Truth: Freud's Suppression of the Seduction Theory* (New York: Farrar, Straus & Giroux, 1984). Van Helsing's drastic 'cure' of the sexually aggressive Lucy resembles some of the brutal but medically approved treatments of women who seemed sexually over-excited, which are described in the nineteenth-century medical reports collected in Jeffrey Moussaieff Masson, *A Dark Science: Women, Sexuality, and Psychiatry in the Nineteenth Century* (New York: Farrar, Straus & Giroux, 1986).

5.   *The Lair of the White Worm* was republished in abridged form (28 chapters instead of 40) in 1925. Stoker's role, if any, in this abridged version is unclear; it may well be by another hand. This 1925 abridgement, reprinted as the 1960 Arrow text, omits a good deal, but also makes curious additions to the original text. In this version, Lady Arabella becomes the Worm after being bitten by a snake in a grove near her childhood home (Stoker, *Lair* (1960) p. 61); she kills, or tries to kill local children by biting their throats (ibid., p. 59); and she is much more breezily informal as she prepares for the male victim whose blood she is apparently to suck:

> She . . . ran down the avenue, and with her small key opened the iron door leading to the atrium . . . In the room beside the atrium, where was the well-hole, she sat down panting . . . She felt that she was excited . . . she felt that she might pause a while and rest. She lay down on a sofa close to the well-hole so that she could see it without moving when she had lit the lamp. In a state of blissful content she sank into a gentle sleep. (*Lair* (1911) pp. 295–6; the omitted matter has to do with lowering an electric wire into the hole, which destroys the lady and the Worm)

> She . . . with her key opened the iron door leading to the well-hole . . . She tore off her clothes, with feverish fingers, and in full enjoyment of her natural freedom, stretched her slim figure in animal delight. Then she lay down on the sofa – to await her victim! Edgar Caswall's life blood would more than satisfy her for some time to come. (*Lair* (1960) p. 179)

Bibliography

Bentley, C. F., 'The Monster in the Bedroom: Sexual Symbolism in Bram Stoker's *Dracula*', *Literature and Psychology*, vol. 22, no. 1 (1972) pp. 27–34.
Briggs, Julia, *Night Visitors: The Rise and Fall of the English Ghost Story* (London: Faber, 1977).
Craft, Christopher, '"Kiss Me with Those Red Lips": Gender and Inversion in Bram Stoker's *Dracula*', *Representations*, vol. 8 (1984) pp. 107–33.
Dalby, Richard, *Bram Stoker: A Bibliography of First Editions* (London: Dracula Press, 1983).
Demetrakopoulos, Stephanie, 'Feminism, Sex Role Exchanges, and Other

58 *Sex and Death in Victorian Literature*

Subliminal Fantasies in Bram Stoker's *Dracula*', *Frontiers: A Journal of Women Studies*, vol. 2, no. 3 (1977) pp. 104–13.

Farson, Daniel, *The Man Who Wrote Dracula: A Biography of Bram Stoker* (London: Michael Joseph, 1975).

Freud, Sigmund, *On the History of the Psycho-Analytic Movement*, reprinted in *Standard Edition of the Complete Psychological Works*, trans. and edited by James Strachey, Vol. 14 (London: Hogarth, 1957).

Griffin, Gail B., '"Your Girls that You All Love are Mine": *Dracula* and the Victorian Male Sexual Imagination', *International Journal of Women's Studies*, vol. 3, no. 5 (1980) pp. 454–65.

Haggard, H. Rider, *She* (1887) reprinted in *Three Adventure Novels of H. Rider Haggard* (New York: Dover, 1951).

Hennelly Jr, Mark M., '*Dracula*: the Gnostic Quest and Victorian Wasteland', *English Literature in Transition*, vol. 20, no. 1 (1977) pp. 13–26.

James, M. R., Introduction to *Ghosts and Marvels: A Selection of Uncanny Tales from Daniel Defoe to Algernon Blackwood*, edited by V. H. Collins (Oxford: Oxford University Press (World's Classics), 1924).

Jones, Ernest, *On the Nightmare* (1931) revised 1951; reprinted (New York: Liveright, 1971).

Joyce, James, *Ulysses*, edited by Hans Walter Gabler with Wolfhard Steppe and Claus Melchior (New York: Random House, 1986).

Lee, Vernon (Violet Paget), *Hauntings* (1890) second edn (London: John Lane, 1906).

Lee, Vernon, *The Snake Lady, and other stories* (New York: Grove, 1954).

Le Fanu, Joseph Sheridan, *Best Ghost Stories of J. S. Le Fanu*, edited by E. F. Bleiler (New York: Dover, 1964).

Le Fanu, Joseph Sheridan, *Carmilla* (1871–2) reprinted in *Best Ghost Stories*.

Le Fanu, Joseph Sheridan, *The Purcell Papers* (London: Bentley, 1880) reprinted (New York: Garland, 1979) three volumes.

Le Fanu, Joseph Sheridan, 'Strange Event in the Life of Schalken the Painter', *Dublin University Magazine*, vol. 13 (1839) pp. 579–91.

Ludlam, Harry, *A Biography of Dracula: The Life Story of Bram Stoker* (London: Fireside/W. Foulsham, 1962).

Machen, Arthur, 'The Great God Pan' (1890) reprinted in Machen, *Tales of Horror and the Supernatural*, Vol. 1 (New York: Pinnacle, 1971).

McCormack, W. J., *Sheridan Le Fanu and Victorian Ireland* (Oxford: Clarendon Press, 1980).

Nandris, Grigore, 'The Historical Dracula: The Theme of His Legend in the Western and Eastern Literature of Europe', *Comparative Literature Studies*, vol. 3, no. 6 (1966) pp. 367–96.

Polidori, John, *The Vampyre* (1819) reprinted in *Three Vampire Novels*, edited by E. F. Bleiler (New York: Dover, 1966).

Prest, Thomas Peckett (or James Malcolm Rymer), *Varney the Vampire, or, The Feast of Blood* (1847) reprinted (New York: Dover, 1972) two volumes.

Richardson, Maurice, 'The Psychoanalysis of Ghost Stories', *The Twentieth Century*, vol. 166 (1959) pp. 419–31.

Roth, Phyllis A., *Bram Stoker* (Boston: Twayne, 1982).

Roth, Phyllis A., 'Suddenly Sexual Women in Bram Stoker's *Dracula*', *Literature and Psychology*, vol. 27, no. 3 (1977) pp. 113–20.

Rymer, James Malcolm, *see* Prest, Thomas Peckett.

Senf, Carol A., '*Dracula*: Stoker's Response to the New Woman', *Victorian Studies*, vol. 26, no. 1 (1982) pp. 33–49.

Showalter, Elaine, 'Syphilis, Sexuality, and the Fiction of the *Fin de Siècle*', in *Sex, Politics, and Science in the Nineteenth-Century Novel* (selected papers from the English Institute, 1983–84, New Series, 10) edited by Ruth Bernard Yeazell (Baltimore: Johns Hopkins University Press, 1986).

Stoker, Bram, 'The Censorship of Fiction', *Nineteenth Century and After*, vol. 64 (1908) pp. 479–87.

Stoker, Bram, *Dracula* (1897) reprinted (New York: Oxford University Press (World's Classics), 1983).

Stoker, Bram, *Dracula's Guest, and Other Weird Stories* (London: George Routledge, 1914).

Stoker, Bram, *The Jewel of the Seven Stars* (sic) reprint of *The Jewel of Seven Stars* (1903) abridged (London: Arrow, 1962).

Stoker, Bram, *The Jewel of Seven Stars* (Scholastic Book Services, 1972); also abridged, but preserving the original ending.

Stoker, Bram, *The Lady of the Shroud* (London: William Heinemann, 1909).

Stoker, Bram, *The Lair of the White Worm* (London: William Rider, 1911).

Stoker, Bram, *The Lair of the White Worm* (London: Arrow, 1960).

Stoker, Bram, *Personal Reminiscences of Henry Irving* (1906) revised edn (London: Heinemann, 1907).

Summers, Montague, *The Vampire in Europe* (1929, New Hyde Park, NY: University Books, 1968).

Todorov, Tzvetan, *The Fantastic: A Structural Approach to a Literary Genre*, trans. Richard Howard (Ithaca, New York: Cornell University Press, 1975).

Twitchell, James B., *Dreadful Pleasure: An Anatomy of Modern Horror* (New York: Oxford University Press, 1985).

Twitchell, James B., *The Living Dead: A Study of the Vampire in Romantic Literature* (Durham, North Carolina: Duke University Press, 1981).

Wasson, Richard, 'The Politics of *Dracula*', *English Literature in Transition*, vol. 9 (1966) pp. 24–7.

4

Tennyson's Sword: From 'Mungo the American' to *Idylls of the King*

Gerhard Joseph

Henry Seidel Canby's *American Memoir* contains an extended definition of what 'Tennysonism', with respect to the sexual impulse, meant to an American at the turn of the century:

> No, the trouble was the Tennysonism of the sexular attitude, the Longfellowism of our morality. The only possible relationship between men and women that is as vital as the relationship between men or between women is the one in which even the married and bechildrened, and the faithful to their spouses, still feel a permanent possibility of sexual awakening. It does not have to be mutual, it is enough that the most settled should know that their nature is still tender, and inflammable by nature if not by will. We, in our middle age, talked to middle-aged women as if they were cinders – agreeable, yes, admirable often, interesting often, yet cinders, good for home walks and garden beds, but long emptied of fire – and like cinders they responded.[1]

In the light of such a passage, an habitual source of puzzlement for me has been the preoccupation with the work of Tennyson, a figure I have returned to again and again in print after the obligatory exercise of the dissertation. Why Tennyson? I do not think of myself as particularly 'Tennysonian', especially in view of the unattractive psychic connotations of the term which the Canby definition captures quite accurately.

By now I have come up with several answers having to do with temperamental affinities, but the germ of the explanation probably lies in a single spot of time, a memory from the day when, in taking a sophomore survey course, I first came upon Tennyson's 'Morte d'Arthur'. There, the image of Arthur's sword Excalibur arching in exquisite slow motion through the moon-drenched night as Bedivere obeys the command to return it to the Lady of the Lake seemed a moment of pure magic:

> The great brand
> Made lightnings in the splendour of the moon,
> And flashing round and round, and whirled in an arch,
> Shot like a streamer of the northern morn,
> Seen where the moving isles of winter shock
> By night, with noises of the northern sea.
> So flashed and fell the brand Excalibur:
> But ere he diot the surface, rose an arm
> Clothed in white samite, mystic, wonderful,
> And caught him by the hilt, and brandished him
> Three times, and drew him under the mere.[2]
>
> (ll.136–46)

I pause here to remember the astonishment of the first-time reader at the 'mystic, wonderful' thing he saw. But, alas, this reader can no longer just stop to admire because he aspires to the condition of critic. For better and worse, the initial untutored response has crystallised into something more complicated – not only the need to analyse the power of the image within the 'Morte d'Arthur'; nor even to experience it as a synecdoche for the rococo splendour of the *Idylls of the King* as a whole; but rather to consider its resonance within the widest Tennysonian frame, his entire corpus.

For the flashing sword was an image that fascinated Tennyson from the very beginning to the very end of his career. And I mean 'beginning' quite literally: when he was thirteen or fourteen years old, Tennyson, in the earliest of his work of which there is record, wrote a brief tale entitled 'Mungo the American'. (The Tennyson children were in the habit of composing tales in letter form, to be slipped under the vegetable dishes at dinner and to be read aloud when it was over. 'Mungo' was no doubt one of Alfred's contributions.) According to the only published account of the tale (in a manuscript now in the Berg Collection of the New York Public Library), it shows how Mungo 'found a sword, & afterwards how it came to the possession of the right owner, after the space of two years'.[3] Generally speaking, in Tennyson's youthful poetry, the martial wielding of the sword leads to unalloyed victory as heroes glory in the bloody devastation of anonymous, unnamed enemies of the tribe. Thus, the weapon addressed in 'The Old Sword' of *Poems by Two Brothers* (1827), Tennyson's first published volume, generates in its wielders 'The cry/ Of triumph's fierce delight, the shoutings of the victory,/ The thunders of the fight' (ll.5–8). In like fashion, the hero of 'The Old Chieftan' from the same volume remembers the lustrous time when he had 'chanted the bold songs of death,/ Not a page would have stayed in the hall,/ Not a lance in the rest, not a sword in the sheath,/ Not a shield on the dim grey wall' (ll.9–12). This blood-lust in the juvenilia is, of course, highly theatrical – such poems are all characterised by what W. D. Paden has called a Byronic 'mask of old age',[4] the world-weary, melancholic pose that the adolescent Tennyson adopted in an attempt to both embrace and fend off manly experience. The feudal world they invoke is entirely an arena of male comradeship and military valour, a society devoid of women. Or if women are present, they are so only as helpless and speechless 'maidens of [the] land' in need of the Old Sword's protection. In a more famous later poem which captures that chivalric ethos, 'Sir Galahad', the exemplary knight's 'good blade carves the casques of men' and 'his strength is as the strength of ten' *because* his 'heart is pure', because he has 'never felt the kiss of love,/ Nor maiden's hand in' his (ll.1–4; 19–20). An insistently non-erotic context for the sword thus makes its triumphant wielding possible, a fact that has implications for Tennysonian aggression more generally.

For it is only in such early works as 'Mungo the American' that the result of aggression is both a joyous and a lasting triumph, and even there the hero is temporarily deprived of the symbol of his masculine integrity. Usually, and certainly in the mature poetry, aggression, whether military or erotic, is full of dangers. Characters in the later work rarely allow themselves hostile actions without immediate remorse, 'passionately melancholic and authoritatively passive' victims of circumstance as they generally are.[5] Only heroes committed to larger causes seem initially exempt from feelings of guilt. Arthur's battles in the *Idylls of the King* are fought 'for the ordinance of God', the equivalent of the 'just' Crimean War to which the dead heroine sends the narrator at the conclusion of *Maud*. This flight from private aggressions into the safe anonymity of national ones would seem to be an important impulse behind Tennyson's poetry. But one is struck by the fact that the best of the military poems are accounts of or reactions to the death of the hero – an

Arthur or a Duke of Wellington – and military disasters rather than victories are usually the occasion of the poems that deal with actual battles. The most famous, 'The Charge of the Light Brigade', describing how six-hundred men perished because 'Some one had blunder'd', appears, appropriately enough, in *Maud, and Other Poems*. It is perhaps misguided to link a short work based upon an important public event with the longer one spun entirely out of the poet's imagination. Still, one is tempted to believe that Tennyson's choice of the doomed charge as a natural subject for poetic treatment indicates that he dimly appreciated the kind of experience the dead Maud is urging her lover toward in the Crimean War. (The prince in *The Princess* had been an earlier hero who had courted a public death inspired by a fiercely martial beloved: 'Yet she sees me fight', he exulted. 'Yea, let her see me fall' (V, 505–6).)

My point is that the Tennysonian sword, which in the juvenilia is merely a martial tool wielded within a world of toy feudal soldiers, becomes threateningly sensual in the later work – becomes, not only the archetypal phallus readily apparent to a post-Freudian/Jungian audience, but is even given that function quite consciously by a pre-Freudian Tennyson. The poem in which such a phallic intention expresses itself most overtly is 'Lucretius', Tennyson's attempt to out-eroticise Swinburne after the publication of *Poems and Ballads*. In Tennyson's work about the revenge of the senses upon the soaring intellect that would transcend both Venus and a human wife, the Roman artist-philosopher Lucretius is beset by a series of maddening dreams: in the second of them, the blood-drenched dictator Sulla appears to the horrified Lucretius slaughtering Roman citizens with indiscriminate abandon, his sword as the military expression of the universal chaos that the atomistic theories of the *De Rerum Natura* can in history's nightmare become. The blood he sheds becomes an obscene distortion of the myth of another 'old chieftan', Cadmus of Thebes. From the blood that Sulla sheds spring up no dragon warriors associated with the founding of Thebes, but rather:

> girls, Hetairai, curious in their art,
> Hired animalisms, vile as those that made
> The mulberry-faced Dictator's orgies worse
> Than aught they fable of the guiet Gods.
> And hands they mixt, and yell'd and round me drove
> In narrowing circles till I yell'd again
> Half suffocated. . . .

This *Walpurgisnacht* of lust, prefiguring nothing so much as the nightmare that undermines the last vestiges of control in *Death in Venice*'s Gustav von Aschenbach, leads directly to Lucretius' third dream, a vision of Helen for whom the Hetairai have prepared:

> Then, then from utter gloom stood out the breasts,
> The breasts of Helen, and hoveringly a sword
> Now over and now under, now direct,
> Pointed itself to pierce, but sank down shamed
> At all that beauty; and as I stared, a fire,
> The fire that left a roofless Ilion,
> Shot out of them, and scorch'd me that I woke.

The significance of that sword as an instrument both of martial destruction and of sexual aggression is masterfully recapitulated a few lines later in the appearance to Lucretius of a satyr pursuing an oread. Lucretius' terrified ambivalence as the nymph threatens to fling himself upon him recaptures in dramatic terms the 'twy-natured' (l.194) force of the Lucretian (and the Tennysonian?) sword:

>   such a precipitate heel,
> Fledged as it were with Mercury's ankle-wing,
> Whirls her to me – but will she fling herself
> Shameless upon me? Catch her, goat-foot! nay,
> Hide, hide them, million-myrtled wilderness,
> And cavern-shadowing laurels, hide! do I wish –
> What? – that the bush were leafless? or to whelm
> All of them in one massacre?
>
>   (ll.200–7)

The sword that hovers above Helen's breasts implies the same double impulse towards sexual indulgence and brutal massacre. But both impulses are frustrated as the sword sinks down, 'shamed at all that beauty'. The counter-thrust of fire from Helen's breasts that leaves a roofless Ilion relates the third dream back to the second: both Sulla and Helen, embodiments of a murderous carnality, destroy entire civilisations. And the swords that razed Rome and Troy are pitted by implication against the sword that founded Thebes, the weapon Cadmus used to slay the dragon.

Of course, the most famous Tennysonian sword, and again one

that is instrumental in the founding and the death of a civilisation, is Excalibur, the phallic sword that the Lady of the Lake bestows upon the king in 'The Coming of Arthur' and that she receives at the end of his life in 'The Passing of Arthur' (the poem that 'Morte d'Arthur' became in the *Idylls of the King*). To be sure, the Lady of the Lake and her sword play minimal narrative roles in the *Idylls*; like the three queens who appear at Arthur's coronation and then again to bear him off to Avilion at his passing, she is a shadowy emanation *behind* the narrative, not a foreground presence like Guinevere who triggers first the creative and then the destructive action of the plot. But in our memory (or at least in mine) the Lady of the Lake and the three queens who become her triplicated expression in Arthur's life have a more potent resonance than many a more fully realised character; and their very amorphousness, the riddling triplication of their meaning (why *three* queens? why *three* flourishes when the Lady receives the sword once more?) haunts us. They demonstrate that 'suggestive indefiniteness of vague and therefore of spiritual *effect*' which made Tennyson for (the admittedly ever extravagant) Edgar Allan Poe 'the *greatest* [poet] that ever lived'.[6] In such vagueness the Lady of the Lake and the three queens supply the supernatural distance, the diaphanous background against which the more palpable women of the poem are set; in the Helio-Arkite mythos of nineteenth-century mythographers, they form the Great Mother archetype, the 'great deep' of the Idylls from which all the male characters, if Arthur most emphatically, receive their swords and to which they must return them upon dying.

If we examine the genesis of the Lady of the Lake and the three queens in Tennyson's mind, we can trace their progress towards an ethereal indeterminacy. In his major source, Malory's *Morte d'Arthur*, the three queens are specific characters – Morgan le Fay, the queen of Northgalis, and the queen of the wastelands (XXX, vi). Characteristically, Tennyson dematerialises Malory's queens and submerges their individuality within the mystery of a collective, triadic archetype in keeping with the dreamlike mistiness of Camelot itself.

In the Welsh works that complemented Malory as sources for the *Idylls*,[7] Arthur is married in turn to three queens rather than the one that Malory allows him, each of them named 'Gwenhwyfar'. That Tennyson was aware of this tradition and meant at one point to follow it is evident from an early sketch of his allegorical intentions which Hallam Tennyson found among his father's manuscripts that mentions a Lady of the Lake and *three* Guineveres. (The first one was to represent primitive Christianity and the second Roman Catholicism.)[8] The next step in the progress of thought, recorded in one of the 1833–40 manuscript books, envisages a 'five-act' structure in which the three Guineveres have given place to one but now there are several 'Ladies of the Lake'.[9] The association of Guinevere(s) and the Lady(ies) of the Lake may have stemmed from the fact that the Welsh derivation of 'Gwenhwyfar' is 'Lady on the summit of the water' – or such at any rate was the etymological theory of George Stanley Faber, the mythographer who may have provided some of the mythic, symbolic and allegorical ideas behind the *Idylls*.[10] While Tennyson eventually compressed the three Guineveres of the Welsh tradition and the several Ladies of the Lake into single figures and replaced them with supernatural versions of Malory's three queens, the existence of interlocking female witnesses to Arthur's rise and fall indicates the transformation of Woman into an all-embracing Other upon whom a civilisation's destiny completely depends. 'The Coming of Arthur' presents three *human* queens – Ygerne, Arthur's mother; Bellicent, his sister; and Guinevere, his destructive wife – who complement the Lady of the Lake and the three phantasmagoric queens in a way that defines the inter-penetration of the natural and the supernatural worlds through the medium of woman. The God who hovers behind the *Idylls* may be literally evoked as male – he is the patriarchal 'high God' who breathes 'a secret thing' into Arthur who in turn inspires his knights.

But surely we must finally see that such an evocation of the Great Father is something of a lip-service, that Tennyson's felt belief in the *Idylls* as elsewhere is in the more substantial power of the Great Mother,[11] for it is she (the '*Isis* hid behind the veil' of *Maud*) and not the Father who bestows the talisman of man's prowess.

Thus far I have been alluding to the phallic sword in a rather old-fashioned Freudian way, as a symbolic constituent buried within the psyche's depth recoverable through dream or literary analysis of imagery.[12] It might at this point be useful to shift to a post-structuralist psychoanalytic model, one that foregrounds language and deconstructs Freud's metaphor of verticality with its psyche composed of a surface consciousness and a subconscious at the depth. To adopt a more recent Saussurean terminology, we can see that the Lady of the Lake's sword is primarily a linguistic tool, a 'privileged signifier' which operates on the level of *langue* and on the level of *parole*. For the words 'Take me' are graven on one side 'in the oldest tongue of all the world', that is, as underlying universal structure, as *langue*; while on the reverse side the words 'Cast me away' are 'written in the speech ye [Arthur] speak yourself', that is, as particular and local realisation, as *parole* ('The Coming of Arthur', ll. 300–4).

Jacques Lacan is the theorist who has given Freud's classical Oedipal formulation its most influential post-Saussurean linguistic cast. Following Freud, he accepts the thesis that the father, as the third party in the Oedipal situation, is the phallic agent whose presence obstructs the unlimited union of mother and child, a threat whose first anguished image emerges in the child's fantasy of being devoured. But Lacan diverges from Freud's 'Metaphysics of Presence' by transforming the father's presence into an absence, one which has an essentially linguistic force in the father's withholding of the power to name. As the great separater, the Father's *'nom'* (both *'le nom du père'* and *'le non du père'*, in French[13]) creates the distance along which will develop the dialectic of presences and absences, the child's speech whose initial form is based on constraints, and, finally, on the relationship of the signifier to the signified which gives rise to the structure of the child's language.

Subverting Lacan's masterful linguistic turn, his 'phallogocentricism', in the matter (with a nod of indebtedness to French feminists such as Cixoux and Irigaray), I would suggest that what Tennyson gives us in the Lady of the Lake's twin enabling messages of 'Take me' and 'Cast me away' is the Mother's *Oui* and the Mother's *Non*. For she combines the phallus-giving power of the imaginary mother (Lacan's 'phallic mother' before the child's discovery of castration) *and* the language-bestowing power Lacan attributes to the father – but now a mother's *'Oui'* rather than a father's *'Non'*. It is not the Father but the Mother tongue which now facilitates and now undermines not only the structure of the individual male psyche but that also governs the fate of an entire civilisation, Camelot.

In short, if women and women's words are largely absent from the martial world of the early Tennyson, in the *Idylls* their influence for good or ill over the Tennysonian sword is total. Man's destiny depends upon the strength of woman to sustain the 'erotic devotion'[14] that he lavishes upon her as an analogue to God. When, like the nun whose speech inspires Galahad in 'The Holy Grail', she can bear the burden of man's idealisation and remain a model of spiritual purity, she keeps him on the high road to the Spiritual City; when, like the Guinevere of the *Idylls* or Helen of 'Lucretius', she refuses to remain the untouchable object into which man tries to crystallise her, she becomes the Tennysonian fatal woman who precipitates the fall of entire civilisations. That, in brief, is the message writ on Tennyson's two-sided sword.

Notes

1.   Henry Seidel Canby, *American Memoir* (Boston: Little Brown, 1947) pp. 88–9.
2.   All quotations of Tennyson's poetry are from *The Poems of Tennyson*, edited by Christopher Ricks (London: Longman, Green, 1969).
3.   As quoted in W. D. Paden, *Tennyson in Egypt: A Study of the Imagery in His Earlier Works* (Lawrence, Kansas: University of Kansas Humanistic Studies, 1942) pp. 73–4.
4.   Paden, pp. 53–6.
5.   The phrase and generalisation are Herbert F. Tucker's in his excellent essay, 'Tennyson and the measure of Doom', *PMLA*, vol. 98 (1983) p. 14.
6.   Quoted by John Eidson, *Tennyson in America: His Reputation and Influence from 1827–1858* (Athens: University of Georgia Press, 1943) p. 43, from an unsigned review in the *Broadway Journal*, vol. 2 (29 November 1845) p. 322, confidently attributed by his biographers to Poe, the 'sole editor and proprietor' of the *Journal*.
7.   See Tom Peete Cross, 'Alfred Tennyson as a Celticist', *Modern Philology*, vol. 18 (1921) pp. 485–92.
8.   Hallam Tennyson, *Alfred Lord Tennyson: A Memoir by His Son*, 2 vols (London: Macmillan, 1897) Vol. II, p. 123.
9.   Hallam Tennyson, Vol. II, pp. 123–4.
10. Paden, p. 156.
11. See Christine Gallant, 'Tennyson's Use of the Nature Goddess in "The Hesperides", "Tithonus", and "Demeter and Persephone"', in *Victorian Poetry*, vol. 14 (1976) pp. 155–60.
12. For a useful discrimination between the two techniques, see David Gordon, 'Dream Symbolism and Literary Symbolism', *The Bucknell Review*, vol. 30 (1987) pp. 19–33.
13. For the full implications of Lacan's pun, see Michel Foucault, 'The Father's "No"', in Donald F. Bouchard (ed.) *Language, Counter-Memory, Practice: Selected Essays and Interviews*, translated by Donald Bouchard and Sherry Simon (Ithaca: Cornell University Press, 1977) pp. 68–86.
14. The term is Arthur Hallam's. See Gerhard Joseph, 'Arthur Hallam and Erotic Devotion', in *Tennysonian Love: The Strange Diagonal* (Minneapolis: University of Minnesota Press, 1969).

5

'Beckoning Death': *Daniel Deronda* and the Plotting of a Reading

Garrett Stewart

Death beds, marriage beds: often in Victorian fiction they end up interchangeable, mere formalities. By their structural role in the conventions of closure, that is, they highlight the fact that, in most novels of the period, death and sex are what happens afterwards. Sex follows marriage as death follows the scene of dying. They brook no representation except as the far threshold of what can be spoken of. With their pre-narrative counterparts in familial lineage and conception, the unenacted poles of marital consummation and death thus lay bare the fact that all narrative ends as well as begins *in medias res*. And Victorian fiction itself, not just its commentary, regularly exposes this fact in and of itself, exposits it, plays with and against the reader's anticipations of such often 'premature' finish. Yet what about the myths of perpetuation that at the same time attend these seemingly opposite modes of closure? Given the varieties of continuance figured separately by marriage and dying – on the one hand generative and generational, on the other elegiac and at times transcendental – the marked overlap in a text of these otherwise divergent last strategies may therefore be more than tautological. Such a closural overload may break open certain questions about the transactive nature of a literary reading: about what readers may be constrained to expect and await, and about their place, or emplacement, when all is done and said. When leaving off, where does a narrative leave the very attention that has sustained it? What are the readers left with – and left to? How, in other words, is a story's implied continuance beyond plot sometimes rendered as our own?

I

As conclusive a stop to the energies of Victorian narrative as is death, and often a day of reckoning and judgment in its own right, marital culmination makes by far the most prevalent and resounding appeal to the paradox of closure as renewal: the wedding bells that knell the end of plot by satisfying its original urge. Given the structural importance naturally accorded to marriage, it would certainly be no surprise to find a reader's investment in such achieved finality actually thematised within Victorian fiction – as a public taste for the written accounts of such private communions. An avid reader about marriages (or for that matter a character evincing a morbid curiosity about death) would thus tend to read our own motives in the desire for narrative fulfilment and stasis. George Eliot, far along in her last novel, stations a particularly complex instance of such a readerly urge rendered by narrative itself. Mrs Meyrick, a minor character in *Daniel Deronda*, is portrayed in passing as 'a great reader of news, from the widest-reaching politics to the list of marriages; the latter, she said, giving her the pleasant sense of finishing the fashionable novels without having read them, and seeing the heroes and heroines happy without knowing what poor creatures they were' (p. 793).[1] In her disinterested fondness for the daily litany of marital celebrations, Mrs Meyrick is addicted to the inherent euphemism of journalistic statistics or the brief reports of the society pages. She stakes her fascination precisely on culmination as closure, on the apogee of marriage cleansed of details, a rite of passage that entails no prologue or aftermath. In this she finds a gratification not won at the price of novel-reading, all reward without the work.

Mrs Meyrick would undoubtedly have neither patience nor stomach for the scarcely 'fashionable' novel in which she is a character, Eliot's virtual parody of the Austenian novel-of-manners, a story including all that outer world of cultural and political action excluded from the precincts of Austen's domestic representations. *Daniel Deronda* is a novel, of course, whose heroine's marriage has occurred (off-stage) thirty chapters before in a typographically marked blank between plotted episodes (p. 403): a tainted ceremony from which narrative has averted its very gaze. Recasting the structural function of the wedding as a depicted but closural ceremony, Eliot's lacunary plotting seems to imply that it is all over for Gwendolen well before the sanctified exchange of vows, her doom sealed from the moment she commits to a loveless match. (Indeed, elided wedding ceremony or not, so strong are the structural conventions of the Victorian novel that almost any marriage occurring this early in a plot forebodes no good; the fact that it opens forward on to a narratable future suggests that there is something other to be said of it, something more specific, restless, troubled, than a formulaic 'happily ever after'.) It happens to be this same marriage, Gwendolen's to Grandcourt, its bitter issue chronicled for hundreds of pages since the undramatised wedding day, about which Mrs Meyrick is momentarily to read on the very morning when we first hear about her thirst for news. She will read of it not in her favoured marriage lists this time, but rather in the journalistic report of a fatal accident – or simply as a death notice in the obituary column. For, a paragraph after we have heard of her reading habits, her son rushes in with the daily paper mentioning Grandcourt's drowning, the dissolution of the marriage by watery death. In this novel's excoriating treatment of the 'fashionable' world, we have heard of everything concerning this marriage for money except its sex, which transpires between the wedding and the death that does them part. Marriage is in fact that emotionally closural death-in-life from which drowning releases the heroine, even as it leads her to suspect herself of murderous complicity in the accident.

This, though, is only half of what by this time we have long been reading. Like Mrs Meyrick, we have given equivalent attention, as in no other novel of the period, to 'the widest-reaching politics', a world-historical rather than domestic agenda adumbrated, meditated, and debated in the 'Jewish half' of this notoriously double-plotted book. In taking this brief description of Mrs Meyrick's reading habits to encapsulate the division of interests to which this novel itself manifestly appeals, the political as against the private, the reader is still left with the structural overtones of her selective reading. One is not likely to assume that Mrs Meyrick, so protectively naïve in her enjoyment of the marital roster, turns to politics with a breadth of comprehension to match its implicit 'reach'. As with her role as a 'great reader' of connubial notices, she can also be presumed to read the political pages out of a genial curiosity that delights in superficial and summary coverage. This of course can only redound to the credit of the writing that represents her, the range and probity of the 'novel' in comparison with what is more loosely called 'news'. But there is more here, and it takes us more deeply into the novel's structural design. In reading of marriage,

Mrs Meyrick has a nose only for closure, for acme and wrap-up, for all that can be condensed, readily typeset, and economically disseminated. It follows logically enough, therefore, that this isolated brief analysis of a single reader's motives, which on the one hand ironises the desire for marital stories only when mythologically distilled to a wedding notice, would on the other serve to establish an ironic stance toward a reading of politics under the same dispensation of precis and closure: politics as digestible. *Daniel Deronda*, as text, envisions an opposite mode of response to the written, one that would resist the foreclosure of facile resolutions, would keep itself always in abeyance, its issues open even when the book is finally closed. To trace out the ramifications of such a tacit plan for its own reception – and to do so partly on the internal footing of other such exemplary reflexive passages that not only conduct the narrative but attempt the conditioning of its response – is the enterprise of this essay.[2]

In regard to the novel's ultimate 'conceit' of perpetuity through interpretation, the modified and ambivalent closural strategies of the Zionist plot are every bit as revealing as the marriage-to-death trajectory of Gwendolen's narrative. In a direct symmetrical reversal of the latter, the marriage of Daniel to Mirah that would seem to bring the 'whole' novel to its finish in the last paragraphs is founded on the death of Mordecai, the latter-day Hebrew prophet, who presides at the wedding as himself the true spiritual bride of the hero. Collapsing upon each other, marital and mortal climaxes thus revise our very notion of closural logic in the contrapuntal plotting of Eliot's ironically braided text. In the one plot: Grandcourt sinking in the sea just when Gwendolen most wishes his death. In the other: Daniel's decision to sanctify his discovered racial origin by marrying the Jewish girl, Mirah, whom he had earlier *saved* from drowning, vowing also his spiritual marriage to her brother Mordecai, self-styled prophet of Zionism, who dies off-stage on the last page of the novel – just as the new couple begins its pilgrimage to the Jewish East. A moribund marriage ending in death in the one narrative path, matched in the other by a death-sanctified commitment figured as marriage and doubled, almost interchangeably, by the conjugal event.

These are the stories. What plots them? In what sense, if any, do they define an interlaced chronology that gives itself over, in closure, to a unifying interpretation? In the divided sense of the term 'end' as finish and purpose, closure and final cause – a difference foregrounded, I will claim, by this one Victorian novel above all – to what extent are the linked structural termini of the two stories plotted to evoke their own interpretation, that destination beyond *finis* of any reading? By the open-ended layering of marriage upon mortality, how does the novel itself move to imagine the event of its own reading – and beyond – a fullness of response at what we might call its receiving end? These are the questions I want eventually to close in upon through a combined confrontation with the novel's most ubiquitous critical topos and its most underworked field of meaning: respectively its emphatic refusal of stable closure and the role therein of Mordecai's attitudes toward writing and cultural transmission.

II

It should be acknowledged from the first that the overtly inconclusive nature of this text, both halves, is very much on the novel's own mind. In an episode that more than one critic has noted[3] as a miniaturised refiguration of the book's open-endedness, the hero discusses with the painter, Hans Meyrick, the five canvases in the latter's pictorial narrative of the legendary Jewish heroine, Berenice. Since neither history nor myth records what happened to her beyond a certain point, the painter's 'story is chipped off, so to speak, and passes with a ragged edge into nothing – *le neant*' (p. 514). In terms of Eliot's novel, this can of course describe the fates of Daniel and Mirah after Mordecai's death on the last page, as well as of Gwendolen after Grandcourt's. To refigure blankness itself as a legible affective tonality, as Meyrick thinks to do by making the truncated series end in a 'pathetic negative' – a negative space to which the viewer's sympathy (or at least interest) is drawn – is an aesthetic manoeuvre that might also describe the indirect representation of the novel's death moments themselves: Grandcourt's going melodramatically unenacted until subsequently replayed in Gwendolen's secondary account, and Mordecai's more elusively displaced from direct narration. At one point in this discussion, Hans alludes to the interlocutor Eugenius in Dryden's *An Essay of Dramatic Poesy*, a theoretical treatise from which Eliot may well have fortified her penchant for 'related' rather than dramatised death.[4] Grandcourt's death is at a certain level redundant anyway, merely epitomising his language and lifelessness all along, just as

Mordecai's concentrated spirituality makes the surrender of his body almost a figurative afterthought. Though by the normal conventions of narrative it would seem that the latter's dying is rendered as part of the main narrative discourse, the actual moment of his demise is in fact suppressed, as we will see, by a grammatical elision that removes it, if not from omniscient purview, at least from specific report. In any case the general rule should stand: that nothing is subtracted from our interest in the deaths of characters by distancing the moment of death from immediate narrative staging; as Dryden puts it, the accumulated 'motion' (Dryden, p. 40) of event propels us beyond the need for direct 'mimesis'. We are thus no more resistant to the indirect narration of a main character's fate 'than we are to listen to the news of an absent Mistress' (Dryden, p. 40).

It is just this suggestion of a quasi-erotic momentum in narrative, theatrical or otherwise, that should help advance our understanding of Eliot's closure, even as it intensifies the problematic of its divisiveness. The most thoroughgoing recent approach to plotting under the aspect of closure is the psychopoetics of Peter Brooks' *Reading for the Plot*.[5] Deriving a comprehensive model from Freud's *Beyond the Pleasure Principle*, Brooks sees the 'eros' that propels a text (the reader's desire for story synchronised with the impetus or ambition of the main character) and the principle of thanatos that prepares for its quiescence (the exhaustion of desire when all is told) to be part of the same narrational curve: the vitality of plot at one with its death drive. What is not clear, though, from Brooks's attempted global theory of narrative is how, exactly, the psychoanalytic model might apply to less linear or monolithic texts than those he takes up for demonstration, concentrating as his argument does either on classic realist narratives in the *Bildungsroman* tradition of the single 'life story', or on frame narratives that neatly encase the telling of one story inside the story of its telling. (This essay will return at the end to the question of the *Bildungsroman* in particular, addressing a recent Marxist attack on *Daniel Deronda* – lodged without sufficient regard to the book's dispersive structure – as a failed version of just this genre, an exposure of its withered ideology.) In the terms of Brooks's schema, we are left to ask: with what in the long run – in the closing upon a *finis* – is the reader's narrational eros identified in a book like *Daniel Deronda*, whose ending is so openly divisive – or at least so manifold and open? How is the quiescence that follows a marriage or a dying, how are sexual relaxation and death, made to figure that hypothetical space beyond the pleasure principle in a novel that seems to leave almost everything unfinished?

Much contemporary investigative energy has of course been directed at the phenomenon of the Victorian multi-plot or counterplot.[6] Yet I wish to pick up a much earlier suggestion, from William Empson's essay on 'The Double Plot', concerning the linguistic pivot point about which such complementary story lines frequently revolve. For Empson, the doubling of one narrative field of action by another is often hinged, in Shakespeare especially, around 'subdued puns' (Empson, *Some Versions*, p. 39) that negotiate, if only by opening a clarifying gap, between 'a personal situation and a political one' (p. 43), just the poles of reference around which *Daniel Deronda*'s stories are made to turn. In respect to its syncopated closural deployment of more or less displaced death scenes, there is indeed such a verbal pun, an instance in fact of Empsonian 'double grammar' (Empson, *Seven Types*, Chapter 2) in Eliot's novel. As the Zionist Mordecai, debilitated by tuberculosis and exhausted by constant declamation, comes under the shadow of his own acknowledged end, language engages in an idiomatic but at the same time arresting way with the divergent vectors of the plot. Mordecai knows he is killing himself with those 'deliverances' (Eliot, p. 605) that are in both senses the end of his very life: the giving out of breath by whose vented wisdom he will be delivered to his immortality. (Indeed, the latter sense of the noun has appeared on the preceding page in the phrase 'deliverance from the dreaded relationship of the Cohens'.) Beyond this operable doubleness of phrase, there is a further verbal biplay that taps more comprehensively into the double plot of the novel. After one of Mordecai's bouts of 'irrepressible utterance', part of a consumptive wasting of vital force that repeats in little the very mechanism of plot as a kind of self-consuming energy, this dispenser of language feels 'as if he had taken a step toward beckoning Death' (p. 848). The thread of not only one but both plots here knots round a perfect, that is unresolvable, ambiguity. With 'beckoning' read as a participial adjective, the phrase calls up the Death that lies greedily waiting for Mordecai when his prophetic breath is entirely expended – the death that we will learn to know as inseparable from closure itself when they coincide in the novel's last sentence. Alternatively, with 'beckoning' taken as a gerund, Death as its object, the phrase names an act of direct invitation to that death toward which Mordecai, in his role as

Jewish martyr, is all but suicidally inclined. But just as soon as the divergence of these two meanings – death stalking and death solicited – is admitted as a functional possibility within the Mordecai plot, the greater relevance of the second meaning throws into relief – not by default but by psychological refiguration – the application of the first to the Gwendolen plot.

Stretched between the political realm, then, where death is welcome(d) as heroic imprimatur, and the personal, where death is feared as annihilation, lies a major structuring differential of the novel. In a prolonged and diffused version of the Vanitas motif, the hypersensitive heroine, ever since being frightened in her family home at Offendene by a secret panel picturing a 'dead face' and a 'fleeing figure' (p. 91), fears repeatedly – as the scourge of her very narrowness and vanity – some ominous, fatal violence. When it comes to her in the form of a blessing, removing Grandcourt from her life, it is the same death anyway: the occasion still of 'spiritual dread' (p. 93) and moral panic, a shameful fear that is in every sense 'mortifying to her' (p. 93). In Gwendolen's phase of the plot, death is always beckoning from some far and unforeseen distance, irrational, relentless, appalling. In the Mordecai plot, on the other hand, death is more and more vigilantly beckoned: an invited destiny. Only the double grammar of the phrase 'a step toward beckoning Death' can capture the simultaneous double-tracking of paired stories plotted toward the ambivalence of mortal closure. Here is language performing in the most circumscribed space what that language act which composes the novel as a whole, that literary plotting, performs in its own highly evasive and, at most, provisional unity – a unity whose guiding principle we are only beginning to detect.

III

In following through this question of unity, it is the interplay, the reciprocal displacement, of those closural tropes of eros and thanatos – death and marriage, marriage and death, marriage as death, death as marriage – that remains our best lead. Mordecai's end, as suggested earlier, will localise these convergent issues around a virtual deathbed vow of passionate commitment from Daniel, a pact conceived as the marriage of blood-brothers. Confronted with such a figurative destination, we may well recall Peter Brooks' sense of fraternal–sororal incest as one of the chief tropes in the nineteenth-century novel for the foundering of the metonymic principle of plot, its differential dynamism, upon the stalling metaphors, the undue equivalences, of over-sameness. What, then, about the case of fraternal–fraternal incest, which removes gender difference altogether in favour of male priority?

Despite her satire of the English patrilineage in the other half of the novel, and elsewhere, the Jewish counterplot of Eliot's narrative involves the moral vitality of such a quasi-familial retrenchment, its tribal necessity as a figure of patriarchal bonding. Daniel and Mordecai testify to a 'willing marriage which melts soul into soul . . . as the clear waters are made fuller' (p. 820). It is built upon an initial intimacy that fuses the two men 'with as intense a consciousness as if they had been two undeclared lovers' (p. 552). The marriage Mordecai eventually consummates with Daniel in the performative mode of its very promise, however, is contracted for with a man whom he thinks of 'as my brother that fed at the breast of my mother' (p. 820). His soul's marriage is thus quite openly imaged by him as an incestuous bonding as well, but one very different, say, from the incestuous *Liebestod* – and drowning – of Maggie Tulliver with her brother Tom at the close of *The Mill on the Floss*. In *Daniel Deronda*, by contrast, a community is sustained rather than renounced by the mutual introversion of desire. It is the two men's disclosed genetic sameness, their racial likeness – their function as 'metaphors' for each other if you will, or 'type' and 'antitype' in the exegetical sense – that is put forward to rectify the metonymical thinning out of the Jewish 'dispersion' (p. 591). The incestuous cast of all homoerotic bonding, mediated here by Mirah as potential midwife (as much as mother) to its presumed communal fruition, is thus meant to emblemise, in this case, a beleaguered and earned consolation, a fending off of the Other, an historically mandated refusal of difference.

Is Gwendolen merely the victim of this vast, this irrevocable difference? Within what dynamic economy of the narrative, in other words, are we to understand that recurrent digression from her desire known as the Jewish plot? As with so many things in Eliot, Henry James is a superb reader of this double-plot structure. One of the fictional interlocutors in James's review illuminates Gwendolen's plight by waxing formalist in a tentative reading of the Jewish section from a strictly structural point of view, its shapeless enormity a counterpoise to Gwendolen's vivid narrowness. It bulks imposingly so that she should shrink the more in recognition. It overwhelms so that she should be dwarfed. 'The very chance to embrace what the author is so fond of calling a 'larger life' is refused to her. . . . The irony of the situation, for poor Gwendolen, is almost grotesque, and it makes one wonder whether the whole heavy structure of the Jewish question in the story was not built up by the author for the express purpose of giving its proper force to this particular stroke' (Carroll, p. 431). James's insight recognises the inalienable link between the polarised sections as reading events, not just in local details. To some degree like Gwendolen herself, we too have to shift gears rather arduously as we turn from one plot to the other. And once caught up in a given stretch of the Jewish plot, once we invest at all in its issues, it is indeed hard to see precisely what 'relevance' our (usually much more immediate) attachment to Gwendolen's plot could possibly still have. The phenomenality of reading, its affective dynamics, supports the weight of a structuring logic – and in turn of a thematics.

When Eliot says in an often-quoted letter, without further elaboration, that she 'meant everything in the book to be related to everything else there' (Haight, p. 290), the formal question is by no means settled. What is the governing mode of such interrelation? It may be that any one piece fits with all the others, taken together, as the part for the whole – so that meaning is not cumulative and reduplicable but, rather, concentrated and intensive. The latter is the principle of integration suggested by another of Henry James's imaginary interlocutors: 'George Eliot's intentions are extremely complex. The mass is for each detail and each detail is for the mass' (Carroll, p. 431). Though unpursued by James, a clue about the particular interaction between mass and detail obtaining here does emerge from the apparent non-sequitur of the very next remark in this dialogue, about Eliot being 'very fond of deaths by drowning. Maggie Tulliver and her brother are drowned, Tito Melema is drowned, Mr Grandcourt is drowned' (p. 431). The frequency of these scenes may well have to do with precisely their enactment of a unique part–whole relationship, their thematising of a structural principle – a fact most apparent in the fully dramatised prototype of Maggie's drowning with Tom in *The Mill on the Floss*. The missing link in James's impromptu roster of such drownings is any allusion to the near-drowning of Mirah in *Daniel Deronda*, rendered from within the consciousness of the sufferer in a way that is ironically denied to the empty Grandcourt. Just as with the summoned archetype of drowning as instantaneous retrospect and review in the double death of *The Mill on the Floss*, so with Mirah's despairing brush with death by water: in the intent rather than the event, nevertheless this manner of death is dramatically prefigured so that it works to replay her life. Even more explicitly than in Maggie's drowning, Mirah's suicidal thoughts 'forced me to see all my life from the beginning' (Eliot, p. 263).[7]

The mechanism of drowning as temporal compression, detached here from the actual moment of death, is nonetheless illustrative. For such is also the mechanism of narrative retrospect and over-view, of plotted duration under the pressure of rereading. In many Victorian novels drowning is thus, as I have argued elsewhere, a synecdochic scene of elapsed narrative, a novel in brief (Stewart, *passim*). The Romantic locus of this idea is perhaps most explicit in Coleridge's reaction to the recitation of Wordsworth's *Prelude*, after which he is morbidly forced to review his own lesser history – 'as Life returns upon the drowned' ('To William Wordsworth', l.63).[8] The link between drowning and *respectus* is further secured in *Daniel Deronda* by a weighted phrase late in Gwendolen's plot. With Daniel's greater mission slowly dawning upon her, a 'great wave' (originally 'shock' in the manuscript) 'of remembrance passed through Gwendolen' (Eliot, p. 876),[9] revealing the crushing flood of the past in a new light (specifically, here, her previously indifferent contact with the Jewish half of the story). By a chilling understate-ment, memory and inundation, previously linked by the melo-dramatics of plot, have passed into the figurative equivalence of a not altogether dead metaphor.

It remains to be explored how this involuntary submission to the currents of the larger world, this submergence in the great tides of history and culture, is connected – through a critique of Gwendolen's paltry reading – to our own retrospective reading of the very novel whose scope she has suffered from not being able to comprehend or encompass. But this connection is complicated in turn by a contrary emphasis in the Jewish plot on the transcendence of any and all writing: Mordecai's rather astonishing wish to leave no written record of his thought. Again the motif of drowning, the threat of death by water, appears (in indirect association with memory and preservation) as a passing exemplum in one of Mordecai's harangues about racial record and cultural perpetuation: 'There is a fable', he recalls to his auditors (never to be readers), 'of the Roman, that swimming to save his life he held the roll of his writings between his teeth and saved them from the waters' (p. 590). Writing in this anecdote seems almost a textualised form of that rehearsed identity, or life's work, recovered from the moment of oblivion itself in the actual scene of drowning. 'But how much more', Mordecai adds, 'than that is true of our race?' – a race that has had all 'visible signs of their national covenant' effaced, a people thus required in part, along with a tireless tradition of sacred writing and scriptural commentary, also to recover and preserve many original traditions through oral transmission – passing them, in other words, between the teeth in a different sense. This is a tragic limitation in Mordecai's view, but also a glory.

Mordecai of course does not drown in the novel. His death from tuberculosis involves a very different sort of introspection, one displaced wholesale on to the mind of his survivor, Daniel. Death completes and insures for Mordecai that deliquescence of identity, that 'melting' of souls, by which 'the clear waters are made fuller' (p. 882). Instead of drowning – indeed by direct figural contrast – he is sustained in death by an 'ocean of peace beneath him' (p. 882). Contriving to transform a racial necessity into a private virtue, as we will see, he is supposedly floated free of the need for any but oral continuance through his acolyte, Daniel. Mordecai thus aspires to no less than a displaced phonocentric salvation from the waters of annihilation – without the need for the very textuality that Eliot in her own right requires in order to envision him for us. A detailed examination of Mordecai's death moment, a moment postponed until the very last lines of the novel, should serve to clarify the relation of writing to the issues of transmission, endurance, and interpretation that – at the very moment of closure – so markedly inflect the status of Mordecai the character (as uninscribed prophetic voice) within the novelistic act of writing and necessitated interpretation that is *Daniel Deronda*. For it is in the nature, or rather the design, of his martyrdom that he dies so that we might survive to read on, read over.

IV

In the speech of his final 'deliverance' a paragraph before his end, Mordecai announces that 'Death is coming to me as the divine kiss which is both parting and reunion', a severance and perpetuation that 'takes me from your bodily eyes and gives me full presence in your soul'. Gasped out to Daniel in particular, his soul's bride (or

partner in the husbandry of his racial dream), Mordecai's last
quoted words are 'Have I not breathed my soul into you? We shall
live together' (p. 891). With Daniel the supposed body to Mordecai's
indwelling spirit, the supernal pact sealed here has its inescapably
ghoulish side: the possession by a tribal incubus from beyond the
grave. Mordecai in fact requires, just before his death, the already
corporeal mediation of those who will survive. This we notice when
'slowly and with effort Ezra, pressing on their hands', – not clasping
or grasping their hands, but leaning *on* them, using the bodies of
Daniel and Mirah as his last earthly support – 'raised himself and
uttered in Hebrew the confession of the divine Unity, which for long
generations has been on the lips of the dying Israelite'. Always
there, waiting, renewed. The divinised unity celebrated in parting is
hereby addressed through a grammatical shift at once into present
tense and general (singular) number: 'for long generations *has* been
on the lips of *the* dying Israelite'. In this last rite of passage, Mordecai
has in every sense *become* his people, the vicar of their nationalist
venture, the one subsumed to the many.

   From this 'confession', Mordecai sinks back in exhaustion, his
rhetorical life over, his prophetic soul anticipating release and
renewal in the communal other – and One. It is only his animal
existence that is still registered by the action of his now worthless
lungs. 'He sank back gently into the chair, and did not speak again.'
In this is his virtual death confirmed, the end of that efficacy by
which he defined his life. 'But it was some hours before he had
ceased to breathe with Mirah's and Deronda's arms around him.' The
staginess and flamboyant improbability of two people embracing a
third for hours on end, in an armchair no less, is easy to miss – and
not just in the swiftness but in the temporal elusiveness of this final
phrasing. By a modulation of tense as muted as the use of the
idiomatic perpetual present of 'for long generations *has been*', the
actual moment of death is memorialised in prospect – as if one were
to have said at the scene: 'It will be some hours before he will . . .
already have been dead'. Within the grammar of a single sentence,
in the slide from '*was* some hours' to '*had ceased*' (instead of 'ceased'),
there passes under suppression the unsaid death moment. In the
rhetoric of the Victorian death scene, the commonplace 'had ceased
to breath' is regularly a euphemism for the last of life. Instead, it
records here the clinical aftermath of a final 'deliverance' of and in
breath. In the shunting from past to pluperfect, Mordecai may seem
to have slipped outside of time altogether. He dies, that is, in the

interstices of syntax rather than in direct mimesis. His unwritten demise thus provides, in the epitome of its elision, a minuscule recapitulation of that foregone conclusion which is his long-beckoning death. At the same time, by never having mentioned death by name, the discourse avoids denominating his removal – as if, at the very moment of closure, Mordecai's spiritual presence may have been displaced elsewhere and preserved.

In the four closing lines (markedly unidentified) from *Samson Agonistes*, we now encounter the familiar format of one of Eliot's epigraphs (as if to the next chapter which never comes) brought forward to the position of epitaph. The adverbial shifter of the first line takes on unexpected resonance: 'Nothing is here for tears, nothing to wail . . .' The grammatical inversion of the idiomatic base in 'There is nothing here (to mourn)' is given an additional spin by detaching the lines from any clear context. Mordecai has after all died declaring that his 'full presence' would now exist only in a realm beyond the spatial and temporal coordinates of 'bodily eyes', that he will be spiritually evaporated into pure meaning without form: that in fact there will be 'nothing . . . here' any longer. But where not, exactly? Unlocated in the voice of character or poet or novelist, wrenched from context without attribution, the mere pendant to a novel that is itself left hanging, the adverb 'here' (with everything else in these supplemental verse lines) is suggestively destabilised. Nothing that merits grief is to be found 'here' in the scene (the consolatory emotional gesture); nor is anything here at all in the discourse, it seems to say, that remains for pain of any kind (the cathartic textual gesture); especially since all is now over and gone, then and *there* (the closural gesture).

V

Yet closure here, just 'here', is possible only because of the promise of continuance: the writing over, the future begun. As we pass from the written and printed text to a realm of reflection and reconsider-ation, to ongoing interpretation, it behooves us to wonder how much the aftermath of our reading is being inferentially linked to Mordecai's abdication from textual embodiment, his desire to die without any written trace available to 'bodily eyes'. One thing is clear: his wish to be remembered without scriptive intervention is pitched against an opposite compact of writing and reading, of epistolary transmission, in the other plot. There, writing begins to make possible for Gwendolen what it would impede for Mordecai from beyond the grave: the most direct possible contact with Daniel. In an obvious parallel to his parting with Mordecai, Daniel will no doubt not lay 'bodily eyes' upon Gwendolen again either, though he does promise her, in effect, 'full presence' (Mordecai's term) in the spirit. 'I will write to you always' (p. 878), he vows, and 'shall be more with you than I used to be'. It is in fact the first instalment of such a verbal communication, Gwendolen's letter to Daniel, that arrives on his wedding day, and that is followed, without further comment, by the last half dozen paragraphs detailing the death – without written legacy – of the man who wants no words of his own to come between his vision and Daniel's instrumentation thereof. Distance, disembodiment, death, perpetuation: these tropes revolve ambivalently around the question of that very textuality to which they lend closural form.

Mordecai's position is borne home in no uncertain terms, though his protestations may seem finally excessive, even suspect.[10] Immediately following his virtual marriage vows to Daniel, that union which 'melts soul into soul', we discover how completely Mordecai desires a transcendence of the body, of materiality, indeed of the material body of his own signifying practice as Jewish historian, philosopher, and poet: 'For I have judged what I have written, and I desire the body that I gave my thought to pass away as this fleshly body will pass, but let the thought be born again from our fuller soul which shall be called yours' (p. 820). Daniel's inspiration from Mordecai would thus devolve upon him untranscribed, a legacy engaged by being wholly internalised. Yet of course hundreds of this novel's paragraphs have offered permanent form to nothing else but Mordecai's pronouncements, laboriously 'transcribed' by Eliot's text. What are we to make of this ironic disjunction? A double-blind? A double-cross? Has the text necessarily flouted the dying wish of its most relentlessly eloquent hero by emblazoning in print just what he had asked to let pass unrecorded? By some curious extra-textual poetic justice, then, do those numerous readers and critics who regret his prominence in the novel as wordy, laboured, and tedious, and who react by skimming and dismissal, only grant him his dying wish by default? But, then again, is this widespread critical indifference not at the same time the mirror reversal, and so symmetrical clarification, of Eliot's design? Flooded with Mordecai's words, could the reader ever have been expected to do much more than carry away from them the spirit rather than the letter of their sentiments?

Mordecai's 'yearning for transmission' (p. 526) seeks in its highest moments of political lucidity no fixed and so potentially dismissible form. He does everything he can to make the mission of his apprentice, Daniel, as epic, originating, and underivative as possible. But the purism of this decision cannot be easily sustained. His own metaphors reveal more of a desire for authorship than he otherwise admits. Though he thinks of his written words 'as the ill-shapen work of the youthful carver who has seen a heavenly pattern, and trembles in imitating the vision' (p. 821), nevertheless this same metaphor of impress and incision is brought to bear on Mordecai's plans to carve, to inscribe or engrave, the lines of his own Hebrew poetry on the memory of young Jacob Cohen. '"The boy will get them engraved within him," thought Mordecai; "it is a way of printing"' (p. 533). When not speaking in metaphor, Mordecai's most compelling reason for seeking an immortality unemcumbered by writing is that, even at the height of his rhetorical power over Daniel, he is very soon too weak actually to transcribe his best thoughts: 'I can write no more. My writing would be like this gasping breath' (p. 557). It would be like those tubercular exhalations: weak, palsied, powerless. Yet in a spurt of logocentric metaphysics, Mordecai at the same time assumes an *inside* to writing, the place of the spiritual voice, indeed the very 'breath of divine thought' (p. 557) descended from the Logos itself. This inspiriting influx can even enter into secondary 'transmission' without the spoiling interposition of script, can pass directly from soul to the body of a spiritual double, a process to be completed at the moment of death.

This mystic bonding and *demise* (in the linked etymological senses of demitting and departure, passing on in passing away) is so often traditionally figured by the notion of a writer's survival by text, however, that this same analogy enters into the narrator's account of Mordecai's very different purposes. Speaking of those who spend themselves through 'deliverances in other ears', the narrator speculates that in death, nevertheless, 'perhaps it may be with them as with the dying Copernicus made to touch the first printed copy of his book when the sense of touch was gone, seeing it only as a dim object through the deepening dusk' (p. 604). The reward of those who die away in the midst of no more than oral transmission, the product of their labour, may well be figuratively 'glimpsed' just before the end, but not in any form that other 'bodily eyes' can, in surviving, hope to inspect. Mordecai wants to leave no book behind him; he does want, though, like Copernicus, to will through the remembered spirit of his words a new view of the world – or at least the spiritual map of a new Jewish world. In this yearning beyond the confines of textuality, his fantasy, we are coming to recognise, is the novel's own.

VI

In a related sense, the associated motifs of drowning, biographical duration, retrospect, and reflection, in their repeated connection with written and remembered record, comment indirectly upon the scene of reading itself. Just as drowning is symbolically deployed as a moment in time that distills all personal history, so are there narrative modules that reduce and illuminate the larger arcs of plot – and even of plot's retrospective processing. One such episode, to which we now turn – though on the face of it a digressive moral exemplum – in fact exemplifies more pointedly the workings of its own inclusion – and, by synecdochic extension, of the entire novel in whose reading it schools us. It goes beyond such earlier *mise-en-abymes* as Mrs Meyrick's reading, Hans Meyrick's narrative painting, Mordecai's anecdote of the Roman saving his scroll from the waters, all episodes that miniaturise in order to reprise the novel's surrounding preoccupation with its representational status. Illustrating again the Jamesian claim of 'each detail for the mass', this late microcosmic episode actually goes so far as to stage a scene of 'reading' without writing, of interpretation in absentia from the text that prompts it – of reading, we might say, the world through text. It thus attempts to let the novel stand back from itself at what could be called an internal remove, emplotting its own organising logic in reduced form, empowering its own rereading from within.

The protagonist of the death-closed narrative in question dies as if presiding over a marriage, which thus seems authorised by the finality of that death – in a doubling of structural logic. It is now the inevitable story of this story – the narrative to be told or at least remembered about such a sacralised dying – which is all that remains: as metanarrative remainder, so to speak. Does the inherited account of the protagonist's death, however, offer a blessing to marital continuance or a more dramatic story meant to eclipse that union, to intrude its own wilful self-abnegation as an ideal more strongly felt than the marriage ties, an ideal and an obligation, a greater bond? As with the novel as a whole, finally, the events of this sequence have become a plot, ready for assessment, a legacy, but an ambiguous one: either a spiritual bonus or an emotional onus. The death of the protagonist, which is necessary to give meaning to the life leading up to it, has in this sense transpired not as the sheer annihilation of self but in the name of the Other, as more a martyrdom than a fortuity, or even a virtual suicide. But where, afterwards, is the place of the vanished self in the wake of that death? Is it not perhaps the case that the myth of selflessness gains in its own a posthumous foothold for self? How, after all, is one to judge the psychology of a simultaneous effacement and canonisation? Is it a contradiction or a ruse, a paradox or an irony, an abnegation or a will to power and perpetuity?

These are questions that do not go away. They return at the end of *Daniel Deronda* to complicate the conclusion of that entire macroplot which this episode so closely resembles in skeletal form: the story of the dying Mordecai ennobling the marriage of Daniel and Mirah, his midwifing of its Zionist issue, the investiture of his sanctifying power in absentia. This is not, though, the story I have just been describing, despite the fact that in moral and psychological outline it corresponds with it at roughly every point. The story I was recounting is instead the one Mordecai himself recounts, in the economy of a single long sentence, as he nears his death: the parable of the Jewish girl who goes to her death in the place of the non-Jewish woman who loves the gentile king with whom she too is hopelessly in love. 'Somewhere in the later *Midrash*' is this story's source, Mordecai recalls, written once but retrievable now without origin or attribution, inherited as part of the wisdom he lives by. 'She entered into prison and changed clothes with the woman who was beloved by the king, that she might deliver that woman from death by dying in her stead, and leave the king to be happy in his love which was not for her' (p. 802). The exemplum is only one sentence long, but it follows a rather full disquisition on the confession of 'divine Unity' which will be on Mordecai's lips at his deathbed, a wholeness explained in a way that all but explicitly invites the application of the following *Midrash* narrative *pars pro toto* to the entire novel: 'Now, in complete unity a part possesses the whole as the whole possesses every part' (p. 802). Advanced as a metaphysical critique of narrowing self-centredness, the heroic alternative to which is supposedly

exemplified by the *Midrash* text, nevertheless this doctrinal sub-
sumption of part to whole is sustained as an article of interpretive
faith as well. Offered up from within the text itself is, again, the
Jamesian notion of the atom for the aggregate, the fraction for the
mass. In becoming a microcosm not merely of the larger plot but of
the plot as interpreted, the *Midrash* parable is a story we are
therefore not left on our own to interpret. Mordecai 'reads' it for us,
translating it into his own words and his own import, even while he
is challenged in his reading by Mirah, one of the two characters who
will be most directly implicated in the closure of his own life, the
bride he gives away so that he can claim her marriage as his own.
One major plotline of *Daniel Deronda* is thus not only miniaturised en
route but submitted to a detailed hermeneutic procedure by the very
characters involved: a novel worrying in advance the psychological
structure of its own closure.

Mordecai, who introduces the *Midrash* tale by appealing to the
gender stereotype that 'women are specially framed for the love
which feels possession in renouncing', believes that the point of the
anecdote is to enshrine a 'surpassing love, that loses self in the
object of that love'. Mirah refuses this reading altogether, insisting
instead that the Jewish girl 'wanted the king when she was dead to
know what she had done, and feel that she was better than the
other. It was her strong self, wanting to conquer, that made her die'
(p. 803). Mordecai the passionate exegete has thus returned to a
cultural parable whose moral he extracts by interpretation, only to
have his reading called into question by a character who is no more
unbashedly projecting on to the heroine her own jealousy than
Mordecai is projecting his coveted aspirations to selfless sacrifice, to
a death with meaning. His own frail person 'framed' like a woman's
for the ultimate renunciation of life itself, he unconsciously identifies
with the female marginal. Excluded from sexuality, he seeks vicarious fulfilment in a way that would somehow transform his fatal
disease into a nuptial gift, a genetic and spiritual legacy. Rescuing
doom from sheer contingency, even if casting himself in the woman's
part of the disappointed suitor to the hand of the kingly Daniel, he
must die not just *of* but *for* something. Yet it is only Mirah in this
scene who appears at all aware of her identification with the *Midrash*
heroine. The catch is that we know by this time (as Mirah does not)
that the racial interdict to her love has been swept away by Daniel's
discovered Jewish birth. Thus the most highly charged connection
between this story and the main plot rests instead with the death it

predicts rather than the desire whose frustrations it temporarily ironises: with Mordecai's gathering self-delusions about the utter surrender of self in a self-dramatising death, that is, rather than with Mirah's false assumptions about Daniel's emotional commitment. And this we can fully know, can fully read, only retrospectively. Such reconsideration is thereby incorporated within this episode's synecdochic model for our ultimate understanding of the whole novel. Even though all the facts are in, as it were, at the story's point of closure, interpretation cannot be simultaneously concluded. It is an act of processing, of retrospect and recombination, of inter-textuality and reading-*in*.

On the score of intertextuality, Mordecai actually charges Mirah with being confused, not to say corrupted, by the theatrical melo-dramas of the day: 'Thou judgest by the plays, and not by thy own heart, which is like our mother's' (p. 803). He might have levelled a more specific charge. In contrast to a character like Mrs Meyrick who avoids fiction, Mordecai might have accused Mirah of reading popular Victorian novels, and one in particular that Eliot may well have had in mind as the other text, besides the *Midrash*, that at once models and complicates the dynamic of her own sacrificial plot. Yet Dickens is never mentioned by the critics in this regard, merely the proleptic connection with Henry James. It is regularly noted that both the Grandcourt marriage in *Daniel Deronda* and the Casaubon marriage in *Middlemarch* are manifest influences on James's con-ception of *The Portrait of a Lady*. If James indeed were reading the 'detail for the mass' in his attention to this last novel of his great precursor, he may well have found in the metanarrative debate over the *Midrash* interpretation a 'germ' for *The Wings of the Dove* as well, encapsulating as it does the influence to be exercised posthumously by Mordecai in coming between the participants of a marriage. For materialised on the last page of *The Wings*, as indeed the symbolic spread thereof, is Milly Theale's post-mortem ability to forestall rather than sanctify a marriage between Kate and Densher, the latter devoted now to the memory of the dead girl. What James offers up at closure is in a sense the culmination of Eliot's Jewish counterplot stripped of its politics – but clarified in its psychology of power.

Such subsequent influence aside, Eliot's own nearest precursor in this theme of coercive immortality is the closure of Dickens's plot in *A Tale of Two Cities*: the supposedly selfless immolation of Sydney Carton in the name of the woman who loves another, his double, and yet whose marriage, saved by his death, produces a child of his

name. What Eliot discovered in the *Midrash* must inevitably have
put her in mind of Dickens's novel, where spiritual peripety also
turns on a surrogate execution. By saying nothing about it, and
recording no last thoughts, Carton achieves that reach beyond
death, that power over the memory, which Casaubon with the
'dead-hand' of his bitter testament, like Grandcourt after him, tries
so monomaniacally to *will in words*. In its own way, however,
Carton's sacrifice of self to something larger and beyond him, like
Mordecai's later, becomes in its own way possessive rather than
relinquishing, acquisitive rather than renunciatory.[11] It takes from
life what it could never gain (or sustain) there: a passionate close-
ness. Like Mordecai, though in privatised and erotic terms, Carton,
who has nothing to live for, dies to envision and accomplish it at one
and the same time. That time is the time of perpetuity, where the
marriage of Darnay to Lucie Manette is inextricable from Carton's
execution, his closure their continuity – and then again his own.
Assuming that this accurately characterises the aggrandisement of
private desire behind the superficially selfless sacrifices both of
Eliot's unacknowledged source in Dickens and her embedded narrative from the *Midrash*, how then can *Daniel Deronda* as a whole
steer free from a critique carried out in this way by synecdoche and
intertext? By this very same logic, Eliot herself risks becoming a kind
of Mordecai or Carton figure, the heroic presiding genius of her own
aftermath, provenance and sponsor of all we read from her once she
is gone, gone silent, gone from the page as eventually she will be
gone – only four years later – from life itself.

VII

It all depends, we must presume, on the degree of coercion versus
freedom to which the interpreter is released at the closure of a story.
A mere guess at the 'right' reading is certainly not the mode of
reflection towards which Eliot's text, in conjunction with Mordecai's
dying retreat from textual fixity, is meant to direct us. The chapter
that closes with the *Midrash* parable happens to open where this
essay did, with the described scope of a character's own reading.
Her son's ominous hints as he delivers to Mrs Meyrick the paper
containing the news of Grandcourt 'set his mother interpreting'
(p. 794). This is that educated guesswork which is, as befits this
superficial reader of prose, the vulgar form of 'interpretation', as is

the case a few pages later with the term's reappearance in 'Hans could not but interpret this invitation as a sign of pardon' (p. 798). Closer to Eliot's purpose, in this chapter and beyond, is the sense conveyed between these two commonplace mentions of 'interpret- ation' (as a figuring out rather than a figuring forth). In a very different sense, Mirah, after defending Daniel before she has quite admitted that she is in love with him, 'was pressed upon by a crowd of thoughts thrusting themselves forward as interpreters of that consciousness which still remained unuttered to itself' (p. 796). Interpretation is there characterised very much as it will appear later in this chapter in Mirah's argument with Mordecai over the meaning of the *Midrash* tale, and as it presumably operates most powerfully for Eliot. The term suggests not the disclosure of encrypted signify- ing, the mere bringing to light, but the actualisation of unwritten or unspoken ramifications (rather than simple 'meaning'). This draw- ing out of implication and association leads, in particular, to the creative act of envisioning a text's force without an exclusive fixation of 'bodily eyes' upon its written words.

Interpretation is an access, in short, to the spirit rather than the letter of a text. This is a distinction which this one text, as we might now expect, works to spell out for itself in yet another of Mordecai's circumscribed anecdotes. When the Gentiles came upon the Hebrew text 'What is yours is ours, and no longer yours', they took it with brutal literalness as a 'dark inscription' (p. 591). They read, explains Mordecai, 'the letter of our law' rather than its spirit. This was in every way an act of usurpation in which they immediately converted the 'parchments' of Jewish writing 'into shoe soles for an army rabid with lust and cruelty': not only an extended pun on the so-called 'march of history' but a grotesque travesty of reducing sacred texts to their material base. All the while, however, such original texts – at times orally transmitted and renewed, no longer bearing material form at all – were passed down through the generations by a tireless cultural rereading of their true spirit. It is in this way that 'our Masters' – our prophets, that is, not our new rulers – were devoted to 'enlarging and illuminating' the sacred heritage with 'fresh-fed interpretation'. If one were searching for a primal trauma which might explain Mordecai's fear of inscription – of a spirit tied to the letter of a text, and imperilled thereby – that fabled racial memory of violent pre-emption and misreading might well provide it. It, and more. For even with Eliot's written and printed text still before us, I want finally to argue, this additional reflexive anecdote about the effects of a too literal reading manages perfectly to inscribe, by ironic reversal, Eliot's envisioned future for her own narrative, renewed at whatever distance from the text by the energies of interpretation.

But first, an admission. It must be said that the kind of reading, or call it interpretation, upon which I have most recently been engaged – bringing together two discrete anecdotal episodes under the aegis of synecdoche – has in this sense submitted to the novel's own indifference to standard plotting. Exactly what readers and critics dislike about the Mordecai section – how, in its amorphousness, it is all random point without plot, shapeless and polemical – has inevitably guided this phase of my reading. About which it might now be asked: In comparing the *Midrash* episode with Mordecai's earlier parable of the letter versus the spirit – under the assumption that the two compressed narratives each testify to, even while analysing, the motive of interpretation – by what *rule* of interpretation is this shared fact about them important to notice? Are the episodes incremental, cumulatively nuanced? Do they build? Add up? Or are they disparate, extractable, in narrative terms supplemental to each other, rather than complementary – and so tautological? If the latter, then they do appear to represent all that may seem expendable in the Mordecai section. The psychological equivalent of the textual *pars pro toto* may indeed be found there, and by many lamented, in the way Mordecai, wanting to make each moment count, goes nowhere. In Peter Brooks's terms, Mordecai's story would seem to be all deferral, all repetition and retardation, without even the transgressive deviance that makes for narrative. Those exemplary or microcosmic moments with which he is associated are brought together by no momentum of plot, but rather by a nexus of common denominators in the philosophical subtext of his story. Yet it is important to recognise that this is not just where they are located but what they tacitly advocate as well. History, the overarching trope of plot, reveals itself in these episodes under the aspect of lesson. The purpose is not decipherment but reactivation, not analytic fixity but furtherance in the world. In the non-narrativity of their concatenation, we might say, these synecdochic moments mark the very conversion of narrative into wisdom. The whole novel would seem in the long run, to ask as much of its own interpretation but only of course after a more complex formal structure, linear as well as recursive, has been worked through.

VIII

More than any Victorian novel before it, *Daniel Deronda* raises questions of reading and interpretation directly through its unorthodox strategies of formal organisation.[12] As we have seen, for instance, duration, retrospect, and closure, three guiding determinants of fictional form, are foregrounded in this narrative respectively by its doubled-plotted chronology, its oblique evocations of drowning as retrospect, and the coincidence of Mordecai's death with the plot's own *finis*. It is under such combined thematic and formal pressures that the *Midrash* story, ending in death and opening upon ambiguity, takes shape as the *pars pro toto* of the whole narrational mechanism. Its divergent interpretations are indeed divided between the larger novel's contrapuntal lines of action. Mirah's reading of the legend attaches to that sphere of desire and frustration centring on Gwendolen, associated first with Mirah's jealousy of her, later with hers of Mirah – and finally with the pangs of remorse that Gwendolen causes Daniel himself when he must desert her. On the other hand, Mordecai's scarcely disinterested interpretation anticipates his own desire for enshrinement in a myth of selfless sacrifice as the destination of the counter-plot, even as it exposes the bid for power that this entails. Once these opposite readings are factored into its structural logic, Eliot's synecdochic parable of reprocessed narrative, the sacred text of her text so to speak, becomes a brief of, and for, interpretation.

This late and consummate high Victorian novel has thus worked to recapitulate – by displacing *en abyme* and at the same time projecting outward beyond textuality – not only the formal cohesion but the very institution of its genre as a public event. Interpretation is a name for this taking up not just of a book but of its ideas: interpretation understood here not as a close analytic reading but as a 'translation' of the text's strained but sustaining unity into a way of knowing the world. 'Zion' is only one name for the scene of that translation, a code word for the readerly covenant. It signifies in spatial terms the temporal field of the book's ultimate action: the extra-textual zone of its effect.

Yet in this sense the novel only ends where it began, off the page and in the mind. Mordecai's death into another and another's 'deliverance' redeems his life in the very terms of its own fictional status in the first place: primarily an idea, an inspiration, a prompting in someone else's mind, first his author's, finally his reader's. In

view of Mordecai's fate, we recognise how the narrative excess of
Eliot's double plot, or more to the point the uncertain exponential
relation of one plot to the other, stages in the space of their (mutually
unassimilable) interplay the text's own attempted transcendence of
mere inscription. Each half of the story, like the novel that binds
them as a printed book, cedes authority and so coherence to the
reader's subjective reprocessing of the two together. It is in this way
that their reverberations outstrip the specified textual sequences
assigned to them by chapters. I am not describing here a dialectical
tension of opposing forces driving at last toward synthesis. What in
the end gets resolved are not the two storylines in relation to each
other. What we find, instead, is that the second plot's theorising of
an exegetical transcendence of textuality (Mordecai's writings
internalised and perpetually rephrased in dissemination) offers
itself as an implicit analogy for the work – the working upon us – of
the whole double narrative taken together. Surrendering his claim
to scriptive immortality (as a mode of stasis), authoring instead
Deronda's commitment to historical time, Mordecai dies never to be
read again, but only in a wider context to become, in memory – and
more or less in the mode of a Biblical exemplum – a text *for*. So in a
sense close both halves of the novel at the moment of his death, a
book always over before we are through with it.

Or so Eliot hopes, a hope dramatised by the very structure of the
novel under the mandate of interpretation. It is also, as with so
many issues in this text, a hope – a fictional programme – confirmed by the book's contrapuntal thematics. The ramifications of
Mordecai's 'sacrifice' are in this sense finally sketched forth by
negation in the penultimate chapter of the novel, the last of the
Gwendolen plot. There we are given specific terms for her failure in
life, her ignorance of all those 'great movements of the world' and
'larger destinies of mankind' that have 'lain aloof in newspapers and
other neglected reading' (p. 874). This is not only the realm of Mrs
Meyrick's interest in political news along with wedding columns,
but the domain – and dominion – of that broader understanding
brought forcefully to bear on domestic life by such neglected fictions as, say, Eliot's own novels. The power of such reading for
Gwendolen, it is clear, would not have been in its momentary
diversion, aesthetic pleasure, or intellectual admiration. It would
have resided rather in its very power to *reside*, to linger in and
redirect her mind, to *take* – and so to give back its influence long after
it is no longer before her 'bodily eyes'. In doing so, it only defines

more explicitly than ever the very ideal of Victorian fictional authority.

Mordecai denies all textual ambitions because he wants less to distill wisdom than to instill the desire for it in his successors. Political in his hopes, he wants others not simply to be moved by, but moved *to*, motivated more generally than any reading could contain. His visionary schemes anticipate, in a strange, short-circuited way, what we might call a phenomenology of reading without the text. In the act of reading, according to Georges Poulet, 'I am the subject of thoughts other than my own' (Poulet, p. 56), impressions that I nevertheless think of (in the sense of consider as well as cogitate) as my own. This is that direct apprehension and internalisation of an expressed belief which, in Mordecai's plan, not only rules out the need for textual mediation but which would only suffer otherwise from a sense of the derivative, the already-read. What Poulet calls the 'dispossession' by that phenomenological 'second self' (p. 57) which takes over in a reading based in 'total commitment', a reading with no 'mental reservation' (p. 57), is just what Mordecai would seem to want from Daniel, while contriving to make the deputised inspiration appear to his alter ego as if moti-vated from within. Along with any reader, but without a text before him, Daniel might therefore find himself following Poulet in charac-terising the nature of his co-option by another's Word: 'I am on loan to another, and this other thinks, feels, suffers and acts within me' (p. 57). Mordecai's 'possessive' immortality might thus be re-thought as the scene of reading displaced from the site of textuality to that of the surviving psyche at large in its life.

After reading Mordecai, that is reading Eliot as Mordecai, where does this leave, not Daniel, so much as ourselves? What, that is, are we left with? Poulet closes his essay by invoking that 'subjectivity without objectivity' (p. 68) which is the abstracted energy of the expressive mind without its normal forms, its inscribed ideas. Between Mordecai the character and the George Eliot of the title page falls that disembodied consciousness of historical trans-formation which is meant to hover free of a text no longer taken as worded, no longer received as sheer words. Poulet's tentative and exploratory conclusions register in this sense a superintending question to which Eliot has implicitly, I think, attempted an answer: 'What is this subject left standing in isolation after all examination of a literary work' (p. 68)? The alternatives for Poulet seem to lie somewhere between 'the individual genius of the artist' and 'an anonymous and abstract consciousness presiding, in its aloofness, over the operations of all more concrete consciousness' (p. 68). Precisely by eschewing any hold on authorship, Mordecai would lay claim to just such a freer mode of presiding over his own aftermath, a genius residual rather than simply constructive: the spirit of an epoch as a potent ghost. The 'egotism' of such a programme, especially as Eliot's own motives attach to it, has been examined from a far more sceptical perspective, though in the same year as Poulet's essay, by Michel Foucault.

In 'What is an Author?' Foucault substitutes the question of 'author-function' for authorship, isolating the 'three egos' (Foucault, pp. 129–30) that form the coordinates of that function. Foucault insists on the strictly linguistic basis of authorial positioning, its dependence on such localising 'shifters' as the adverb and tense structure we found operating, for instance, in the unattributed Miltonic citation, 'Nothing *is here* for tears'. Deployed as the novel's own last inscription, these Miltonic lines orient the closure of a text that finds itself passing both back as well as forward into literary history.[13] Apart from its thematic suggestion of the presence-within-absence of the dead prophet, Mordecai, in discursive terms 'who' can be said to 'author' this utterance in Milton's (onetime) words? Who is speaking – and from where? Is it Manoa, father of Samson? Milton, father of Samson? Eliot, author of neither but having the words of both in her keep? Eliot's narrator, the reader as perpetuator? And what kind of authorial ego is this? Effaced by tradition? Elevated on its crest?

In Foucault's view, the divergent 'egos' determining the author-function are given play among, roughly speaking, the signator, the narrator, and some position that we might call the projector. There is on the one hand the writing subject who signs and entitles (Mary Ann Evans inscribing her copyright as 'George Eliot,' for example) and on the other the subject – or in Foucault's (like Poulet's) phrase the enunciating 'second self' – who does the speaking (an omniscient persona, say, or first-person narrator). For Foucault, the '"author-function" arises out of their scission – in the division and distance of the two' (p. 129). The equivalent of this constitutive tension between 'I's in a scientific discourse would be, he explains, the subject who identifies the project embarked upon and completed as distinct from the 'I' that conducts the logical steps of the demonstration. 'It is also possible to locate a third ego: one who speaks of the goals of his investigation . . . and the problems yet to be solved' (p. 130). In conjunction with the ego that enters upon, and then the one that subsequently defines, the enunciation of its text, this putative third ego is the one that enters the text itself into a broader field of discourse. As against the 'I's that initially fix and then construct the discourse, this third 'I' situates it beyond itself. The quasi-biographical (even if pseudonymous) ego – that starting point (itself a point of no return) for all representations – is thus matched at closure by the ego of extrinsic destiny.

Apart from the clear case of an ongoing scientific (or, we might add, political or religious) project, it is not at all clear whether, or where, Foucault would find such a 'third ego' in fiction. But it should by now be apparent where this essay would be inclined to locate such an authorial function in *Daniel Deronda*. Indeed, to follow Foucault's emphasis on adverbial shifters, my claim would be that it is implicit at closure across that now *three*-way 'scission', demarcating the most obvious (the second ego's) 'here' of the omnisciently rendered dramatic scene ('Nothing is here for tears'); the supervisory 'here' (and now) of intentional vantage, whose purpose is to effect just this discursive retreat from undue sentimentality; and the 'here' (as well as temporal 'now then') of a cathartic and reflective reading under the auspices of authorial inspiration: the 'here' of looking back and going forward. This final (ad)version of the ego localises the always displaced present of a reading that includes the evaluation of its own response. When, in the very moment of closure, the middle (mediating) ego of the discursive voice is annihilated, vanishing into the gap opened by the very transaction with literary history involved in the Miltonic quotation, the bracketing egos of narrative intent and cultural motive may resolve themselves like vectors into the force field of inspired reception. Understood as a field of action rather than of passive acceptance, as the realm of an eventuation, this version of reading – as an entrance upon the conditions of intellectual, and hence, social empowerment – is very far from the idealised and abstracted notion in Poulet of a sheer consciousness of consciousness, a subjectivity without objectivity. What Eliot's text would seem rather to leave us with is indeed an objectivity, a cultural object, as easy to recognise as it is difficult to describe or circumscribe: the vast humanist programme of her art, her always moralised imagination of the 'larger life'. Rather than offering a reified image of the conceiving and constructive mind, that is, her text *puts us in mind*: of all that is left to be done by the work of thought in action.

To account for the ideological privileging of transmitted cultural wisdom in Eliot's fictional strategy, one might wish to modify a famous early pronouncement of Roland Barthes's about texts in reception with one of his subsequent propositions about narrative fiction in particular. Barthes's maxim that 'the birth of the reader must be at the cost of the death of the Author' (Barthes, 'Death', p. 148)[14] needs qualification – in its radical externalisation of the site of meaning – by his later emphasis in *S/Z* on the (still internally) 'pensive text' (Barthes, *S/Z*, pp. 216–17). This is that equilibrated closure of 'replete' narrative which always suggests a thematic (hence interpretive) residue or supplement, something not quite used up by plot. Instead of the scenario of usurpation by which obliterated author is sacrificed to the freedom of an inseminated reader, we might rather say that in *Daniel Deronda* the evoked institution of reading, the subjection of a text to the terms of its own reception, provides the virtual parthenogenesis of the reader from the tireless brain of the author's third ego.

Emerging near the close of *Daniel Deronda*, then, is Eliot's dream for the 'full presence' of her ideas in perpetuity, ideas embodied in reader rather than text, incarnate in the action they motivate instead of the action they emplot. It is this that the text insinuates when it has Mordecai speak of an unbound (and boundless) 'fuller volume' (Eliot, p. 802) of cultural engagement, punning on – while out-stripping – the textual limitations of just that multi-volume genre of Victorian writing that has paved the way for his intended heroic out-reach. From the perspective of her last work, Eliot implies that the authorial function is to provide fictions not just as aesthetic achieve-ments but as rhetorical instruments, novels not just huge but enlarging, novels that always – and only the more blatantly here – close by opening out. The truly 'novel' is that whose freshness, whose force, is renewed in each reading, a power that follows upon, in part by coming after, its plot. *Daniel Deronda* is Eliot's production in much the sense that its eponymous hero is coopted as Mordecai's production. The hero, in his promised survival beyond the text, is thus one indispensable proxy of the text named for and containing him. Like Mordecai's cultural masterplan, Eliot's writing also con-stitutes a work 'authorised' by being perpetually re-worked in the mind of the reader, inconclusive and thus endless, in short re-readable – in that brand of reactivation, that form of remembrance, known as interpretation.

There is no denying, however that the novel's abrupt, splayed

'closure' can easily be taken for a symptom (of internal and irreconcilable contradictions) rather than an asymptote (of extrinsic
destination). The most unflinching rejection of *Daniel Deronda* has
come recently from the Marxist perspective of Franco Moretti, who
reads the 'terrible' failure (Moretti, p. 226) of the book as the last
gasp of that already depleted genre, the European *Bildungsroman*.
For Moretti, George Eliot had already come up against the in-
adequacy of such a canonical format to address her culture's attenuated models of youth and maturation, well before the bankrupt
fabrications of *Daniel Deronda*. An irreparable rent in the conceptions
of personal destiny – between self-culture and vocation, private and
social fulfilment – is already apparent in *Middlemarch*, exposed in the
interrelated motivations of Dorothea and Will and travestied respectively by those of Rosamond and Lydgate. By the time of her
last novel, all chance for the generic energy and momentum of a
potential *Bildung* is squandered from the outset, where Gwendolen
is closer to the ineducable *belle* and the hero is all latent vocation to
begin with – just waiting for the invocation. When Mordecai points
the finger, it is as if Daniel is by that very fact already marked as one
of the 'chosen people', fulfilling a destiny spiritually nurtured long
before it turns out to be genetically prescribed. He need not grow
into his role, nor even go looking for it; it descends on him *ex
machina*, the whole Romantic dramaturgy of youth levelled in the
process. This is, in rough outline, the novel Moretti is bent on
dismissing.

I would argue rather that the generic impasse of the *Bildungsroman*
form in *Middlemarch* has redirected Eliot's efforts in *Daniel Deronda* in
a way that attempts the revival of such a narrative format on new –
and formally articulated – grounds. Moretti is right that 'Eliot shifts
literary genres' early on in the divergence of Daniel's plot from
Gwendolen's, from realistic novel to 'melodramatic fairy tale' – or in
other terms from novel to romance. But this leaves unclear the
continuing hold of the *Bildungsroman* (subgenre? mode?) on either
or both of these narrational options. Against Moretti's claim of
defaulture and obsolescence, it is one last implication of the present
essay that Eliot, still with the psychological trajectories of this format
of maturation in mind, is attempting to resolve novel and romance
together into a third narrative genre: a prophetic epic. But this is not
first and foremost an epic of Jewish tribal consolidation. She is
instead prospectively mounting, by setting its stage, primarily the
epic of her own readership, the founding of a newly empowered

tribe of moral activists and cultural interpreters. In this sense the generic expectations of 'growth' or 'education' are shifted outward to emplot the growth and edification of her own audience. Between Gwendolen's disaster and Daniel's triumph, that is to say, between her unequipped life and his vocational fervour (the latter replacing, by subsuming, the usual marriage trope that closes off the exigence and contingency of the *Bildungsroman* form), between her falling short and his forging on, lies (open) all that reading which she has not – but he has, and we in part will have – accomplished when we move on from this book to yet another. The model of evolving mentality has become less an effectual literary form than a form of literary effect. Openness, promise, potentiality: these now characterise not a hero's field of action so much as the space of reading. Out of the very dead end of the genre's romantic operability (that exhausted narrative pattern diagnosed by Moretti), Eliot has ended up essaying the *Bildungsroman* of her own ideal reader, imagined en masse: the reader as social subject.

Whatever declines in a given fictional genre – as genre – this novel might be taken to witness, it therefore remains – as structural provocation – an undaunted monument to the Victorian fictional agenda as a whole, the constitution of a readership as a secular congregation. As such, this quintessential Victorian masterwork is not primarily a work at all, fixed and finished, over when the two entwined plots have been played out, and not just an act of writing either. It dreams, by dramatising, its own visionary transcendence of mere material signification – to become that ultimately bodiless thing, a public 'text'. By such a concerted mystification of its own effect, this novel moves to exceed inscription, to be less citation than incitation. In this sense it is a work sent into production only after the fact, a story whose full reach is achieved only in the event of a reading. And whose unity is therefore always *ex post facto*, always provisional.

In all this it should be obvious that Eliot designs to summon from the unsaid blank at the premature close of her novel something more palpable and felt, more motivating, than Poulet's generalised and incorporeal 'subjectivity without objectivity'. The text's appeal must be directed instead at the specific subjectivity which the reading of such a text is meant to anchor, confirm, and unify. Here we encounter, for and in ourselves, a second intended proxy of Mordecai's devolved vision. The reading subject is not so much positioned by the narrative, pinned down, as commissioned by it to win its own wholeness and authenticity from the fracturing of the text before it, the overt challenge of cleft emphasis and allegiance. Closural form is revealed once and for all in its affective dimensions: in what we might now call the psychopoetics of a structured *response*. To read in this way is not a reading-in but a reading-*out*.

Certainly the book does nothing to mask its own self-divisions. It all but flaunts its contradictory and wrenching claims on us, right through to the doubly truncated 'finish'. The text knows full well that we cannot 'accept' equally its two halves, that we cannot 'identify' with Gwendolen and Mordecai at the same time, in any intuitive 'oneness' of response. It knows that its polarised subject matter is written with different subjects in mind – but held together in the *one mind* of a narrating consciousness whose powers, if the text does its work, will eventually refashion the consciousness of all that is – and all who are – subject to it: of my reading, of me reading. The text thus attempts to render its own formal extremity redemptive. In my always trying encounters (even in retrospect) with an only apparent textual divisiveness, it is not it, finally, but I who should be made one: the continually split subject held (together) in suspension between the contrary sways of reading. Interpretation stabilises me rather than the text's plurality. And the horizons of this interpretation are foreshadowed here, as we have seen, under the name of Zion. As the cultural code word for a political aggregate, of course, this promised land is also the eventual secular site of that Unity wrested from dispersion which characterises the theological (and nationalistic) impulse itself. This unity is, in turn, the transcendental ideal not only of the novel, and of the epic consciousness for whom it is named, but of the ideologically circumscribed 'I' who is supposedly returned strengthened to myself somewhere in the temporal space following on from closure.

To meet the challenge of Eliot's novel, to put its pieces together in contemplation and interpretation, to find its principle of unity, I must, in other words, pull myself together. The Victorian novel becomes here the acknowledged *pars pro toto* of itself as social institution. It goes public in me. What other major fictions of the period ask of me but call giving, what other stories offer up to the process of reception, this story moves to process while my response is still only in the offing. Straining to override its very textuality in the foretelling of its effects, *Daniel Deronda* attempts nothing less than the reading of its own reading.

Notes

1. References given in the text are to the titles and editions listed in the Bibliography following these notes.

2. In an article on Eliot's allusive invocation of contemporaneous debates within Biblical hermeneutics over 'The Apocalypse of the Old Testament', Mary Wilson Carpenter's subtitle, *'Daniel Deronda* and the Interpretation of Interpretation', may sound deceptively close to the interests of my own essay. Like the reading by Cynthia Chase, however, to which her work is cast in part as a rejoinder, Carpenter's essay concentrates upon the internal linkages of narrative event by which a comprehensive reading is made possible, rather than upon the largest ramifications of the novel as a whole under pressure of the reader's interpretive compulsions. Where Chase takes the novel to be deconstructing the narrative logic of cause-and-effect by generating the former out of the latter, Carpenter sees this, less sceptically, as the reconstructive work performed by any process of historical analysis, a process which has no choice but to read causality backward from its manifested effects. Whereas for Chase the unmentioned circumcision of the hero, sign of his vocation as a genetic cause, is what we might call the structuring absence around which the narrative turns, for Carpenter the place of this absence is taken rather by the Feast of the Circumcision, the new year's day of both Hebrew and Christian prophecy. On either reading, the materials of interpretation (or its undermining) are examined as provided by and in the narrative, primed for a hermeneutics of textual uncovering. The present essay is preoccupied instead with the open-ended interpretability of the text after its formal closure: a structuring absence, one might say, at the point of reception. One cause behind the novel's constructed effects is thus in another sense the social, political, and moral 'cause' – Zionism, broadly conceived, or at least its attendant libertarian sensibility – which, in various existential forms, these narrative constructions are meant to *effect* in the mind of the reader. It is in this sense that my reading is more nearly related to D. A. Miller's punning central claim for the Victorian novel as 'the very genre of the liberal subject, both as cause and effect: the genre that produces him, the genre to which, as its effect, he returns for "recreation"' (Miller, *The Novel*, p. 216).

3. Barbara Hardy's note to her edition of the novel reads simply: *'The story is chipped off.* Like *Daniel Deronda'* (p. 895 n. 4). In *Tradition Counter Tradition,* Joseph Boone includes *Daniel Deronda* among the 'form-breaking' structural experiments in Victorian fiction in which marital ideology comes into tension with a resistance to ordinary domestic closure and consolidation. Without citing Hardy's note, Boone too sees this episode as exemplary. On his account, 'the end of book 8 has been self-reflexively foreshadowed in the fable of Berenice that Daniel's artist friend Hans tells' (Boone, p. 184).

4. Dryden's fictional disputants achieve a rare moment of unanimity in agreeing that an unenacted death succeeds by drawing on the audience's previous investment in the fated character. What goes

unsaid in Dryden, though, is an acknowledgement of the deepest fitness of this approach: its parable of the mind's access to death. It may be argued that the chief impact of death on life is never in the event but in its reflection, in what there is to say about it before undergoing it. Such a dramatic structure as advocated by Dryden thus encodes by hiatus the blank of death and processes by discourse its affective force. In Eliot's novel, the meaning of Grandcourt's end lies almost entirely in its after-effects on the heroine, who can clear neither memory nor conscience of her failure to rescue him from the sea. Other motives, though not unrelated as we will later see, remove – just barely – the moment of Mordecai's death from direct 'mimesis' in omniscient narrative.

5. See especially the fourth chapter, 'Freud's Masterplot: A Model for Narrative' (Brooks, pp. 90–112). A related approach to the way in which each novelist 'motivates the narratable with different kind of content' is found in D. A. Miller's argument that 'the drift of desire . . . and the drift of the sign' represents the 'erotic' and 'semiotic' motivations of narrative (Miller, *Narrative*, p. xi), its alternative push-and-pull toward closure.

6. Following a tendency descended from the earliest reviewers of *Daniel Deronda*, Peter Garrett, for instance, sees the novel divided between 'novelistic' and 'romance' treatments of the Gwendolen and Deronda plots respectively (Garrett, p. 168). In this regard, however, the disjoint plots function (as the title of his chapter on Eliot would have it) as 'equivalent centers' in the novel.

7. Whereas Maggie explicitly evokes the river that will end her in her brother's arms when insisting that 'the first thing I ever remember in my life is standing with Tom by the side of the Floss while he held my hand' (*The Mill on the Floss*, Chapter V, i), Mirah, who thinks 'my life began with waking up and loving my mother's face' (Eliot, p. 250), believes, after her mother's death, that the virtually amniotic reversion of drowning 'was the way to her' (p. 262) once again. I consider Maggie's earlier drowning at some length in *Death Sentences* (Stewart, pp. 113–22). More recently, Judith Wilt discusses both the 'drowning woman topos' and 'the unnarrated drowning scene' familiar to Victorian fiction in connection with Grandcourt's death in *Daniel Deronda* (Wilt, p. 331).

8. In the concluding book of *The Prelude*, Wordsworth recalls the origination of the poem in his apostrophe to that life which had already elapsed by the inaugural point of departure: 'I said unto the life which I had lived, / Where art thou?' (XIV, ll.379–80). The answer is sought in a kind of retroactive spatialisation of temporal existence in which Wordsworth 'saw beneath me stretched' – like a corpse waiting to be anatomised – 'Vast prospect of the world which I had been / And was' (ll.383–4). In hearing the whole of a memorial narrative thus brought to a close in the recapitulation of its sponsoring impulse, Coleridge at one remove recalls 'awakening as a babe / Turbulent' (ll.65–6), moving again through the subsequent stages of 'Youth' and 'Manhood'. Inundated by Wordsworth's genius, he is submerged in his own past,

figured as an unwanted recuperation, a story renewed again at peril of regret.

9. Hardy's gloss takes no note of the thematic overtones of this change: 'An interesting small instance of George Eliot's careful revision: she first wrote "shock" and then must have decided that "wave" was more suitable for the gradually spreading mental and physical reaction' (Eliot, p. 903).

10. Gillian Beer has recently dropped in passing the intriguing hint that the relation of Grandcourt to his obnoxious minion Lush is a 'sick parody' (Beer, *George Eliot*, p. 227) in one plot of the relation of Mordecai as prophet to Daniel, his acolyte or priest, in the other. If so, the force of this satiric redoubling and demotion might be carried further by Grandcourt's peculiar relation to writing and his use of Lush as a perverse mechanism of transmission. Even when having to convey some disagreeable aspects of his last will and testament to Gwendolen, Grandcourt remains one of the class of men who hated 'to write letters' and who would never 'rush into manuscript and syntax on a difficult subject in order to save another's feelings' (Eliot, p. 657). Whereas Mordecai commissions Daniel for the instrumentation of his posthumous dream, Grandcourt recruits Lush, 'as much of an implement as pen and paper' (p. 657), to transcribe the intent of his Casaubon-like 'dead hand', his posthumous will to power.

11. John Kucich's treatment of Sydney Carton as an exemplary Dickensian case of a 'desire' that 'seeks its fulfillment outside the limits of selfhood, in the death of the individual' (Kucich, p. 204) – in Carton's case by a 'semisuicidal act' of supposed 'self-negation' (p. 210) as the culmination of an 'opposition of passion to repression' (p. 241) – suggests to my mind connections with Eliot's novel that Kucich himself does not draw out. In considering the dialectic of self and other in *Daniel Deronda*, Kucich's interest in the 'surprisingly dependent egotists' (p. 199) of Eliot's career leads him to concentrate on Gwendolen rather than Mordecai, even though it is in the latter's relation with Daniel that the 'general fraternal intention' (p. 116) of Eliot's societal ethic and the 'erotic element in repression' (p. 286) might most problematically coalesce. Mordecai seems to function in this last novel as a fictional construct designed by Eliot to overcome, even at the cost of his life, just the double-bind that Kucich diagnoses in her work: a recurrent tendency for the self to 'protect autonomy' by preserving 'the balance of self-negation and self-affirmation in an asocial, inward dialectic' (p. 200). Mordecai's schemed projection of his ego outward into Daniel, and through him to a tribal apotheosis – advancing a nationalist venture by his own paradoxically hubristic effacement – is in this sense Eliot's most troubled and illustrative, her last and most explicit, address to the crisis of dual motive at the root of desire.

12. In *Darwin's Plots*, Gillian Beer sees the angling of *Daniel Deronda* towards an unwritten evolutionary future as evidence that 'descent and extension are the ordering principle – and finally its unsolvable problems' (p. 182). I follow Beer in thinking that the encyclopaedic

mythological ambitions of the work 'form part of an argument which
is conducted for the most part covertly, expressed almost as much
through structures as through semantics' (p. 196). Part of this
structuring is for Beer a matter of chronology, the way 'George Eliot
draws upon a spatial model of time' (p. 209). Reading the novel's
opening in these terms, Beer notes that, though we meet Gwendolen
before Mirah, Daniel's encounter with the latter actually precedes the
opening scene by a year, '*chronological* time' is thus overshadowed by
'narrative time' (p. 207) in its claims upon the reader's sense of
priority. In remarks that verge intriguingly close to those of Cynthia
Chase on the confounding – or deconstruction – of causality, Beer
speaks of an 'ordering' in this episode that 'does not rely upon cause
and effect, not upon moral discrimination, but poises itself exactly at
the point where chance and intention intersect' (p. 208). I would then
look to the end of the novel for the relaxation of intentionality
towards contingency once again. This may be true of all novelistic
closure, but it is a fact made active, structural, in *Daniel Deronda*,
where the subordination of chronological to narrative time is
chiastically reversed in the novel's closural thrust beyond plot.

13.   In the final chapter of *The Sense of an Audience*, called 'Severing
Relations,' Janice Carlisle, arguing for Eliot's self-conscious divorce
from her previous popular readership, interprets Eliot's recourse to a
Miltonic coda in *Daniel Deronda* as a deliberate surrender of continuous narrative voicing and authority: 'Storytelling as a source of
relation and mediation is no longer the powerful force it has been'
(Carlisle, p. 218). What I am suggesting is rather that the content of
the coda, grammatical as well as thematic, together with the formal
disjuncture of voice it introduces, operates more complexly – guiding
what Eliot imagines as a more strenuous, participatory, and elitist
engagement with her text on the part of its ultimately *authored* reader.

14.   Foucault comes to his discriminations of the 'author-function' after
considering more 'traditional' ideas about the 'kindship between
writing and death' (Foucault, pp. 116–17): the notion both that
writing immortalises the self – witness Poulet's mention of an author
'saving his identity from death' (Poulet, p. 58) – and that it at the same
time voluntarily obliterates that self, in one sense defeating but in
another merely repeating the work of death. We might thus read
Mordecai's attempted escape from textual memorialisation as a
stratagem designed to break this deadlock, to achieve a perpetuity
that will not at the same time entirely annul him. Though Foucault
does not return to this motif of 'death' via 'perpetuation' (or vice
versa) later in his essay, it is tempting to think of the 'third ego' of
authorship as an envisioned shoving-off from scriptive entombment
into that continuous renewal incident to interpreted discourse.

Bibliography

Barthes, Roland, 'The Death of the Author', *Image—Music—Text*, translated by Stephen Heath (New York: Hill and Wang, 1971).

Barthes, Roland, *S/Z*, translated by Richard Miller (New York: Hill and Wang, 1974).

Boone, Joseph Allen, *Tradition Counter Tradition: Love and the Forms of Fiction* (Chicago: University of Chicago Press, 1987).

Beer, Gillian, *Darwin's Plots: Evolutionary Narrative in Darwin, George Eliot, and Nineteenth-Century Fiction* (London: Routledge and Kegan Paul, 1983).

Beer, Gillian, *George Eliot* (London: Harvester, 1986).

Brooks, Peter, *Reading for the Plot: Design and Intention in Narrative* (New York: Knopf, 1984).

Carroll, David (ed.) *George Eliot: The Critical Heritage* (London: Routledge and Kegan Paul, 1971).

Carlisle, Janice, *The Sense of an Audience: Dickens, Thackeray, and George Eliot at Mid-Century* (Athens, Georgia: University of Georgia Press, 1981).

Carpenter, Mary Wilson, 'The Apocalypse of the Old Testament: *Daniel Deronda* and the Interpretation of Interpretation', *PMLA*, vol. 99 (1984) pp. 56–67.

Chase, Cynthia, 'The Decomposition of the Elephants: Double Reading *Daniel Deronda*', *PMLA*, vol. 93 (1978) pp. 215–27.

Dryden, John, 'An Essay of Dramatic Poesy', *The Works of John Dryden: Prose 1668–1691*, Vol. XVII, edited by Samuel Holt Monk (Berkeley: University of California Press, 1971).

Empson, William, *Seven Types of Ambiguity* (New York: New Directions, 1947).

Empson, William, *Some Versions of Pastoral* (New York: New Directions, 1947).

Eliot, George, *Daniel Deronda*, edited by Barbara Hardy (Harmondsworth, UK: Penguin, 1967).

Garrett, Peter K., *The Victorian Multiplot Novel: Studies in Dialogical Form* (New Haven: Yale University Press, 1980).

Foucault, Michel, 'What Is an Author?', in Donald F. Bouchard (ed.) *Language, Counter-Memory, Practice*, translated by Donald Bouchard and Sherry Simon (Cornell: Cornell University Press, 1977).

Haight, Gordon S. (ed.) *The George Eliot Letters*, Vol. 7 (New Haven: Yale University Press, 1955).

Kucich, John, *Repression in Victorian Fiction: Charlotte Bronte, George Eliot, and Charles Dickens* (Berkeley: University of California Press, 1987).

Miller, D. A., *Narrative and its Discontents: Problems of Closure in the Traditional Novel* (Princeton: Princeton University Press, 1981).

Miller, D. A., *The Novel and the Police* (Berkeley: University of California Press, 1988).

Moretti, Franco, *The Way of the World: the 'Bildungsroman' in European Culture* (London: Verso, 1987).

Poulet, Georges, 'Phenomenology of Reading', *New Literary History*, vol. 1 (October 1969) pp. 53–68.

Stewart, Garrett, *Death Sentences: Styles of Dying in British Fiction* (Cambridge, Massachusetts: Harvard University Press, 1984).
Wilt, Judith, '"He would come back": The Fathers of Daughters in *Daniel Deronda*', *Nineteenth-Century Literature*, vol. 42 (1987) pp. 313–61.

6

Against Completion: Ruskin's Drama of Dream, Lateness and Loss

Mary Ann Caws

. . . I never can enjoy any place until I come to it the second time. Tomorrow – what shall I do tomorrow. Anything but think. (*Diaries*, 11 March 1841)[1]

I cannot understand why my dreams are not nobler, nor consistent; must watch this. (*Diaries*, Saturday 10 August 1867)

I TOO PASSIONATE

To Ruskin we come, whether for enjoyment or puzzlement, as to a place beloved and perplexing, always, at least for the second time. An immense sorrow seems often to radiate from the man Henry James thought 'the author of the most splendid pages in our language', who had spent his life, James continued, in a 'too passionate' endeavour to right what he found wrong, to establish his 'rigid conception of the right' (Hunt, p. 5). The sorrow has partly to do with the non-establishment, finally, of that right, and the vivid incompletion of his work – as even his massively regretful *Praeterita* took on its appendaged *Dilecta*, and cross-references began to, and never ceased to, abound everywhere.[2] It has no less to do with the waning of the passion and, of course, of its objects. Hoping to do so much with every day, as Ruskin wrote to his mother (12 July 1869), he always found the ends of things sorrowful, days, voyages, projects: always he would have done so little, he felt, building up such accumulations of failure. Thus, the 'anything but think' by which he cautioned himself, a useless cushion intended as buffer against meditating on that failure and on a certain loss of everything.

For he tried so dreadfully hard. His diary reveals his efforts, his distress, and his re-solutions. On 6 June 1841: 'I have formed resolutions to be always trying to get knowledge of some kind or other, or bodily strength, or some real available, continuing good. .' But by the next day, he would slip out of the temper of that being 'good', and thus berate himself, as James reminds us, for his timidity and irresolution, across from his 'selfishnesses, prides, insolences, failures'. But over and over he tried: on 5 July 1849: . . . 'really my Chamouni work has been most disappointing to me – and humiliating. I can't do it yet, but I have the imagination of it in me, and *will* do it yet, someday' (*Diaries*, p. 401). The images of nature and those of the self mingle, depressingly: in October 1858: 'I have had cloud upon me this year, and don't quite know the meaning of it; only I have had no heart to write to anybody', he says in a letter to Elizabeth Barrett Browning, continuing the lament: 'I am not able to write as I used to do nor to feel, and can only make up my mind to the state as one that has to be gone through, and from which I hope some day to come out on the other side' (14 October 1858, Clark, p. 55). Whether or not he ever could come out to the other side is debatable – but his struggle is surely sensed, and it is that that moves us.

Bizarrely, his sense of mental power and his sense of sadness were, eventually, to coincide. Thus, a far later diary entry, on 17 August 1873: 'Got up this morning with good resolutions. Odd, that 're' should give such force to 'solve'. But it may be 're' too often' (*Diaries*, p. 751). It is in his own mind that the trouble arises and this is, naturally, what appeals to the modern Ruskin reader, who is likely to listen with special sympathy to the recounting of the inside/ outside split: witness this entry, from 3 May 1877:

> Everything going well (but so slowly!) except my own mind, which is in a quite discomfited and disgraced state . . . except only in taking shame to itself for all failure, and resigning itself to what of distress it has to bear, and to what pleasure it can take; my clear duty being now to be as happy as I can, so redeeming what I can of the past which has been so lost or miserable – happy for the sake of others always, without wanting, for pride's sake, that they should know how hard it costs to be happy. (*Diaries*, p. 950)

The shame is always taken unto himself, the reprimand to the self absorbed unquestioningly. The distress and disorder seem to radiate from the self outward, from the person to the work which was, perhaps, to have saved the person.

We listen, then, as, repeatedly, his cry echoes: 'I *cannot* get into order' (*Diaries*, February 1854). 'I cannot get to my work in this paper, somehow; the web of these old enigmas entangles me again and again' (*Crown of Wild Olive*, p. 149). Things uncompleted all about him, 'violent little fragments of undelivered lecture' (*Queen of the Air*, p. 157). Everywhere, incoherence threatening this greatest of minds until silence finally takes over altogether – how can our picture of Ruskin, or, most often, his of himself, be other than tragic? 'I cannot speak, to purpose', he maintained, 'of anything about which I do not care' (*Crown of Wild Olive*, Lecture II on 'Traffic', p. 51). Caring about too much, speaking and thinking of too much, far from unsung, this great hero of genius and madness is a reliable cornerstone for what too much passionate feeling and thinking can lead to: 'anything but think' indeed.

II LESSONS

In better times, thinking and focus and caring and seeing attentively were entirely his aim, held up against a flagging sense of the tiresomeness of so much attention paid to everything. Reflecting upon a simple Sunday walk in Switzerland, in June 1849, he notes in his diary his ascent to Blonay (over which walk, however, the sunset was to sink upon him 'like the departure of youth' – no one is quite so hauntingly time-haunted as Ruskin). He notes, and we with him, how his hot march between the vines and 'dead stone walls' begins to seem tiresome until his wonderfully puritanical will takes over and focus returns. The passage is emblematic of his almost desperate intention to control and to pay attention in one of its moments of total success – a recapturing of a 'boy's soul' in himself by an ageing scoutmaster of the eye and notepad. That all this should be noted in his diary puts it at yet another remove from the instantaneous reaction of the walk itself and yet closer to what serves the reader as, precisely, a *lesson* about reading places with mind, heart, imagination, and eye. 'I have not insisted enough on this', he will say – as if in his preaching to himself, he were also speaking for us:

. . . then I put my *mind* into the scene, instead of suffering the body only to make report of it; and looked at it with the possession – taking grasp of the imagination – the true one. It gilded all the dead walls, and I felt a charm in every vine tendril that hung over them. It required an effort to maintain the feeling – it was poetry while it lasted – and I felt that it was only while under it that one could draw or invent or give glory to any part of such a landscape. I repeated 'I am in *Switzerland*' over and over again, till the name brought back the true group of associations – and I felt I had a soul, like my boy's soul, once again. I have not insisted enough on this source of all great contemplative art. The whole scene without it was but sticks and stones and steep dusty road. (*Diaries*, p. 381).

Thus he instructs himself to repeat, like some incantation, the name, until attendant associations restore the soul, once again. There follows a lesson on focus, learned on the way back down from Blonay, which he notes for future reference: he longs to draw a 1609 tower with its conical roof mingling with the distant mountain peaks of Meillerie seen through an open window, but refrains because of the fence and field beneath it, which might have seemed to detract from that upper register. The specific details of date and place bring all this into clear focus, and then, as he corrects himself by 'throwing' his mind 'full into the fence and field' as if there were only those details to deal with, he finds the enviable trinity of 'light and power and loveliness' in his own sketch.

A double lesson emerges from this reflection: that even over the most focused and successful of creation scenes, brought about by the most carefully-attentioned and intentioned intelligence and imagination, the sunset inevitably sinks; but that nevertheless, in spite of the perpetual too-lateness and the eventual loss of sight, its moment of non-illusory presence was or can have been – because of its precise focus – real.

Among the numerous recalls of Ruskin's mastery by Proust, that quite unforgettable and justly celebrated moment of the recapture of the steeples of Martinville as they are noted down by the young Marcel as they recede from his sight in the distance – the beginning of his writing work – seems to recapture this scene. In similar fashion, the older Marcel's rapt concentration on the way a tree trunk divides its part of shadow and its part of light, among other tree scenes – seems to recapture the wonderful passage in *Praeterita* of branches, sky, and vision held in tight and creative focus.

Repeatedly, the narrowness of the focus is stressed, with a certain regret about what is *not* seen: 'nothing to see but . . .', 'no prospect whatever but . . .', 'when there were sandstone rocks to be sought for', 'today, I missed rocks, palace, and fountain. . . .'. The passage holds the reader's focus in much the same precise way as does the tower scene in its details, and the focus is sharpened by the regret for what is not included:

> . . . getting into a cart-road among some young trees, where there was nothing to see but the blue sky through thin branches . . . the branches against the blue sky began to interest me, motionless as the branches of a tree of Jesse on a painted window . . . How I had managed to get into that utterly dull cart-road, when there were sandstone rocks to be sought for . . . And to-day, I missed rocks, palace, and fountain all alike, and found myself lying on the bank of a cart-road in the sand, with no prospect whatever but that small aspen tree gainst the blue sky.
>
> Languidly, but not idly, I began to draw it; and as I drew, the languour passed away: the beautiful lines insisted on being traced, – without weariness. More and more beautiful they became, as each rose out of the rest, and took its place in the air. With wonder increasing every instant, I saw that they 'composed' themselves, by finer laws than any known of men. At last, the tree was there, and everything that I had thought before about trees, nowhere. (*Praeterita*, pp. 283–5)

The discovery about trees themselves, in all their presence, abolishing previous suppositions and traces of weariness, seems increasingly wondrous; through sketching, he learns the composition of nature and how to retain its knowledge. Yet this serves as yet another cause of regret for Ruskin's characteristic attitude: his manservant carried his sketchbook around for him, but unused: 'in the evening there was too much always to be hunted out, of city; or watched, of hills, or sunset; and I rarely drew, – to my sorrow, now. I wish I knew less, and had drawn more' (*Praeterita*, p. 325). So nature has to be transformed through human design to be preserved; how art saves is another Proustian lesson drawn from Ruskin's drawing and not-drawing.

In preservation, nature was really precious little help, according to Ruskin. The sunsets she sent were bound to fade – 'It is going fast – fading fast – fading – gone' (*Praeterita*, p. 201) – and her clouds bound to grow dark, in parallel to the Storm Cloud of the Nineteenth Century which Ruskin felt about him and gave objective evidence of, outside as in himself. 'The deadliest of all things to me is my loss of faith in nature', he writes to Charles Eliot Norton on 13 February 1875 (Clark, p. 119): 'No spring – no summer. Fog always, and the snow faded from the Alps.' One of the great depressive geniuses of the Victorian age, says a recent article by Casillo, thus placing Ruskin in the same family of thinkers as Adrian Stokes, so influenced by Melanie Klein. In this position, the acceptance of loss precedes a compulsion to restore, says Stokes (Casillo, p. 5), and indeed as we watch Ruskin watching sunsets or gathering clouds, we see the immense effort of a man trying to put back together positively what seems to be working out its own *via negativa*, to labour towards the valuable, as in the definition he proffers in *Unto this Last*: 'To be "valuable", therefore, is to "avail towards life". A truly valuable or availing thing is that which leads to life with its whole strength' (p. 168).

But the intensity of the negative vision was so strong as to make impossible such restoration as he longed for, and everything seemed to come at the wrong time. 'But all this I have felt and learned, like so much else, too late', he exclaims in *Praeterita* (p. 326). Each thrill of happiness of which he is conscious he strives to retain, with the result that each of us knows: 'Which, if I had been able to keep! – Another "had been" this, the gravest of all I lost; the last with which I shall trouble the reader' (p. 346). So many desires stated so often, and so many regrets and losses; his dreams, simply stated and never analysed, offer a quite extraordinary catalogue of horrors: imprisoning places, images of faces twisted by wires in the nose, laden with wrinkles until they resemble death's heads, of serpents, of impotence: keys lost, or deformed, wives beaten, dogs with their legs crushed, and the like. In them, true drama seems often to lie, and a more clear statement of his problematic relation to his interior life.

III DRAMATIC FADING

'It was poetry while it lasted . . .' (*Diaries*, p. 201). A diary entry for early June, 1841, is illustrative of the Ruskinian vision of natural beauty, both in its intensity of waxing and waning and its correlation with the human heart. He is describing, at some length, the brightness of the snow, shining like the full moon and pouring light over lake Leman and the Pays de Vaud, and – detail by detail – the redness of the hills in the sunset, with grey above and below them, the snow red to bursting with conflagration, over shades of purple, then the light moving, leaving, going. The description is breathless with exclamation points at its inception, diminishing in excitement to dashes, question marks, and incompletions of interrogation and statement – like the sunset itself on the wane, the natural with hesitations and wondering humanly intertwined, in some great correspondent tragedy sensed and communicated by dramatic style, never entirely devoid of self-pity:

> Now the light has left the bases, but it is far along to the left on the broad field of snow, less and less but redder and redder. Oh, glorious! It is going fast; only the middle peak has it still – fading fast – fading – gone. All is cold but the sky, whose gray clouds are red above, and a soft clear twilight still far down the lake with the Voirons and Saleve against it. When shall I – Nay, now there is a faint red glow again on the snow fields to the left. It must have been a cloud which took it off before – When shall I see the sun set again on the lake Leman and who will be with me, or who not? All is cold now. (*Diaries*, p. 201)

The rhythm is remarkable as it seizes on the high points and pulses along to the lonely conclusion, from conflagration to cold, from red to gray, from communion between lyrical transcriber and spectacle to utter aloneness:

> Now the light
> but it is far
> less and less
> Oh, glorious
> going fast
> fading fast
> fading
> gone
> all is cold
> down the lake
> when shall I
> nay
> it must have been

when shall I
who will be
who not
all is cold now.

From the now to the now, the presentness of the spectacle could scarcely be more emphasised. From question to question: when, who, who not? the stress is shared and pushed on, in a consciously dramatic, even melodramatic style that precisely translates Ruskin's vital identification with the world exterior to him.

Like some set piece, this prose poem of an artist's observation works in its very brevity towards a completion which compensates in some sense for the incomplete entries, such as the one of January 1846 on the Mont Blanc and its 'great and glorious pyramid of purple in the evening light', like a lesson given only to him by his favourite mountain. To this entry there is a footnote of 19 January 1847, expressing surprise that he should never have completed this particular entry; it then continues to recount the events of that day, compares the lake in its calmness to a path towards Bunyan's celestial city: 'Her ways are pleasantness and all her paths are peace', describes his continuing in prayer and determination, and ends the addendum with a Nota Bene saying: 'A full year intervened between this entry and the last' (*Diaries*, p. 322).

Such urges towards completion are characteristic of Ruskin, as is the attendant depression at the incomplete. So the lament at the inconsistency of his dreams enters this system – they, too, should be completely inscribed in something seizable, understandable, finishable, ennobling. They too should be poetry.

IV   DRAMATIC DREAMING

'But all of this I have felt and learned, like so much else, to late' (*Praeterita*, p. 326). The lament that his dreams are not 'nobler, nor consistent', and the self-admonition to pay attention to that lack, comes directly after a dream whose bizarre nature does not hide – any more than do most of Ruskin's dreams – the intense eroticism of his sleeping imagination. It is, of course, as we would suspect, given his well-documented attachment to little girls, generally aroused in relation to them. (As for the lack of consistency, it is not so apparent as all that; far, indeed, from it.)

A dream in August 1867, for example, is signalled by Ruskin as being 'most singular', and so it is. He is laying out a garden, and a little monkey-like child brings him a bunch of keys to sell, of precious material, but he 'could not make out on what terms they were to be sold'. Then, in a theatre, an exotic girl is dancing, who had never shown her face or neck before, and is ashamed of doing so; behind her, the first little child who had brought the keys is with others in a little gallery, with Ruskin's father. So far, the reader would surely jump to certain not difficult conclusions, about little-ness, about keys and young exotic girls and, on top of it, as it were, one's father. I quote the rest of the dream, verbatim, since it is clearly marked as concerning the keys above all, in the mind of the dreamer and in his reported conversations as well as deeds, and conse-quently – consistently, I would say – goes on to deal with entrance, attainment of treasures and keys, and – in particular – since it will end with the same regret that incompletion brings to this 'great depressive Victorian genius'.

> And then it came back – the dream – to the keys, and I was talking about them with some one who said they were the keys of a great old Arabian fortress; and suddenly we were at the gate of it, and we could not agree about the keys; and at last the person who held them said; 'Would it not be better no one should have them?' and I said, 'Yes'; and he took a stone, and crushed them to pieces, and I thought no one could now ever get into the fortress for its treasures, and it would all moulder into ruin; and I was sorry, and woke.
>
> Except that my watch-key had got awkwardly entangled with my other keys, when I wound up my watch, I have no clue to this ridiculous dream, at all. (*Diaries*, p. 628)

No clue at all. Less ridiculous than watchful, this dream, and more interesting still in the light of the next entry, marked as taking place in WATERHEAD, and telling of a dream of Rose, which was dreamt not 'worthily, though not painfully', a statement followed by the one already quoted: 'I cannot understand why my dreams are not nobler, nor consistent; must watch this' (*Diaries*, p. 628). Every-one's dreams, runs the Freudian story, bear some watching, hold out some key, get awkwardly entangled, if we can stand to have a clue to their very consistency, not always noble.

A subsequent dream in February of 1868, depicts Russian

chambermaids (exotica are definitely part of Ruskin's dreaming dish) supplying four serpents in the tub to be fed, before he stumbles over an umbrella stand, with people in the passage thinking how awkward he is to take a pretty girl out walking. Ruskin's serpents writhe everywhere, throughout his dreams and lectures, figuratively a vivid part of the same system as the umbrella, and the pretty girl, chambermaids, exotica, and the rest.

It all fits. Try another dream of this same month, that of 26 February 1868, for example. This time, keys return, but in a different mode, as it were. He dreams of being in a large room eating, with a piece being played on a double-width piano at the side of which a square hole is cut just wide enough . . . but I should let John Ruskin tell the rest:

> just enough for a little girl-baby to sit in, who played on about seven keys, set across the other keys, all for herself. Then the grandmama played the great keys and the mama played on a deep soup-plate, with a knife handle, all very prettily; and I was standing leaning against a sort of kitchen dresser, with my knife and fork stuck out awkwardly at the musicians till I thought I had better put them down; so I did, on the dresser; and then the cook, behind me, began finding fault with my coat collar and asking leave to put it right and brush it, and as he was brushing he cried out at something, and I looked to see what he meant, and the lappet of my waistcoat was all stained with blood, and I thought I had been going about all the evening like that, and so I woke. (*Diaries*, p. 643)

Yes. The reader thinks, too, that he would have done better to put the knife and fork down, instead of having them sticking out rather suggestively at the family of women, girl-baby and all, even if it has to be on the dresser – never, it seems, too late for the bloodstain to get in the picture.

Bloodstains on the collar, as if in some deep sense he felt he deserved punishment for the protrusion in the dream of the utensils which are his own: the cook's 'finding fault with my . . . collar' occasions a dream which ends by a semi-castration, deserved by his fault. Here again, the accent and the climax – the crying out – are on what cannot be 'put right', no matter how much it is brushed at, brushed away, brushed into. His only declared thought in the dream is one of duration and ignorant behaviour: he had indeed been going about all evening like that, and all night, and probably some preceding nights too. All, really, that can be observed in such massively overdetermined understatements is that they might as well be waked from. Ruskin, declares the dream, hasn't a clue.

One further note on snakes in dreams: on 9 March, still in 1868, shortly after the last dream recounted, he takes too much wine and dreams of taking all the short cuts while sending Joan and Connie around by the road,

> and then came back with them jumping up and down banks of earth, which I saw at last were washed away below by a stream. Then of showing Joanna a beautiful snake, which I told her was an innocent one; it had a slender neck and a green ring round it, and I made her feel its scales. Then she made me feel it, and it became a fat thing, like a leech, and adhered to my hand, so that I could hardly pull it off – and so I woke. (*Diaries*, p. 644)

He may, of course, have told her it was an innocent one, and may himself have believed it; but Ruskin's imagery, and his imaged grasp, are rather more forceful than his apparent grasp of dream imagery – in that, above all, lies the drama.

One last dream of this same year will suffice to make the point or at least to illustrate the backdrop for it: he dreams of going to court, at the French emperor's, and getting one foot crossed over the other when he sits talking to the Empress,

> so as to crush her dress a little, and some Frenchman came in and was ready to faint with horror and amazement – and I couldn't uncross my foot, do what I would; and, afterwards, I was to go somewhere with the emperor, and he told me to wait ten minutes for him, and just as he was coming, I woke. And tonight, I was going to the English court in carriage following others rolling over a rumbling drawbridge, and just as I got to the palace door, couldn't find my ticket of entrance, or at least couldn't separate it from two others, each a quarter of a yard wide, tumbling about in bottom of carriage. (*Diaries*, p. 657)

It doesn't take a Frenchman to faint with amazement over that crossing and that crush – such a loud-speaking gesture it is – or over the fact that one wakes just as one is, or the other is, finally, coming. To say nothing of the way those tickets of entrance really swell up large when they are tumbling about, inseparable, in the bottom of the carriage. The dreams are still relatively full of the exotic, the swollen, the overdetermined and not really understated.

Elsewhere, and at other times – although 1868 seems a particularly rich year for this kind of closet drama – girls bathe in pools, give kisses that make the bullrushes quake around them, narrow glaciers are shut in soft ridges of snow, there is a bit of dwelling on six-inch long things, all this mixed with injunctions as to the dreadfulness of being too free with colour: 'License, and its evil'. Even Turner's colours led to abuse, in their too much of black and vermilion, and then all those fish and that red flesh, leading in their turn to 'foreground figures, and all that came of them', as Ruskin says, most incompletely (*Diaries*, p. 657). In the picture of everything dreamlike and daylike being so abundant, this particularly wonderful ellipsis sets us to filling in the details, like another drama incomplete, out of control, and definitely to be watched.

For Ruskin has that effect generally and specifically upon the reader, who eventually learns to project some sort of dramatic consequence and consistency into all his ellipses, wrongly or – does it make any difference – rightly? If it seems to other readers that this reader has been rather narrow in her focus, staring in particular here at one aspect of what is recuperated within the drama to offset the restatements of loss, I will end with one final passage from a dream of 2 November 1869. It takes place in Verona, or then not, 'some place that was and wasn't Verona. Met an Englishman, who said he "had been staring at things". I said I was glad to hear it – to stare was the right thing, to *look* only was no use' (*Diaries*, p. 685).

Notes

1. All references in the text are to titles and editions given in the Bibliography following these Notes.

2. See John Dixon Hunt's remarks on Ruskin's ever-expanding, never-completed work, in *The Wider Sea*.

   Elizabeth K. Helsinger, in 'The Structure of Ruskin's *Praeterita*', in *Approaches to Victorian Autobiography* calls the autobiography a strangely self-destructive work, written, to all evidence 'by a man who did not like himself. He measures his achievements, professional and personal, and concludes he is a failure.' She believes that we expect exactly what he refuses to offer:

a retrospective account which discovers some order, consistency, and purpose in past actions, a progress towards his present self. *Praeterita* lacks focus . . . The absence of introspection in all his memories is striking. Regret for lost opportunities is so frequent that it becomes obtrusive. The tone of discontent is pervasive. *Praeterita* is hardly adequate as personal history or apology. It is an apparently perverse undertaking, almost a sabotage of the self . . . These experiences do not . . . form a pattern of growth, a progressive development toward the achieved self of the moment of writing . . . but instead a series of repetitions and returns. (Landow, p. 87)

In short, his autobiography does not give us what we expect: this may reflect as badly on what we are assumed to expect as on what Ruskin offers – something different, to be sure. Precisely, I would maintain, this self-sabotage, this unself-congratulatory model, this refusal to try to order the self in a neat progress overlying what is, most frequently, not that, is what endears Ruskin to a twentieth-century mind. He has, she says, a peculiar sensibility rather than an achieved identity, is more attached to places than persons, digresses widely – are these not exactly the characteristics of our own sensibility when it is most honest with itself, most spontaneous with its own rhythms?

Bibliography

Casillo, Robert, 'The Stone Alive: Adrian Stokes and John Ruskin', *Journal of Pre-Raphaelite Studies*, vol. VII, no. 1 (November 1986) pp. 1–28.
Clark, Kenneth (ed.) *Ruskin Today* (Harmondsworth: Penguin, 1982).
The Diaries of John Ruskin, selected and edited by Joan Evans and John Howard Whitehouse (Oxford: Oxford University Press, 1956).
Hunt, John Dixon, *The Wider Sea – A Life of John Ruskin* (London: J. M. Dent, 1982).
Landow, George P. (ed.) *Approaches to Victorian Autobiography* (Athens, Georgia: Ohio University Press, 1979) especially Elizabeth K. Helsinger, 'The Structure of Ruskin's *Praeterita*'.
Letters of John Ruskin to Charles Eliot Norton, Vol. I (Boston and New York: Houghton Mifflin, 1904)
Proust, Marcel, *On Reading Ruskin*, translated and edited by Jean Autret, William Burford, and Phillip J. Wolfe; introduction by Richard Macksey (New Haven: Yale University Press, 1987).
Ruskin, John, *The Crown of Wild Olive, and the Cestus of Aglaia* (London: J. M. Dent, n.d.)
Ruskin, John, *Praeterita: The Autobiography of John Ruskin* (Oxford: Oxford University Press, 1949).
Ruskin, John, *The Queen of the Air* (Orpington, Kent: George Allen, 1883).
Ruskin, John, *Unto this Last. The Political Economy of Art. Essays on Political Economy* (London: Dent; New York: Dutton, 1968).

7

Controlling Death and Sex: Magnification v. the Rhetoric of Rules in Dickens and Thackeray

Carol Hanbery MacKay

Shall I believe
That unsubstantial Death is amorous,
And that the lean abhorrèd monster keeps
Thee here in dark to be his paramour?
(Shakespeare, *Romeo and Juliet*, 5.3.102–5)[1]

He held her, almost as if she were sanctified to him by death, and kissed her, once, almost as he might have kissed the dead.
(Dickens, *Our Mutual Friend*, p. 764)

Perhaps because sex and death involve such intense, primal emotions, the rhetoric of each often comes to resemble that of the other – that is, an intense poetic rendering of death may assume an erotic cast, while a rhetorical amplification of sexual desire frequently evokes images of death and dying. From Cupid's arrow to the Elizabethan slang term for sexual climax, 'to die', we witness this melding. My point here is primarily a rhetorical one, borne out especially well by Victorian fiction, but we can recognise a similar psychological tension existing in both desire and death – the tension between attenuation and completion – and presume that rhetoric, faced with the problem of expressing such opposite extremes in human experience, might be forced to conflate the two. Georges Bataille pursues the connection one step further in his basic formulation: 'eroticism is assenting to life even in the face of death' (Bataille, p. 11). By eroticising death, an author makes of death not an ending but something that is a part of the life process, itself endlessly repeated. And when death is rendered at moments which otherwise impose closure, this strategy becomes especially tempting, for it permits an author to resist an ending that implies the 'death' of his or her connection with the reading audience; in effect, this treatment allows the author to seduce the reader into a living, ongoing relationship.

But the desire to embellish death also presented a challenge to Victorian novelists, who – on some level of consciousness – sought to make death an aesthetic act without giving free rein to its erotic component. Garrett Stewart's full-length study of death scenes in British fiction confirms this concern with 'styles of dying' – or dying 'aestheticized' – while John Kucich's close analysis of Charles Dickens' *The Old Curiosity Shop* points equally well to how 'the eroticizing of death' can establish a conjunction that still keeps sexuality in check (Kucich, 1980, p. 64). Thus, our goal is to be alert to forms of control or distancing of death in Victorian fiction. Note, for example, how often Victorian novels focus on childhood mortality or death in old age. Even when these deaths are introduced primarily for mimetic purposes, they also provide Victorian novelists with a relative degree of asexuality or, at the very least, with a way of apparently introducing eroticism more safely.[2]

The favoured method for attempting this de-eroticisation involved a manipulation of time, which could reduce the tension between attenuation and completion. Besides making the victim very old or very young, the novelist could attenuate death in such a manner that the sexual element apparently disappears – as is the case in Dickens' *Great Expectations* with Miss Havisham, who seems to be living a perpetual, attenuated death-in-life, its erotic component buried in the dust and decay of time. Of course, to twentieth-century minds – aware of unconscious psychological mechanisms such as transferral, sublimation and repression – these efforts may sometimes seem less than wholly successful.[3] At the same time, however, such efforts and our attention to them can equally well remind us of our continuity with our Victorian predecessors regarding both obsession with and repression of sexuality, as the work of Michel Foucault and the recent collections edited by Martha Vicinus, Donald Cox, and Catherine Gallagher and Thomas Laqueur have attested.

Through Miss Havisham we can also read another major means of restraining the sexual aspect of death, often employed in conjunction with manipulations of time: the use of social rules and boundaries – power and powerlessness – to pre-empt the erotic through depersonalisation, isolation, and the dampening effect of ethical considerations or religious language.[4] One can try to lose the sexual element of death either through the powerlessness of the masses or through the extreme isolation of status, both of which are depersonalising. Specifically, Miss Havisham's powerlessness – her isolation and position as a social outcast – denies her sexual possibilities. At the same time, however, she exercises power by perpetuating through Estella her death-in-life, transferring the contained erotic component so effectively that Estella becomes the cold-hearted temptress, who in turn manipulates social rules and boundaries to self-destructive ends.

Social boundaries likewise de-eroticise death in Thomas Hardy's *Jude the Obscure* and Anthony Trollope's *Barchester Towers*. In Hardy's novel, eroticism is dispersed: Little Father Time commits murder and suicide 'because we are too menny' (Hardy, p. 266). And in Trollope's text, Bishop Grantly's all-too-unique social status dilutes the emotional component of his death by blending it with power machinations, as his son tries not to hope too fervently for the old man's timely demise (Trollope, pp. 1–9). Here we can recognise another example of eroticism transferred. Although the son's emotional intensity almost parallels the energy of sexual desire, his emotions are confused, ambivalent, and ultimately denied. Both of these cases also convey strong moral or ethical considerations – variations on the theme of social power – whose presence tends to defuse erotic potential.

With George Eliot and the ending of *The Mill on the Floss*, we witness a typically aesthetic treatment of death that reveals an almost overwhelming erotic component. Up until this point in the novel, the erotic has been kept fairly well in check, emerging briefly in the imagery of the Red Deeps and in Maggie Tulliver's 'electrical' response to Stephen Guest. Only at the moment of closure is the erotic allowed to dominate – in this case in an image of dissolved boundaries, of brother and sister dying in each other's arms. Maggie and Tom Tulliver are at the mercy of the raging floodwaters of the river Floss, its fatal vehicle inevitably 'hurrying on in hideous triumph'. Suffused with foreboding, the scene is rife with erotic overtones, which Eliot tries to control:

They sat mutely gazing at each other: Maggie with eyes of intense life looking out from a weary beaten face – Tom pale with a certain awe and humiliation. Thought was busy though the lips were silent: and though he could ask no question, he guessed a story of almost miraculous divinely-protected effort. But at last a mist gathered over the blue-gray eyes, and the lips found a word they could utter: the old childish – 'Magsie!' (Eliot, pp. 455–6)

At this intimate moment, Eliot evokes the power of time to contain the erotic element. Maggie's 'weary beaten face' and the reversion to childhood both offset the building intensity, while 'awe and humilation' suggest a degree of social and religious distancing. The erotic bursts forth in the line, 'Maggie could make no answer but a long deep sob of that mysterious wondrous happiness that is one with pain', but it is immediately suppressed by her invocation of duty: '"We will go to Lucy, Tom"' she says; '"we'll go and see if she is safe, and then we can help the rest."' The wooden machinery, 'clinging together in fatal fellowship', also serves as a social image, pointing back toward the social boundaries that constrain Maggie and limit Tom's capacity to accept her freely.

The sexual implications of this scene are so strong that Eliot's rhetorical attempts at control barely restrain them. Even Victorians had to bow to the conflation of the rhetorics of sex and death during times of great emotional intensity, as in the flood scene, or when the moment of death itself was at hand and needed to be given a full poetic treatment. One solution to this dilemma seemed to involve the use of religious language and imagery, in which the sensual qualities were sanctioned – 'de-psychologized', as it were – by time and longstanding tradition. Eliot seeks to control the flow of eroticism by a sustained use of this Victorian technique of last resort:

[The full meaning of what had happened to Tom and Maggie] came with so overpowering a force – it was a new revelation to his spirit of the depths in life, that had lain beyond his vision which he had fancied so keen and clear – that he was unable to ask a question.

Ultimately, this technique depicts brother and sister reliving together 'one supreme moment', their tandem death transforming the physicality of 'two bodies that were found in close embrace' into the transcendent epitaph: 'In their death they were not divided' (p. 457).[5]

As might be expected, we find some of the most intriguing examples of rhetorical attempts to control sex and death in the work of the two leading male novelists of the Victorian era, Charles Dickens and William Makepeace Thackeray. Whereas Dickens magnifies and then tries to de-eroticise death through extreme attenuation, displacement and isolation – of either character or psychological conflict – Thackeray puts boundaries between sex and death from the outset by setting up ironic parallels between them. In this manner, he plays on the social rules and power relationships themselves, employing them as a form of parodic negation. In particular, Thackeray replaces the usual rhapsodic rhetoric of death with the rhetoric of his own rules, which allow him to 'put away' his puppets and draw lines between layers of the text.

I

Dickens typically magnifies death through an extreme attenuation of time, only to de-eroticise it through a process of rhetorical or psychological dispersal, which separates and isolates the erotic elements. *Dombey and Son* enacts for young Paul a very sensual death, its attenuation emblematic of erotic death in literature – making it an especially fitting climax to Dickens' public reading, 'The Story of Little Dombey'. In fact, this reading so condenses the rendition of Paul's death as to make it appear even more erotic than it seems to be in the novel. In this case, Dickens could perhaps be adjudged a fairly conscious manipulator of his elements, for we know how carefully he revised and shaped his public readings from their published originals. And in this respect, he was already building on what many readers of his letters have concluded was a highly calculated incident: in *Dombey and Son*, with the death of Little Dombey, Dickens was attempting a 'repeat performance' of the 'popular' death of Little Nell. As George Ford observes, elements of Dickens the rhetorician blend with those of Dickens the artist in the conscious manipulation of this death scene.[6]

Through Paul's impressionistic view of time slowly passing, Dickens renders his death attractive, even beautiful. Spatial con-figurations and posture set up and frame the erotic imagery, which pours in just before the moment of death:

> Sister and brother wound their arms around each other, and the golden light came streaming in, and fell upon them, locked together.

'How fast the river runs, between its green banks and the rushes, Floy! But it's very near the sea. I hear the waves! They always said so!' (*Dombey and Son*, p. 297)

Here Dickens reaches the height of sensuality, his rhetorical energy infused by typical erotic imagery in the conjunction of rhythmic waves, rocking boat, and golden light. Thus, we should not be surprised to discover that when a popular song of the day, 'What Are the Wild Waves Saying', drew upon this imagery, its lyricist was quick to counter the eroticism with his own brand of religiosity in the refrain: 'The voice of the great Creator/ Dwells in that mighty tone!' (Glover, p. 9) And as Alexander Welsh notes about Florence Dombey's role in this intimate scene, it too creates an antithetical effect: Dickens has been grooming her to be one of his 'Angels of Death'.[7]

But most significantly, extreme attenuation in this version of death enables Dickens to disperse the sensual elements, temporally and spatially (in effect, Paul can be said to be 'dying' over the space of some 100 pages.) If we take key words and phrases from a single extended passage towards the end of this process – about two pages of the text – we can see the erotic element only too clearly: 'quivered', 'rolled', 'resistless, he cried out!', 'leaning his poor head upon her breast', 'rising up', 'reviving, waking, starting into life once more', 'glistening as it rolled', 'roused', 'the flush', 'again the golden water would be dancing on the wall' (*Dombey and Son*, pp. 292–4). Yet Dickens not only dissipates these sensual terms over time; he also shunts them aside by making them poetic descriptions of the environment as the boy perceives it. All the while, death is spoken of and treated as part of nature, implying the conjoinment of sensual and morbid qualities, despite their rhetorical dispersal. At the same time, the isolation of Paul reveals Dickens' characteristic use of psychological and social isolation to de-eroticise his scenes. When death finally does arrive, it comes to the old-young boy who epitomises – through the aesthetic power of repeated parallelism – the 'old old fashion – Death!'[8]

Any discussion of death in Dickens' fiction must eventually address his presentation of Little Nell in *The Old Curiosity Shop* and the immense interest her death has generated – in both the author and his reading public. Little Nell's death also disperses and displaces the erotic – this time into both the framing narration and her grandfather's romantic rhetoric, which dramatises the lover's insistence that he is not separated from his beloved:

'You plot among you to wean my heart from her. You never will do that – never while I have life. I have no relative or friend but her – I never had – I never will have. She is all in all to me. It is too late to part us now.' (*The Old Curiosity Shop*, p. 652)

These words asserting love's union occur in the context of a novel which has portrayed the villainous Quilp as relentlessly pursuing Nell – the eroticism of his pursuit barely concealed – and they were written by an author who admitted to the childhood desire of wanting to marry Little Red Riding Hood when he grew up.[9] Trying to deny fourteen-year-old Nell's sexuality by direct ascription throughout the novel, Dickens finally protests too much. At this point, it is impossible to resist the temptation to read into this scene some of Dickens's own biography. Writing to John Forster about the difficulty of performing what he would two months later call his 'Nellicide', he comments, 'Dear Mary died yesterday when I think of this sad story' (*Letters*, vol. 2, pp. 228 and 182).[10] Mary is, of course, Mary Hogarth, Dickens' teenaged sister-in-law who died in his arms in 1837; not only did he wear her ring for the rest of his life, but he hoped to be buried next to her as well. Given this insight, we would not be amiss to read into the rhetoric of Nell's grandfather some of Dickens' own sentiments.

As Dickens approaches Nell's death – not something absolutely demanded by the plot – he succumbs to another form of rhetorical attentuation and temporal avoidance: he presents her death after the fact. Nonetheless, the surrounding rhetoric of the characters extols and glorifies Nell, each character jealously vying with her grandfather to apotheosise her the more. Finally, based on Dickens' explicit instructions, George Cattermole's illustration presents us with the pubescent 'bride' on her death-'bed': 'upon her breast, and pillow, and about her bed, there may be slips of holly, and berries, and such free green things' (*Letters*, p. 172). Flirting with necrophilia as he earlier has with paedophilia, Dickens' interest here may seem inappropriate to our twentieth-century readership, but it did not seem so to his Victorian audience, for many of whom personal connotations (and perhaps suppressed eroticism) were released. While we might expect such a popular incident to result in one of Dickens' public reading texts, we can also recognise that – for both author and auditor – the emotional intensity might well have been excessive.[11]

But Dickens also tries to delimit the erotic element by setting

Nell's grandfather in conflict with other characters and isolating him through his apparent insanity. Her grandfather's denial of death – 'She is sleeping soundly' (*The Old Curiosity Shop*, p. 648) – is further contradicted by the narrator's litany, 'She was dead. . . . She was dead' (pp. 652–4). Moreover, we can actually see the physical separation of the fulminating old man and Nell herself during the height of his rhetoric: not only is she already dead, but she is also sealed off in another room. Once again, Dickens illustrates for us the twin motifs of excess and restraint that Kucich has so appropriately employed in his full-length study to characterise the opposing forces of Dickensian energy.

In *Oliver Twist*, with the overt sexual overtones of Sikes killing Nancy, we uncover a treatment of death which is strikingly atypical for Dickens. A violent murder leaves no scope for languid attenuation or sentimentalisation of death. Victorian authors generally favoured the erotic over the merely lustful side of sexuality, and the spiritual over the violent aspect of death – but here those preferences cannot hold sway. At the same time, Sikes's murder of Nancy employs in concentrated form some of the same rhetorical techniques we have recognised in other fictional scenes of death. This passage gains its phenomenal intensity precisely because of the pressure it places on the very Victorian desire to keep things discrete. The rhetorical tools used to offset the sex–death conflation must be economical and powerful, eschewing the sort of slow dispersal that Dickens generally espoused.

Although time is limited, Dickens still tries to keep his characters' sexuality in complete isolation – from one another as much as possible, and from the Victorian reader as well. Note, for example, that the violent death itself occurs between two members of the lower classes, to some degree isolating it from its presumed Victorian audience. The graphic description of Sikes as he blindly rushes home to do the deed – with his blood-engorged muscles fairly bursting through his skin – presents a rare glimpse of murderous lust:

> Without one pause, or moment's consideration; without once turning his head to the right or left, or raising his eyes to the sky, or lowering them to the ground, but looking straight before him with savage resolution: his teeth so tightly compressed that the strained jaw seemed starting through his skin; the robber held on his headlong course, nor muttered a word, nor relaxed a muscle, until he reached the door. (*Oliver Twist*, p. 421)

But this vividness is altered when Sikes comes upon Nancy and their physical separateness ends. The descriptions of Sikes are greatly reduced and depersonalised. He douses the only candle in the room and prevents Nancy from opening the curtain on the faint light of day, and what we see of him from then on are murky glimpses of hands and arms committing the murder. He is depersonalised – referred to as 'the man' and 'the housebreaker' – while Nancy's words enhance the negative quality, as she cries, 'You cannot have the heart to kill me. . . . I will not loose my hold, you cannot throw me off' (p. 422).

The murder itself is rife with forms of isolation. Sikes and Nancy speak in ways that indicate their contrasting perceptions – like a meeting of two opposite worlds – the social and perceptual boundaries rendered all the more emphatic because they are *not* dispersed or attenuated. Once these separate beings begin to talk and interact, Nancy's words take on some of the spiritual or aesthetic quality we have witnessed in more typical death scenes, but her attempts to 'aestheticise' the scene only isolate her further. The rhetoric negates light and time, typical aesthetic images and motifs of natural death. Knocking down the candle, Sikes denies even its faint light. Time, too, is negated – an inversion of Dickens's usual technique to de-eroticise death – as Nancy helplessly pleads for time: 'It's never too late to repent. . . . We must have time – a little, little time!' Finally, Dickens completes this complex and difficult isolation of murderer from victim as Nancy breathes 'one prayer for mercy to her Maker!' (p. 423) – so that Sikes becomes the profane representative of death, Nancy the transcendent victim.

Yet this is not the final word on this infamous murder, for Dickens resurrected it for his reading audiences. Recast as 'Sikes and Nancy', the reading text develops through a series of parallel structures, thus attempting to highlight the aesthetic as a counter to its eventual acts of violence. Then, as he begins to recount the murder scene, Dickens almost reproduces it from the novel exactly. This in itself is unusual, for it points to the highly condensed nature of the original – creating the intensity that has already challenged the author to offset it. But Dickens also performs several key acts of omission, which force us to return to the novel and to read its murder more as an implicit rape. Unlike the reading text, the novel's text continues to affirm Nancy's sexuality as it describes her greeting Bill 'with an expression of pleasure at his return' (p. 421).[12] The novel further provides Nancy with the very words a rape victim might utter to pacify her attacker: 'I—I won't scream or cry—not once—hear me—speak to me—tell me what I have done!' (p. 422) Deleting these sexual overtones from his reading text hardly left Dickens with an expurgated passage, but he did reduce some of its over-charged nature. There would be difficulty enough in his re- peatedly performing the roles of murderer and victim – the very performance which from most reports constituted his self- murder.[13]

II

Dealing more overtly with the erotic than Dickens, Thackeray in *Vanity Fair* draws a satiric contrast between the rigidified, death- oriented (i.e. military and legal) rules of male society and the diffuse, unspoken rules of the suppressed subculture of women. Here the parallels between sex and death are consciously depicted and constitute part of the novel's structure, yet the very highlighting of the parallels emphasises their separateness and distinction. Thackeray recognises that he cannot talk about either male or female sexuality directly, so his viewpoint is distanced, avoiding, by and large, aestheticisation. In the preface to his next novel, *Pendennis*, he would make his famous pronouncement on the limits dictated by middle-class morality: 'Since the author of Tom Jones was buried, no writer of fiction among us has been permitted to depict to his utmost power a MAN' (*Pendennis*, p. xi). Thackeray tends to be blunt about death – recall the sudden, anti-erotic revelation of George Osborne 'lying on his face, dead, with a bullet through his heart' (*Vanity Fair*, p. 315) – and ambivalent about sex, rather than en- gaging in the rapturous time-dilation and dissolution of boundaries that we encounter in Eliot, Dickens and many other Victorian novelists. We do not, in other words, uncover in Thackeray a rhetorical struggle against the conflation of sex and death, but rather an intellectual acknowledgement and manipulation of their paral- lels. Instead of invoking rhetorical forms of isolation, Thackeray depicts the two elements as occurring in different spheres and according to different rules from the outset: isolation exists as the fabric of his fictional world.

When Becky Sharp appears in the charade as Clytemnestra, Thackeray seems willing to concede the connection between sex and death, but he carefully encapsulates the scene, almost parodying his own aestheticising of it: it is a tableau – outside the temporal flow of the plot and with no causal relationship to the rest of the story:

> Aegisthus steals in pale and on tiptoe. What is that ghastly face looking out balefully after him from behind the arras? He raises his dagger to strike the sleeper [Agamemnon, played by Rawdon Crawley, Becky's husband], who turns in his bed, and opens his broad chest as if for the blow. He cannot strike the noble slumbering chieftan. Clytemnestra glides swiftly into the room like an apparition – her arms are bare and white, – her tawny hair floats down her shoulders, – her face is deadly pale, – and her eyes are lighted up with a smile so ghastly, that people quake as they look at her. (p. 494)

At the height of the murderous illusion, someone shouts out his recognition that Clytemnestra is indeed Becky, and then 'scornfully she snatches the dagger out of Aegisthus's hand, and advances to the bed'. The scene has sensational power – 'a thrill of terror and delight runs through the assembly' (p. 492) – but we end up feeling that Thackeray, as usual, remains relatively free of these disturbing forces and is using them intellectually as a discrete comment on his text, rather than as a symbolic statement of what really goes on at the heart of his novel.[14] This scene is to *Vanity Fair* what Sikes killing Nancy is to *Oliver Twist*: in Dickens, the result is shattering, a release of repressed emotional power; in Thackeray, it is an entertainment, once again deliberately highlighting the boundaries that keep sex and death separate in his world. This is Thackeray's intellectual means of isolating these elements. Cooler and more distanced than Dickens in his approach, he draws parallels and keeps his forces – like puppets – under control.

Thackeray can even be blunt about death when he chooses to attenuate its presentation. Chapter 61 of *Vanity Fair* – 'In Which Two Lights Are Put Out' – juxtaposes the deaths of the two patriarchs, Mr Sedley and Mr Osborne.[15] In the first case, a dissolution of old emotional boundaries and an expansion of time occur, as they frequently do in Dickens. But when death finally comes, the sexual angle is more anti-erotic than anything else, for Thackeray treats death almost wholly in terms of satiric negation – i.e. by the setting up of ironic parallels:

So there came one morning and sunrise, when all the world got up and set about its various works and pleasures, with the exception of old John Sedley, who was not to fight with fortune, or to hope or scheme any more: but to go and take up a quiet and utterly unknown residence in a churchyard at Brompton by the side of his old wife. (p. 587)

Moreover, as Mr Osborne's death is compared with Mr Sedley's – and we realise that there will never be a reconciliation between the two former friends – we recognise that Thackeray has consciously set up this contrast, again maintaining his intellectual control: 'One day when he should have come down to breakfast, his servant, missing him went into his dressing-room, and found him lying at the foot of the dressing-table, in a fit' (p. 591). Indeed, Thackeray's use of parallelism could be said to constitute his rhetorical manipulation of time – his technique for allaying the sex–death conflation.

Elsewhere in Thackeray's canon, when he magnifies death, as in the case of Helen Pendennis or Colonel Newcome, he continues to exert his control through satirical framing or drawing an actual line between death and imaginary sexual fulfilment. For example, as Helen's impending death leads to a mother–son reconciliation, the narration leaps ahead in time to observe, in the context of religious discourse, that ever after, in his best moments and worst trials, Pen would know that 'his mother's face looked down upon him, and blessed him with its gaze of pity and purity' (*Pendennis*, p. 213). Time also stretches backwards, to encompass Pen's youthful repetition of his 'Our Father', recited 'at his mother's sacred knees' (p. 214). On the one hand, when this earlier period is recalled, the alert reader can hardly deny the incestuous overtones at both periods, for Helen has ever desired of Pen that she be 'his all in all' (p. 196). On the other hand, these overtones also provoke a more incisive narrative commentary that undermines both Helen's death scene and the sexual connotations of her 'poor' individual story.[16] In the chapter immediately preceding the one that narrates her death, Helen's 'devouring care' prompts the narrator to turn her into a representative 'type', who perpetuates – in co-conspiracy with her male partner – the tyranny of gendered role differentiation:

Is it not your nature [Delia] to creep about his feet and kiss them, to twine round his trunk and hang there; and Damon's to stand like a British man with his hands in his breeches pocket, while the pretty fond parasite clings round him? (p. 197)

In many ways, Colonel Newcome's death recalls Little Nell's: it is Thackeray's old-age counterpart to Dickens' treatment of death claiming the innocence of youth.[17] In fact, when the Colonel becomes a poor brother at Grey Friars, time expands to encompass him as both 'a youth all love and hope' and 'a stricken old man, with a beard as white as snow covering the noble care-worn face' (*The Newcomes*, p. 443). But any sexuality raised by his excited, romantic rhetoric is displaced by Thackeray's rhetorical handling of the attenuated death scene: the Colonel's age and delirium isolate him from the other characters (as they do Nell's grandfather); his repeated reunions with Madame de Florac recall only unfulfilled love; and we are further distanced from his courtly discourse because it is not directly quoted. Moreover, the conclusion itself cuts both ways:

> And just as the last bell struck, a peculiar sweet smile shone over his face, and he lifted up his head a little, and quickly said, 'Adsum!' and fell back. It was the word we used at school, when names were called; and lo, he, whose heart was as that of a little child, had answered to his name, and stood in the presence of The Master. (pp. 444–5)

Here we can recognise emotional magnification as time expands to convey the old man once again as a young boy. Yet 'Adsum' also recalls rules, and 'Master' implies hierarchies. Then the 'real' conclusion appears as Thackeray draws a literal line across his text, thereby foregrounding his own artistry and reminding us that he can make his own rules: now we are in the author's, not the narrator's, time frame, where the fulfilment of erotic passions is merely a speculative venture – 'for you, dear friend, it is as you like' (p. 446).

Such boundarylines and rule-making return us to *Vanity Fair*, where we can note that even when Becky is depicted as a mermaid – as a death-in-life siren – and Thackeray evokes some of the disturbing, unconscious disgust at the conjunction of death and sexuality, his whole rhetorical approach involves drawing ironic parallels, playing on the dividing line that the water makes – and on his intention to keep clear of it:

Those who like may peep down under waves that are pretty transparent, and see [the monster's tail] writhing and twirling, diabolically hideous and slimy, flapping amongst bones, or curling round corpses; but above the water line, I ask, has not everything been proper, agreeable, and decorous, and has any the most squeamish immoralist in Vanity Fair a right to cry fie? (*Vanity Fair*, p. 617)

The passage that follows continues to deliver negations. Whenever Thackeray touches on this sort of charged material, he launches into either controlled, intellectual parallels or else a series of parodic denials: now we learn that 'we had best not examine the fiendish marine cannibals, revelling and feasting on their wretched pickled victims'. Cannibalism combines with sexuality to suggest all the attendant horrors of vampirism raised by Nina Auerbach in *Woman and the Demon*, yet Thackeray still maintains 'the laws of politeness' and invokes the power of his own negating rhetoric.[18]

Given his usual separation of death and sex, it is intriguing to note that in order to illustrate how Becky refuses to confront the implications of her own sexuality, Thackeray uses a metaphor of death: 'But, – just as the children of Queen's Crawley went round the room where the body of their father lay; – if ever Becky had these thoughts [of leading a straightforward life], she was accustomed to walk round them, and not look in' (pp. 410–11). In fact, she pointedly avoids examining thoughts about an alternative existence: 'She eluded them, and despised them – or at least she was committed to the other path from which retreat was now impossible.' But Becky circling round a corpse at a great distance is equally an appropriate symbol for the author's own reluctance to confront death *or* sex, his distanced, manipulative treatment of both contrasting with Dickens' tendency to immerse himself in the magnification of death, while concurrently trying to de-eroticise the subject. Thackeray's enforced 'bachelorhood' due to his wife's mental illness, and Dickens' attraction to younger women, made sexuality a highly charged subject for both of them – and hence something they were more comfortable positing in their female characters. In this respect, both also evince a fear of female sexuality. Yet while Dickens kills off or deports a number of his most erotic female characters, Thackeray persists in examining Becky Sharp – his epitome of female eroticism – from the admittedly safe distance implied by ironic parallels with death and destruction.

Finally, at the end of *Vanity Fair*, death once more occurs within a context that seems to invoke sexuality. In stark terms, Jos Sedley is reported to have died. But instead of learning any details about his demise, we are confronted with speculation, innuendo, and insurance companies – death and sex completely bureaucratised, which at the same time might be considered as the most extreme form of dispassionate separation. In the midst of this controversy, Thackeray makes it clear that the insurance companies are very suspicious about the cause of Joseph's death, with foul play on Becky's part being the implication. On this occasion, for such a specific insinuation about sex and death, Thackeray employs some of his most powerful negating rhetoric: 'it was the blackest case'; Becky's lawyers, 'of Thaives Inn', are named after three notorious murderers; and they in turn declare her 'the object of an infamous conspiracy' (pp. 664–6). Yet Thackeray does not stop with the power of language: he carries his argument into the visual arts, where his accompanying illustration depicts Becky lurking behind a curtain while Jos pleads with Dobbin not to reveal his intention of leaving her. Entitled 'Becky's second appearance in the character of Clytemnestra', this illustration is teasingly ambiguous: does Becky hold a knife in her hand, or is that just a trick of the light? Thackeray obviously intends this ambivalence to extend to her sexual power over Jos as well: she may be using her (and his) sexuality to bring about his death, but we will never know for certain since she is always allowed to operate 'below the water line'.

The whole subject of *rules*, especially social and artistic ones, is central to this topic. Victorians were very involved with social regulations – particularly those involving sex and death – yet the foregrounding of either sex or death tends also to involve a questioning or loosening of rules. This condition created another link (besides what I have been calling 'aestheticisation') between the rhetorics of sex and death. It provided Thackeray with a perfect fulcrum for dealing with both sex and death, not in terms of the usual rapturous rhetoric, but in terms of *artistic* rules – disposing of puppets ('Come children, let us shut up the box and the puppets, for our play is played out', p. 666) and drawing lines between layers of the text. And Becky Sharp works in the limbo between these two realms (which may be the true import of the mermaid symbol, a sexually enticing yet sexually censored figuration) as does the novelist himself. If neither Dickens nor Thackeray could articulate sexuality without invoking controls (after all, neither could transcend both personal and societally imposed proscriptions), Thackeray's artistry was the more daring, allowing him to layer private and public sublimation in ways that are particularly amenable to twentieth-century narrative analysis. Ultimately, it is Thackeray's use of his own artistic rules to explore societal rules that makes *Vanity Fair* one of the most innovative Victorian novels on the twin subjects of sex and death.

Notes

1.   All references given in the text are to titles and editions given in the Bibliography following these Notes.
2.   Kucich's article provides a good introduction to how the literature of the period reflected the Victorian 'climate' of death (see especially pp. 58–9), while Kincaid's paper, as well as his work in progress on paedophilia, alerts us to how Victorian discourse on child sexuality operates within and exposes models of play and power.
3.   For example, David Lean's film of *Great Expectations* (1946) justifies its 'happy ending' by having Pip save Estella – who has just been jilted by Bentley Drummle in the rewritten script – from becoming another Miss Havisham. Polhemus develops his argument by concentrating on Pip's symbolic 'rape' of Miss Havisham, finding in it 'the tension and energy latent in the nineteenth-century drive to reconcile the desire and the prohibition [against incest] without diminishing the power of either' (Polhemus, p. 1). And Eigner's study demonstrates how David Copperfield's suppression of both death and sex results in the formulation of his doubles, Steerforth and Heep.
4.   The contributors to the collection of Gallagher and Laqueur, originally published as *Representations*, No. 14 (1986), build especially on the work of Foucault to illustrate how Victorian agencies of power began to redirect their energies to evidence concern about and then control of various aspects of sexual behaviour.
5.   Stewart's book is certainly required reading for anyone studying about death in Victorian fiction, while his article is of particular interest on the subject of death by drowning.
6.   Ford continues: 'Even on Dickens' own terms, there was an ironical aftermath to his bid for favor. . . . After the death of Paul, the later numbers of *Dombey* seemed anti-climactic' (Ford, p. 59).
7.   In his chapter, 'Two Angels of Death' (Welsh, pp. 180–95), Welsh presents Florence Dombey and Agnes Wickfield in the context of nineteenth-century allegorical representations of the female angel of death. This presentation is a prelude to the argument that 'sexuality in a heroine biologically implies the hero's death as an individual' (p. 210). Thus, the strategy of Dickens and his contemporaries was 'to domesticate death, to wrest it from the city and take it in by the

fireside' (p. 212). As a result, Welsh concludes, 'the institution of marriage and the institution of the novel deserve credit for so adroitly converting the sexual relation that implies death into a relation that saves from death' (p. 228). Of course, Florence as a representative of woman's regenerative power can produce another Little Paul; in Bataille's terms, 'Reproduction leads to the discontinuity of beings, but brings into play their continuity; that is to say, it is intimately linked with death' (Bataille, p. 13).

8. As I argue in my article on the rhetoric of soliloquy, Dickens is particularly adept at utilising structural and imagistic parallelism at moments that transcend closure. The concluding words of *A Tale of Two Cities* speak this point eloquently, creating foreshadowing that crosses the boundaries of time and consciousness: 'It is a far, far better thing I do than I have ever done; it is a far, far better rest that I go to than I have ever known' (*A Tale of Two Cities*, p. 403).

9. Kucich cites the Little Red Riding Hood anecdote as taken from Dickens' short story, 'A Christmas Tree' (Kucich, 'Death Worship', p. 71 note 20). He goes on to discuss *The Old Curiosity Shop*'s 'explicit experience of violence' as a project that dramatises violation as eroticised death (p. 68). Mark Spilka, on the other hand, reads the text as releasing 'neurotic rather than erotic violation'. 'How else', he argues, 'can we explain such related phenomena as the cult called Love of Little Girls . . . or the increased popularity of child-prostitutes . . .?' (See p. 175 of his article, 'On the Enrichment of Poor Monkeys by Myth and Dream; or, How Dickens Rousseauisticized and Pre-Freudianized Victorian Views of Childhood', in Cox, pp. 161–79.)

10. Letters to and from Dickens during the months preceding and following Nell's death confirm his shared preoccupation with the death of this girl-child. Ford devotes an entire chapter to the Nell phenomenon, 'Little Nell: The Limits of Explanatory Criticism' (Ford, pp. 55–71).

11. William Macready's letter of 25 January 1841 may be representative of this degree of feeling: 'This beautiful fiction comes too close upon what is miserably real to me [the death of his own daughter two months earlier] to enable me to taste that portion of pleasure, which we can often extract (and you so beautifully do) from reasoning on the effect of pain, when we feel it through the sufferings of others' (*Letters*, p. 193). Weinstein picks up on the recurrence of father–daughter relations in Dickens within a context of illicit sexuality (Weinstein, p. 32), noting that he is 'unable to abandon or endorse this fantasy-desire [of father/husbands]' (p. 39).

12. Langbauer's article demonstrates that Dickens grounds erotics in woman – making *her* the seductress.

13. Collins' introduction to 'Sikes and Nancy' describes how Dickens developed this last addition to his repertoire – how he revelled in its horror, passion and drama. His friends and family found such 'outright histrionic violence disquieting' – and he went on to become obsessed by it, to the point of jeopardising his health (Dickens,

The Public Readings, pp. 465–71). We must not forget, either, that the murder of Nancy serves as a prelude to the pursuit and death of Sikes, rendered subjectively in the rewritten version. Thus, Dickens' most dramatic tie with his living audiences was also intimately linked on multiple levels with acts of dying.

14. Of course, the charade does provoke Lord Steyne's intense admiration of Becky and foreshadows elements of the triangular confrontation scene that follows their interlude. DiBattista also argues persuasively that the Clytemnestra myth 'serves as a psychological and *historical* commentary on the unexamined delusions of the Victorian's sexual ideology' (DiBattista, p. 833). But both points simply confirm my assertion that Thackeray has moved our considerations to an intellectual plane.

15. Another old patriarch's death deserves comparison here because it is so totally negated and anti-eroticised: Thackeray completely elides the death of Sir Pitt Crawley; it apparently occurs within the interstices of the text: 'there was a great hurry and bustle'; 'lights went about'; 'a boy on a pony went galloping off' – and then the Bute Crawleys arrive to ascertain that no one falsely lay claim to family property (*Vanity Fair*, pp. 390–1).

16. Bledsoe's article makes a good case for the novel's careful balancing between 'Helen the self-styled middle-aged martyr' and 'Helen the sympathetic young wife' (Bledsoe, pp. 871–2), but she finally devolves into an embodiment of all pure but possessive women (p. 875). In this respect, she rather accurately reflects Thackeray's intense ambivalence about his mother. In contrast, Dickens tends to create split characters to represent his mother, e.g. Mrs Micawber and Miss Murdstone.

17. Stewart's discussion of Colonel Newcome's death also suggests its affinities with Dickensian death scenes by raising the issue of sentimentality but then qualifying it with reference to contrivance and irony (Stewart, p. 132); in general, Stewart's study demonstrates how much less sentimental both of their death scenes are than is usually presumed. In this respect, Barickman *et al.* have not analysed the specific conjunction of death and the erotic when they too easily generalise about 'the eroticism that is diluted into sentimental rhetoric in Dickens' (Barickman *et al.*, p. 93).

18. Mermaids and serpent-women, vampires and monsters blend angel and demon in Auerbach's discussion of characters like Becky Sharp and Beatrix Castlewood (from Thackeray's *Henry Esmond*); see *Woman and the Demon*, especially pp. 88–101. The figures of angel and demon inform Auerbach's earlier studies of Florence Dombey and Maggie Tulliver as well; see her reprinted essays in *Romantic Imprisonment*, pp. 107–29 and 230–49. For his last completed novel, *Philip*, Thackeray was prepared to conjoin motherhood, self-sacrifice, and cannibalism within his opening pages (*Philip*, p. 106).

Bibliography

Auerbach, Nina, *Romantic Imprisonment: Women and Other Glorified Outcasts* (New York: Columbia University Press, 1985).

Auerbach, Nina, *Woman and the Demon: The Life of a Victorian Myth* (Cambridge, Massachusetts: Harvard University Press, 1982).

Barickman, Richard, Susan MacDonald, and Myra Stark, *Corrupt Relations: Dickens, Thackeray, Trollope, Collins and the Victorian Sexual System* (New York: Columbia University Press, 1982).

Bataille, Georges, *Death and Sensuality* (New York: Walker, 1965).

Bledsoe, Robert, '*Pendennis* and the Power of Sentimentality: A Study of Motherly Love', *PMLA*, vol. 91 (1976) pp. 871–83.

Cox, Don Richard (ed.) *Sexuality and Victorian Literature. Tennessee Studies in Literature*, vol. 27 (1984).

DiBattista, Maria, 'The Triumph of Clytemnestra: The Charades in *Vanity Fair*', *PMLA*, vol. 95 (1980) pp. 827–37.

Dickens, Charles, *Dombey and Son*, introduction by Raymond Williams (Harmondsworth: Penguin, 1970).

Dickens, Charles, *Great Expectations*, edited by Angus Calder (Harmondsworth: Penguin, 1965).

Dickens, Charles, *The Letters of Charles Dickens*, edited by Madeline House and Graham Storey, vol. 2: 1840–1841 (Oxford: Clarendon Press, 1969).

Dickens, Charles, *The Old Curiosity Shop*, introduced by Malcolm Andrews (Harmondsworth: Penguin, 1972).

Dickens, Charles, *Oliver Twist*, introduced by Angus Wilson (Harmondsworth: Penguin, 1966).

Dickens, Charles, *Our Mutual Friend*, edited by Stephen Gill (Harmondsworth: Penguin, 1971).

Dickens, Charles, *The Public Readings*, edited by Philip Collins (Oxford: Clarendon Press, 1983).

Dickens, Charles, *A Tale of Two Cities*, edited by George Woodcock (Harmondsworth: Penguin, 1970).

Eigner, Edwin, 'Death and the Gentleman: Charles Dickens as Elegiac Romancer', unpublished essay, 1985.

Eliot, George, *The Mill on the Floss*, edited by Gordon Haight (Boston: Houghton Mifflin, 1961).

Ford, George, *Dickens and His Readers: Aspects of Novel-Criticism Since 1836* (New York: Norton, 1965).

Foucault, Michel, *The History of Sexuality. Vol. 1: An Introduction*, translated by Robert Hurley (New York: Random House, 1978).

Gallagher, Catherine, and Thomas Laqueur (eds) *The Making of the Modern Body: Sexuality and Society in the Nineteenth Century* (Berkeley: University of California Press, 1987).

Glover, Stephen, 'What Are the Wild Waves Saying'. Lyrics by Joseph Edwards Carpenter (London: Robert Cocks, [1850]).

Hardy, Thomas, *Jude the Obscure*, edited by Irving Howe (Boston: Houghton Mifflin, 1965).

Kincaid, James, 'Dickens, Discourse Analysis, and the Sexuality of the Child', MLA Convention, Chicago, 30 December 1985.

Kucich, John, 'Death Worship among the Victorians: *The Old Curiosity Shop*', *PMLA*, vol. 95 (1980) pp. 58–72.

Kucich, John, *Excess and Restraint in the Novels of Charles Dickens* (Athens: University of Georgia Press, 1981).

Langbauer, Laurie, 'Dickens's Streetwalkers: Women and the Forms of Romance', *English Literary History*, vol. 53 (1986) pp. 411–31.

MacKay, Carol Hanbery, 'The Rhetoric of Soliloquy in *The French Revolution* and *A Tale of Two Cities*', *Dickens Studies Annual*, vol. 12 (1983) pp. 197–207.

Polhemus, Robert. 'The Burning of Miss Havisham: The Oedipal Dickens and the Victorian Incestual Bias.' MLA Convention. New York, 29 Dec. 1986.

Shakespeare, William, *Romeo and Juliet*, in John E. Hankins (ed.) *The Complete Works* (New York: Viking, 1969) pp. 855–94.

Stewart, Garrett, *Death Sentences: Styles of Dying in British Fiction* (Cambridge, Massachusetts: Harvard University Press, 1984).

Stewart, Garrett, 'The Secret Life of Death in Dickens', *Dickens Studies Annual*, vol. 11 (1983) pp. 177–207.

Thackeray, William Makepeace, *Vanity Fair: A Novel Without a Hero*, edited by Geoffrey and Kathleen Tillotson (Boston: Houghton Mifflin, 1963).

Thackeray, William Makepeace, *The Newcomes* (London: Smith, Elder, 1878).

Thackeray, William Makepeace, *Pendennis* (London: Smith, Elder, 1878).

Thackeray, William Makepeace, *Philip* (London: Smith, Elder, 1879).

Trollope, Anthony, *Barchester Towers*, introduced by Robin Gilmour (Harmondsworth: Penguin, 1983).

Vicinus, Martha (ed.) *A Widening Sphere: Changing Roles of Victorian Women* (Bloomington: Indiana University Press, 1977).

Weinstein, Philip M., *The Semantics of Desire: Changing Models of Identity from Dickens to Joyce* (Princeton: Princeton University Press, 1984).

Welsh, Alexander *The City of Dickens* (Oxford: Clarendon Press, 1971).

8

Evolution and Information, or Eroticism and Everyday Life, in *Dracula* and Late Victorian Aestheticism[1]

Regenia Gagnier

In 'A Manifesto for Cyborgs', Donna Haraway signals three boundary breakdowns causing considerable stress in late twentieth-century life, in which the meaning of life – that is, of the word 'life' – is part of the stress.[2] These boundary breakdowns are between the human and animal, the human/animal and machine, and, a subset of the second, the physical and non-physical. Biology and evolutionary theory have claimed that human and non-human animals share language, tool use, social behaviour, and mental events, and that nothing really convincingly settles their separation; and advocates of animal rights have repudiated the need for such a separation. The distinction between organism and machine has disappeared with organicism in post-modern life: pre-cybernetic machines were not self-moving, self-designing, autonomous, says Haraway, they were not selves at all, but only a caricature, like Frankenstein's monster, of the masculinist reproductive dream. Today, machines challenge the difference between natural and artificial, self-developing and externally-designed; moreover, machines are near the hearts of many of us, prolonging our lives mechanically. The distinction between physical and non-physical is further eroded by modern machines, which are quintessentially microelectronic devices, nothing but signals, but are nonetheless, as Haraway says, 'a matter of immense human pain in Detroit and Singapore' (p. 70). Sherry Turkle, the anthropologist whose fieldwork is among Hightech Society at the Massachusetts Institute of Technology, argues that in the nineteenth century when machinery was transparent, when as if in a Chaplin film one could see the wheels and gears and shafts, the worker could distinguish herself from the machine and see the machine as no more than a mechanical threat; today, workers in artificial intelligence have great plans for the machine: because AI is invisible but everywhere (like God) they imagine that the soul inhabits it, that it represents our own Unconscious, the limits of cognitive possibility, our omniscience.[3]

This boundary breakdown, one of the material sources of what is called the post-modern condition, signals changing concepts of the self and personal identity beyond the literary intelligentsia's wildest nightmares. (Turkle's training in psychoanalysis in Paris, she tells us, was rendered obsolete at MIT.) It has also, apparently, made scholars sensitive to cultural variation in boundary construction. Some, concerned with the Gothic and Gothic moments, have written extensively about the psychological state of abjection, or loss of self and absorption by the Other, often in terms of class, race, or gender instability.[4] Others, like Evelyn Fox Keller, Arnold Davidson and Roberto Mangabeira Unger, have explored the consequences to personal or social identities of epistemic disruption, or historical shifts in legitimating discourse in religion, science and philosophy.[5]

This essay looks at an historical instance of boundary construction between self and Other, Britain and the world, men and women, organisms and machines, and 'Art' and life. The time is the late Victorian period, when prosperity at home and abroad was pro-tected by recent developments in management and technology, which were in turn supported by recent developments in boundary construction in the social and natural sciences. My main text is the source of one of the enduring myths of sex and death, Bram Stoker's *Dracula* of 1897. The Count Dracula's protracted cultural status is attributable at least in part to Stoker's having brought together a number of boundary-defining cultural oppositions with eroticism and the machinery of everyday life.

My argument will be divided into three parts. The first is on eroticism in *Dracula*. Others have pursued this topic at greater length, psychoanalytic critics for some time in terms of sublimated sexuality, and feminist critics more recently in terms of male vio-lence against women, male bonding and homoeroticism by way of the mediation and victimisation of women, and the unconscious threat and mythic power of Victorian femininity.[6] I provide this initial section for readers unfamiliar with criticism of Stoker and the late-Victorian sex-gender system and to give a sense of the period's

peculiar combination of excess and banality in popular representations of everyday life between the genders. For in *Dracula* the
problems of the everyday will be displaced on to a figure alien to it, a
properly 'aesthetic' figure. I also provide the section because it is
necessary for my main argument in part two, which establishes the
second everyday scene from which eroticism in the form of the
Count erupts. Part two establishes the discourse of machinery and
operations – as organised and pervasive as the sex-gender system,
and as antagonistic to everything the Count represents – and shows
the technical implications of the thematic struggle. The third part
addresses the historical and aesthetic significance of the findings in
parts one and two.

I   EROTICISM AND EVERYDAY LIFE

From Polidori's *Vampire* of 1819 to contemporary film, the popular
fascination with vampirism has been related to its alleged expression
and distortion of an originally sexual energy. Although in Montague
Summers' classic work, *The Vampire: His Kith and Kin* (1928), violent
sexuality was only one – and by no means the defining – characteristic of the vampire, Summers quotes sources from Havelock Ellis to
Sicilian peasants on 'the definite connexion between the fascination
of blood and sexual excitation' (pp. 184–92).[7] According to this view,
Dracula may be read as the surrogate release of the Victorian Unconscious. The Count is introduced, entertained, and expelled (or
repressed). He expresses what the men in the novel, and by
extension the readers, want and distorts it by transferring their
desires to a surrogate. Thus the popular reading or viewing public
may revel in vamping while saying, it's this foreign aristocrat, not
us.

Werner Herzog's extraordinary film *Nosferatu* (1979) presents this
'surrogate' interpretation. It is reported that Herzog hypnotised his
actors in order that they better dramatise Unconscious processes,
and from the thousands of tiny white rats that he liberated on site to
the continuous gentle sucking sounds of Klaus Kinski, Herzog
exploits the customary phobias and obsessions of a European
audience. A clerk in Delft in Holland – a town that visually in-
carnates clean, bourgeois order – Jonathan Harker longs to escape
from the insanely monotonous city of 'canals that circle back on
themselves'. As he proceeds into the Count's territory, he is warned

by the innkeeper, 'whoever ventures too far into the land of phantoms is lost'. By the end of the film, the city of tedious canals is destroyed; the clean quiet streets have made way for the plague and *danse macabre*; and Harker, now a vampire, has internalised the phantoms. All social bonds are obliterated with the boundaries between life and death. The camera fades men into rodents, psyche into psyche.

True to the psychology of the novel if not to its Victorian ending, the Herzog also represents the obliteration of gender roles as a kind of death. Stoker provides numerous associations of gender instability and danger. An effeminised Harker lies squirming and coy before the three aggressive female vampires, 'feeling in my heart a wicked, burning desire that they would kiss me with those red lips. . . I lay quiet, looking out under my eyelashes in an agony of delightful anticipation. . . . There was a deliberate voluptuousness which was both thrilling and repulsive. . . I closed my eyes in a languorous ecstasy and waited' (*Dracula*, pp. 37–8).[8] Even the paternal Van Helsing is tempted to subject himself to their 'sweet fascination': 'Yes, I was moved – I, Van Helsing, with all my purpose and with my motive for hate. . . Certain it was that I was lapsing into sleep, the open-eyed sleep of one who yields to a sweet fascination' (p. 370).

One of the major ideological impetuses of Stoker's text is the re-empowerment of endangered gender roles. References to 'manhood' pervade the novel, which is one of the early sources in England of the North American slang expression 'true grit' (p. 228). In its course, the New Woman is ruthlessly domesticated and weak men progressively gain strength. Harker is 'propped up with pillows' (p. 105) when Mina marries him. Seward is embarrassed when Van Helsing 'gave way to a regular fit of hysterics. . . he cried till he laughed again; and laughed and cried together, just as a woman does' (p. 174). Every major male character in the novel cries, usually in a woman's lap. 'The tears rained down his cheeks. . . With a sob he laid his head on my shoulder, and cried like a wearied child. . . . I stroked his hair as though he were my own child' (p. 230).

One corollary of gender instability and containment in *Dracula* is sexual violence. After the marriage proposals of three men in one day Lucy Westenra impulsively confides to her girlfriend Mina, '"Why can't they let a girl marry three men, or as many as want her, and save all this trouble?"' (p. 59). Greedy Lucy pays for her enthusiasm: she is violently sexualised, or vamped, by the Count – surrogate for male violence against women – and destroyed for her sexuality. She is represented as a perversion of maternity – 'With a careless motion, she flung to the ground, callous as a devil, the child that up to now she had clutched strenuously to her breast, growling over it as a dog growls over a bone' (p. 211) – and a Medusa: 'The beautiful colour became livid, the eyes seemed to throw out sparks of hell-fire, the brows were wrinkled as though the folds of the flesh were the coils of Medusa's snakes. . . If ever a face meant death – if looks could kill – we saw it at that moment' (p. 212). The active woman is finally pacified by her fiancé in a scene that reads less like salvation than violent sex. Amid much writhing, screaming and wild contortions on Lucy's part, 'Arthur never faltered. . . . his un-trembling arm rose and fell, driving deeper and deeper the mercy-bearing stake, whilst the blood from the pierced heart welled and spurted up around it. . . . the sight of it gave us courage. . . . And then the writhing and quivering of the body became less. . . . Finally it lay still' (p. 216).

When Lucy pays for her abuse of chivalry (wanting any number of men to adore her), the three suitors and the ever-faithful Van Helsing transfer their professedly 'platonic' love to Mina, who is in turn victimised in a male contest for power. The Count invades her bedroom and, while her stupified husband and the other four gape on, initiates a scene of symbolic fellatio (p. 282) that she later recounts, '"When the blood began to spurt out, he took my hands in one of his, holding them tight, and with the other seized my neck and pressed my mouth to the wound, so that I must either suffocate or swallow some of the – Oh, my God, my God! what have I done?"' (p. 288). Her husband's hair turns white and the wafer burns into her forehead, signifying that she has been desecrated. In the denouement she is purified and bears a child, the proper function of female sexuality and proper product of sexual encounter: her son's 'bundle of names links all our little band of men together' (p. 378).[9]

The linking of the little band of men together, or male solidarity, occurs through the mediation – or, again, victimisation – of women.[10] The first hint of male bonding through blood precedes the advent of the Count and the narrative proper: the foundational friendship was initiated when Seward sucked the gangrenous tissue from a knife-wound of Van Helsing's that had been caused by Holmwood (p. 112). Within the narrative proper, Lucy is the com-mon pool of the four men's blood injections that ultimately empower the Count, who sucks the blood as determinedly as they pump it in. The blood transfusions of Holmwood, Seward, Van Helsing, and Morris serve as antidote to the blood-sucking of the Count, incorporating the metaphor of substantive 'red-blooded' masculinity as antidote to foreign aristocratic anaemia. As with the vamping, the serial transfusions are dominated by sexual imagery, now accompanied by voyeurism and male jockeying for position:

'No man knows till he experiences it, what it is to feel his own life-blood drawn away into the veins of the woman he loves' (p. 128)

The Professor watched me critically. 'That will do,' he said. 'Already?' I remonstrated. 'You took a great deal more from Art.' To which he smiled a sad sort of smile as he replied: – 'He is her lover, her *fiancé*' (p. 128).

'A brave man's blood is the best thing on this earth when a woman is in trouble. You're a man, and no mistake' (p. 150).

Apparently sensing that there is more at stake (as it were) than saving a woman's life, Van Helsing admonishes Seward not to tell her fiancé of the 'transfusion': '"It would at once frighten him and enjealous him"' (p. 128). In a joke that Seward considers in poor taste, Van Helsing suggests that the transfusions were adulterous:

'Just so. Said he not that the transfusion of his blood to her veins had made her truly his bride?' 'Yes, and it was a sweet and comforting idea for him.' 'Quite so. But there was a difficulty, friend John. If so that, then what about the others? Ho, ho! Then this so sweet maid is a polyandrist, and me, with my poor wife dead to me, but alive by Church's law, though no wits, all gone – even I, who am faithful husband to this now-no-wife, am bigamist.' (p. 176)

During this metaphorical gang-rape vengeance, presumably, for wanting three men at once – Lucy functions as the conduit through which the men's blood reaches the Count, who duly claims the English women as his link to the men: '"Your girls that you all love are mine already; and through them you and others shall yet be mine"' (p. 306).

Yet despite such female and foreign threats to the paternal, bourgeois family, the good men triumph through arms, money and power. '"How can women help loving men when they are so earnest, and so true, and so brave!"' enthuses Mina, '"And, too, it made me think of the wonderful power of money!"' (p. 356). The novel concludes with Van Helsing's praise of valiant 'Men who so loved [woman], that they did dare much for her sake' (p. 378). Godalming and Harker inherit fortunes; the gallant Quincey Morris – sacrificed for reasons that will become clear below – like all Texans in British fiction of the period, was always rich. The novel that began with a New Woman who wanted to marry three men at once concludes with three happily married couples and a grand-fatherly Van Helsing 'with our boy on his knee' (p. 378). The banality of this conclusion – and indeed of the predictable gender dimorphism that has preceded it – reinforces the Count's exoticism and eroticism.

II   INFORMATION AND EVOLUTION

In addition to the disturbance of middle-class gender roles, the late-Victorian period saw the disturbance of middle-class aesthetics in the beginnings of mass society.[11] Although the first disturbance is evident throughout late Victorian cultural production, from classics like Hardy's *Jude the Obscure* (1895) and Gissing's *Odd Women* (1893) to numerous lesser-known works by women and men on the New Woman or the New Culture (i.e., anachronistically, homosexuality), the second disturbance comes to the fore in popular works like *Dracula* and may be analysed in terms of 'information' and 'evolution', rubrics representing two different descriptions of order within disorder. The *fin de siècle* frequently represented the two systems as engaged in competition; the rise of systematic methods of intelligence was accompanied by a whimsical nostalgia, often seen in terms of genealogy, history, or evolution, for all that the modern age had abandoned or repressed.

We may describe this reactionary response in terms of Walter Benjamin's discussion of the aura in 'The Work of Art in the Age of Mechanical Reproduction'.[12] Let aura be defined as the lost pro-vince of connoisseurship, the work's history, 'its presence in time and space, its unique existence at the place where it happens to be'. What withers in the age of mechanical reproduction is the aura of the work of art. Canonical works have generally preserved some of the aura by repressing the mechanical appurtenances and technical operations of everyday life, including the production of writing itself. Popular literature, on the other hand, is frequently obsessed with the machinery of modern life. Yet despite its fidelity to technique and technology, late-Victorian popular literature produced a longing for the lost original, which was likely to be aestheticised – that is, separated from everyday life – and eroticised.

The competing systems appear in Stoker's epigraph to *Dracula*. Here we are told that the ordered array of papers (i.e. the novel itself) constituting the case of the Count do not rely on memory or belief (the superstition associated with the Count) but on the collation of independent accounts, or 'facts': 'All needless matters have been eliminated, so that a history. . . may stand forth as simple fact. There is throughout no statement of past events wherein memory may err, for all the records chosen are exactly contemporary, given from the standpoints and within the range of knowledge of those who made them.' Stoker's note suggests the late Victorians' attitude to two modes of production: the evolutionary or genealogical mode on the one hand, here represented as 'memory', and the non-rooted, non-unique operations of modern science, technology and bureaucracy, or information, on the other, here represented as 'fact' and 'records'.

In *Dracula*, information, science, and technology triumph over a mode of production that has a particular and unique genealogy, took centuries to evolve, and is tied to a particular place. The operation of stopping the vampire enlists the aid of scientists, scholars and clerks, and exploits an international information industry, drawing upon institutional collaboration across public and private lines in business, family, law, government and modern technology. Yet although the epigraph insists upon the triumph of information over evolution, and the plot consists of this triumph, the Postscript – written by one of the victors – denies that the record bears any weight, as it includes 'hardly one authentic document' (p. 378). This paradoxical denial corresponds to Benjamin's loss of the original in the reproduction of many copies. Even while Van Helsing denies that that loss is significant, claiming a domestic moral – '"We want no proofs; we ask none to believe us! this boy will some day know what a brave and gallant woman his mother is. . . he will understand how some men so loved her, that they did dare much for her sake"' (p. 378) – the loss is insistent, sexy, attractive.

The authentic story that is lost is the Count's, and, like his story, he cannot be duplicated. The Count embodies Walter Pater's 'modern idea' or evolution, 'the idea of humanity as wrought upon by, and summing up in itself, all modes of thought and life': his blood-sucking is a form of history. La Gioconda's image, 'what in the ways of a thousand years men had come to desire', is in Pater's terms the vampire's evolution. 'She is older than the rocks among which she sits; like the vampire, she has been dead many times, and learned the secrets of the grave.' The Count promises his zoo-phagous victim Renfield, who 'desires to absorb as many lives as he can' (p. 70), the future of Britain. The Count himself embodies the past. He has been present at every Transylvanian battle; his house 'seemed to have in it a whole history of the country'; his veins contain 'the whirlpool of European races' (p. 28). As Dr Van Helsing learns from his scholarly friend Arminius of Buda-Pesth University, the Count was in former lives 'that Voivode Dracula who won his name against the Turk' with that warrior's 'mighty brain' (p. 240) and accumulation of knowledge. An image of evolution, the Count cannot be created, evolved, or duplicated in a day.

The evolutionary model Stoker associates with Eastern Europe includes superstition, oral tradition and mythic heroes. ('It is hardly too much to say', wrote Summers in *The Vampire in Europe* in 1929, 'that in Roumania we find gathered together around the Vampire almost all the beliefs and superstitions that prevail throughout the whole of Eastern Europe' (Summers, p. 301).) Stoker's 'source', Dracula, Prince Vlad of Wallachia (1431–76), had represented the great medieval struggle between the Eastern and Western Churches; Stoker's Dracula represents an imperial struggle between Eastern and Western Europe.[13] In preparation for his trip, Jonathan Harker 'had visited the British Museum, and made search among the books and maps of the library regarding Transylvania' (*Dracula*, p. 1). He has learned that he is dealing with a primitive race, that 'every known superstition in the world is gathered into the horse-shoe of the Carpathians'; that science has not yet found an entry into that 'imaginative whirlpool'; that nothing there is rational or regu-lated; and that the trains in Eastern Europe are notoriously un-predictable, hence the Count's fascination with Bradshaw (pp. 2, 22). In transit, Harker dutifully takes notes in shorthand on all he sees, including dinner recipes, telling himself that 'imagination must not run riot with [him]', that he must be 'prosaic so far as facts can be', thus establishing the antagonism between the threatening irrational realm of the Count, and systematic intelligence, the British system.

England casts the net that catches the Count and defeats the forces of myth and superstition by enlisting an international network of scientists and scholars, reflecting contemporary methods of 'research' and the progress of professionalisation. Van Helsing, MD, DPhil, DLitt, is 'a philosopher, metaphysician, and one of the most advanced scientists of his day' (p. 112); he can draw upon the expertise of his friend Arminius of Budapest University for a history of vampirism (p. 240) and his friend Hans Andersen for appropriate folk wisdom (p. 340); he is also an accredited lawyer (p. 163) with 'an absolutely open mind' (p. 112). He has apparently trained the distinguished research physicians of the period, including Seward. (Critics like Nina Auerbach have explored the similarities between him and Freud or Charcot, see n. 6.) Seward holds the post of Head Physician at an asylum; Professor Arminius, the Chair of European History and Myth at Budapest; and Jonathan Harker is, like Stoker himself, a clerk. Their research is further aided by international networks of law, business and government: the Incorporated Law Society, Lloyd's of London, the British Consulate, MacKenzie and Steinkoff of Galatz, Godalming's 'people' (i.e. the aristocracy), the police, and numerous other 'connections'. The institutional collaboration of business, law and government reflects the late-Victorian consolidation of management techniques with technology.

In his *Society of the Spectacle*, Guy Debord defines the spectacle as the self-portrait of power: in the spectacle, one part of the world represents itself to the world and is superior to it.[14] The English deploy their technology as spectacle. Eastern European peasants are awestruck by Mina's travelling typewriter, Dr Seward's phonograph, the telegraph, and English electric lamps. They marvel at their steamships, and are consumed in all their 'quaintness' and 'picturesqueness', (pp. 3, 360) by Harker's Kodak. (In advertisements of the period, the camera was often represented in the act of being 'drawn' from the pocket like a gun, to be pointed toward picturesque – that is, non-threatening – Others, i.e. indigents; and English schoolboys were taught to replace guns with cameras in their confrontations with small animals. Charles Darwin discovered on the *Beagle* 'that the pleasure of observing. . . was a much higher one than that of skill and sport'.)[15] The gypsies have their superstition, and the British have 'a kind of belief' in their Winchester rifles (pp. 324, 354). Mina records the forms of transportation by means of which the British, in the cowboy denouement, cut off the

Count at the Borgo Pass: steam launch, carriage and train, all purchased with 'a good deal of ready money' (p. 356) from obliging friends in international banking. As rapid transport converges on him from all sides, the Count's coffin can only drift down the river guided by knife-bearing gypsies.

With technology the English deploy new intelligence techniques. I have mentioned Harker's graphomania. In preparation for her marriage to him, Mina learns stenography and typing (p. 53) and practises to 'remember all that goes on or that one hears said during a day' (p. 54). Entire chapters of the novel are marked as newspaper clippings she has pasted in her journal (pp. 75, 136). Van Helsing urges Seward to record everything he hears (p. 119), then reads Lucy's, Mina's and Harker's journals to the company (p. 186). They begin to read one another's diaries (p. 236), finally finding this more expedient than spontaneous communication (p. 267). As deduction becomes essential to their campaign, they read their logical con- clusions in the shared intimacy of a reading circle (p. 350). Renfield is said to be 'mixed up with the Count in an indexy kind of way' (p. 248).

All of the characters except the Count keep scrupulous records. Van Helsing writes his memoranda in the 'cumbrous old fashion', but Seward uses a phonograph to record diary entries, and both Jonathan and Mina Harker use shorthand in preparation for Mina's transcription on to her typewriter. Godalming and the American Quincey Morris take 'accurate notes of the various addresses' (p. 301) of the locales where the Count deposited the *soil* – Benjamin's 'unique existence' – of his beloved Transylvania imported to England. The Count attempts to destroy these records, but for- tunately 'there is the other copy in the safe' (p. 285). These repro- ductions, which finally consist of 'hardly one authentic document' (p. 378), make up the text of *Dracula*, recorded, collated and dupli- cated by the characters themselves.

Stylistically, this obsession with record-keeping is duplicated by Stoker's ethnographic obsessions, such as dialect. Quincey Morris is always 'laconic' in the informal American style, proposing to 'Miss Lucy' that she 'hitch up alongside of me and let us go down the long road together driving in double harness' (p. 58). It is pointed out that he is the only one of the company who does not speak any foreign language (p. 347). Mina records Van Helsing's broken accents summarising a conversation with two British sailors whose favour- ite term – significantly for the Count's campaign for new blood – is 'bloody': '. . . Then the captain replied that he wished that he and his box – old and with much bloom and blood – were in hell . . .' (pp. 317–18).

Within the text, this style indicates teamwork and shared communication; for the reader, the paratactic structure emphasises the disjunctiveness of the data and the absence of the one story – the Count's – that is the powerful source – Benjamin's lost original – of the rest. The Count can tell his entire genealogy in three pages in Jonathan Harker's journal, but his adversaries piece together a four-hundred page 'mass of typewriting' (p. 378) to erase that original source. In the paratactic ruptures the reader misses the insistently coherent narrative of the Count.

Dracula responds by trashing the study, where he burns the manuscripts and melts the phonograph cylinders (p. 285); yet he had previously stacked his castle library with books, magazines and newspapers on English history, geography, political economy, botany, geology and law; and he had studied the London Directory, Red and Blue books, Whitaker's Almanack, the Army, Navy, and law lists, and Bradshaw train timetables (pp. 19–22).

Yet needless to say, the Count's self-educated, gentle, ultimately 'amateurish' mastery of British ways cannot compete with the modern systematic data processing of the English. He himself is categorised, assigned a place in the order of organised knowledge and culture as a 'child-brain' and 'criminaloid'. Initially, the English allow the mystery of vampirism (p. 192); then through a detailed (inductive) exposé of the powers of *nosferatu* (p. 237) they specify the particularity of the Count and his 'mighty brain' (p. 302); and finally labelling him a criminal ('Nordau and Lombroso would so classify him'), they deduce that he is instinctual, habitual, selfish, 'and therefore small' (pp. 340–2). Once the forces of the information industry assign the Count the label of 'child-brain' (a contemporary term from ethnology) and 'criminaloid' (from criminology) – in late-Victorian terms, atavistic, at a lower stage of evolution – he can only instinctively return home to the land of superstitions. A similar reduction and containment befalls his 'index' Renfield, who symbolically waivers between the Count ('absorbing as many lives as he can', p. 70) and the English ('keeps a little notebook in which he is always jotting down something', p. 69). Renfield is finally diagnosed as suffering a 'homicidal and religious mania' (p. 100).

III   HISTORICAL AND AESTHETIC SIGNIFICANCE

In the battle between Transylvania's genealogy and history and the mobilised British State, as we know, the British win. They have the 'powers of combination' (p. 238) (or networks of power), science, technology and daylight, or longer work hours. As we have shown, this theme is consistent with the rise of 'research', the social sciences and professionalism in Britain. It is also consistent with British entrepreneurial activity in Romania. It may be coincidence that the *Texan* Quincey Morris is alone among the little band of men to be sacrificed on Transylvanian soil, or it may not. Although Romanian petroleum allegedly carried a higher percentage of pure oil than American and African deposits, American competition had nearly destroyed the industry between 1873 and 1895. After 1895 improved methods and legislation favouring the introduction of foreign – including British – capital, enabled it to recover. At the beginning of the twentieth century, Romanian petroleum deposits were among the most important in the world. The defeat of the Count also signals the colonising of the Other through tourism – human circulation as a leisure form of consumption. Although initially Harker found Transylvania strange, 'not like England', after the recipe-collecting, picture- and note-taking, the British return there as tourists (p. 378), and the reader foresees the further touring of Mina's grandchildren – and of future generations who would mystify an historically-embedded and complex popular hero as an aristocratic vampire.

Yet beyond the Count's textual defeat, and long after the banalities that beat him down have been forgotten, Dracula remains in readers' imaginations. Defeated by the modern age, he yet lives on with all the 'aura' – presence through time and space – of art.

This effect of ambivalence is hardly surprising when one remembers that Stoker spent ten years as a civil servant; entitled his first book *The Duties of Clerks of Petty Sessions in Ireland* (1878); worked as clerk, newspaper editor, reporter and writer on the Dublin *Mail* and London *Telegraph*; and after 1878 managed the Lyceum Theatre in London. To his penchants for sexual fantasy and sensational fiction he opposed what he knew best, management and information technique and technology. His monument to modern industry nonetheless reveals a longing for a mythic and imaginative art. As Harker, 'sitting at a little oak table' in Dracula's castle, writes in his shorthand diary, 'It is nineteenth-century up-to-date with a vengeance. And yet, unless my senses deceive me, the old centuries had, and have, powers of their own which mere "modernity" cannot kill' (p. 36).

In late-Victorian writing, such nostalgia *vis-à-vis* the encroaching phenomena of the modern age generally surfaces in the fetishising of place – the imputing to the East, or the village, or the farm, the ability to magically fulfil the wishes threatened by the modern age, the new woman, modern science, or the anonymous city. These magical places are the site of art with its aura, its presence in time and space, its unique existence at the place where it happens; they include Pater's Italy, Ruskin's Gothic, or Morris's crafts-mystery London in *News from Nowhere*. But the greater writers suppress the machine in their works. They connect evolution – Pater's 'modern idea', which he locates in Leonardo da Vinci – with the feudal, and treat modernity like the plague. As Strother Pardy has observed, technology has played little historical part in literature.[16] But as Norman Holland and Anthony Niesz write in an article on compu-novels, popular works like *Dracula* always exhibited the machine.[17] We can say that this foregrounding of operations, even to the point that it transformed traditional literary form, as in *Dracula's* paratactic structure, aestheticised the auracular narrative art it threatened. For Benjamin that auracular art was the bourgeois art then in transition toward art for the masses – the art of the future that he would weigh as potentially democratic or potentially fascist, that Orwell would fear as 'totalitarian literature', and that we call 'the media'. In their conspicuous production, still-bourgeois writers like Stoker left a place for modernity's opposite, an auracular, evolutionary 'art', an enclave of desire, relegated – like disturbing developments in the sex-gender system and Eastern peoples – to the realm of alterity.

This unexplored aspect of late-Victorian aestheticism is significant in that it represents aestheticism beyond elite circles. I shall con-clude with two more, very different, examples. In Arthur Machen's very popular horror story *The Three Impostors* (1895), the detective story of information-retrieval is interrupted by self-contained nar-ratives that are conspicuously marked as 'novels' within the framing text and are supernatural variations on the theme of evolution. (One, for example, is concerned with 'protoplasmic inversion'.) These self-consciously artificial 'novels' are pointedly set in the country as opposed to the primary detective setting of urban crime, and they thus bear the qualities of the Benjaminian auracular: uniqueness, local specificity, evolutionary history. Like the Count's imaginative force in *Dracula*, these evolutionary tales evoke the lost beauty of organic, uninterrupted narrative, or auracular 'art'. Yet within the frame of the detection plot, the transformation of the archaeological scholarship that preserves and protects precious antiquities into a conspiracy network begins in the British Museum with a scholar's avaricious betrayal of his avocation. In the shocking end of all the stories, the neo-Faustian drive to know and codify inscribes itself murderously upon the organic scholar's living body.

Max Beerbohm's satiric *Zuleika Dobson: Or An Oxford Love Story* (1911), read by generations of undergraduates, rings the death knell of the evolutionary mode of production. Beerbohm's prefatory note of 1946, like Stoker's, contrasts the sacred store of knowledge with the new ways of technology: 'Let me assure [my young readers] that my fantasy [of Oxford life in *Zuleika Dobson*] was far more like to the old Oxford than was the old Oxford like to the place now besieged and invaded by Lord Nuffield's armies.'[18] What was the old Oxford? A place whose movements, reminisces the reverent narrator, 'have been no more than protests against the mobility of others' (*Zuleika Dobson*, p. 138). Like Lord Nuffield's armies of Morrises, the first cheap mass-produced automobiles in Britain, Zuleika invades Oxford, with the result that the entire undergraduate population commits mass-suicide in the most absurd case of mimetic desire in literature, but one foreshadowing the mass march to war three years later. (The mobilisation of mass society in war concludes Benjamin's essay.) The culprit is the world of the supermarket, Nuffield's Armies, the superstar femme-fatale, and the mass hypnosis that these forces inflict upon the sacred and sleepy province of Oxford. Zuleika, the quintessence of mass society, is the victor on the battleground of privilege and history.

The foil to Zuleika Dobson, daughter of a circus-rider and herself a travelling public performer, is the dandiacal Duke, a work of art with an aura, meaningless outside of his particular history, an original, irreplaceable, and clearly Beerbohm's imaginative centre in the text. In longing to reproduce the Duke's inimitable heroic action, hundreds of undergraduates copy it to their demise. Like the Count Dracula's, the Duke of Dorset's genealogy takes two pages to trace. His evolutionary history is opposed to Zuleika's journalese: a mobile magic act accompanied by advertising slogans. (By 1911 the advertiser rivalled the engineer.) Against the Duke's accumulated knowledge, acknowledged with every prize in Oxford, Zuleika stacks her library: a Bradshaw covered in semi-precious stones and an A.B.C. Guide. Just as Mina Harker and the Count competitively memorised the train tables, the end of *Zuleika Dobson* shows Zuleika timing the trains to Cambridge with a 'thought about the power of example', or duplication. Glamour triumphs over Beauty ('Zuleika was not strictly beautiful', Beerbohm tells us, p. 12), operations over eros and aesthetics.

This erotic aestheticising of evolution in the beginnings of modern mass society returns me to my initial discussion of late twentieth-century boundary construction. In the most recent of the ongoing discussions of what computers cannot do, the most oft-named incapacities are sexual reproduction and bodily intelligence, which always in such discussions have something to do with the erotic. Whereas the offspring of animal (including human) parents blend the traits of two individual partners, machines make only exact copies; they imitate rather than reproduce. Beyond the role of reproduction, the distinction between machine intelligence, which is abstract like mathematics and logic, and human intelligence lies precisely, some humanistic philosophers claim, in the human body and its bodily intelligence, such as that displayed in the Count's hypnotic gaze, or in the way the Duke of Dorset wears his robes. Thus we have a mass technological age's unending fascination with Stoker's ancient image of erotic evolution, which it aestheticises and mechanically reproduces.

Notes

1. This paper has profited from my conversations with Kelly Hurley, Elizabeth Bohls and Lydia Fillingham, and was first presented at the North East Victorian Studies Association Annual Conference, April 1985, in Providence, Rhode Island. I am grateful to these and, once again, to Regina Barreca.
2. Donna Haraway, 'Science, Technology, and Socialist Feminism in the 1980s', *Socialist Review*, No. 80 (March–April 1985) pp. 65–107.
3. Sherry Turkle, 'A New Romantic Reaction: The Computer as Precipitant of Anti-Mechanistic Definitions of the Human', paper presented at 'Humans, Animals, Machines: Boundaries and Projections: A Conference on the Occasion of the Centennial of Stanford University,' April 23–25 1987.
4. Julia Kristeva, *Powers of Horror: An Essay on Abjection*, translated by Leon S. Roudiez (New York: Columbia University Press, 1982).
5. Evelyn Fox Keller, 'Language and Ideology in Evolutionary Theory: Reading Cultural Norms into Natural Law', and Arnold Davidson,

'The History of Horror: Abomination, Monsters and the Unnatural', papers presented at Humans, Animals, Machines Conference (see n. 3). Roberto Mangabeira Unger, *Passion: An Essay on Personality* (New York: The Free Press, 1984) and *Knowledge and Politics* (New York: The Free Press, 1984).

6. For a summary of the psychoanalytic tradition see James B. Twitchell, *The Living Dead: A Study of the Vampire in Romantic Literature* (Durham, North Carolina: Duke University Press, 1981) especially p. 135n.*ff.* Also Franco Moretti, *Signs Taken for Wonders* (London: New Left Books, 1983). For the feminist tradition, see Nina Auerbach, *Woman and the Demon* (Cambridge: Harvard University Press, 1982); Carol A. Senf, '*Dracula*: Stoker's Response to the New Woman', *Victorian Studies*, vol. 26 (1982); Kelly Hurley, 'Seduction by Surrogate: Stoker's *Dracula*', *Sequoia*, vol. 28 no. ii (Spring 1984) pp. 24–36. Other references to specific arguments are included in notes below.

7. See Twitchell (n. 6); R. B. Kershner, Jr, 'Degeneration: The Explanatory Nightmare', *Georgia Review*, vol. 40 (Summer 986) pp. 416–44; Montague Summers, *The Vampire in Europe* (New York: University Books, 1961; first published 1929); and *The Vampire: His Kith and Kin* (London: Kegan Paul, Trench, Trubner, 1928).

8. *Dracula* (Oxford: Oxford University Press, 1983). All subsequent references in the text are to this edition.

9. For a full analysis of sexual surrogatism in *Dracula*, see Kelly Hurley (n. 6).

10. For the theory of mediated desire see René Girard's *Violence and the Sacred* (Baltimore: Johns Hopkins University Press, 1977); as applied to male bonding through the mediation of women, see Eve Kosofsky Sedgwick's *Between Men: English Literature and Male Homosocial Desire* (New York: Columbia, 1985); and as applied specifically to *Dracula*, see Christopher Craft, '"Kiss me with those red lips": Gender and Inversion in Bram Stoker's *Dracula*', *Representations*, vol. 8 (Fall 1984) pp. 107–33.

11. I discuss this at length in my *Idylls of the Marketplace: Oscar Wilde and the Victorian Public* (Stanford: Stanford University Press and London: Scolar, 1986).

12. Walter Benjamin, *Illuminations* (New York, 1969) pp. 219–54.

13. Stoker probably saw the print of Vlad Tepes ('the impaler') – a Romanian popular hero – on exhibition in London in the early 1880s. For the historical Dracula, see Twitchell, p. 133n (n. 6). For another political interpretation of *Dracula*, see Twitchell, p. 139n (n. 6).

14. See Guy Debord, *Society of the Spectacle* (Detroit, 1977) pp. 24, 42.

15. See Eastman Kodak 'Pocket Kodak' advertisements of the period and Edward Lyttleton, *Memories and Hopes* (London: John Murray, 1925) p. 9. For Darwin, see *The Autobiography*, edited by Nora Barlow (New York: Norton, 1969) p. 79.

16. Strother Pardy, 'Technopoetics: Seeing What Literature Has To Do With The Machine', *Critical Inquiry*, vol. II, no. i (September 1984).

17. Norman Holland and Antony Niesz, 'Interactive Fiction', *Critical Inquiry*, vol. II, no. i (September 1984).

18. All citations are from Max Beerbohm, *Zuleika Dobson: An Oxford Love Story* (Harmondsworth: Penguin, 1983).

9

The Plot of the Beautiful Ignoramus: *Ruth* and the Tradition of the Fallen Woman

Hilary Schor

In 1849, while visiting prisoners in a Manchester jail, Elizabeth Gaskell met a sixteen-year-old prostitute named Pasley who had been incarcerated for theft, a career she had fallen into after having been seduced by a doctor, abandoned, and sent off in the care of a neglectful female procurer. In 1852–3, Gaskell wrote *Ruth*, a novel described in contemporary reviews as having an 'unfit subject for fiction', which takes up the story of an abandoned fallen woman who moves to an English village, redeems herself and dies. In a letter Gaskell wrote to Dickens describing her meeting with Pasley and asking for his help resettling the girl, she comments that Pasley is 'a good reader[,] writer and a beautiful needlewoman':[1] but what Gaskell constructs in her novel is a Wordsworthian story of a daughter of nature, passive, simple and good, whose beauty marks her for a fall and whose docility is both redemptive and fatal. Out of this range of elements comes a novel in which generic conflicts, gendered poetics and aesthetic debates connect to challenge the assumptions of Victorian narrative itself, and which marks the novelist's own challenge to (male) narrative authority.

The novel has been most often treated as a work of moral outrage and moral courage, in which the gentle but angered novelist forces her resistant Victorian audience to face the consequences for one woman of a fall from purity, and allows that heroine to work out her salvation before killing her off prematurely.[2] But Gaskell is playing off readers' expectations about fallen women to create her own female passion play, one worked out in more specifically

158

Christological terms than have been noted, and one which portrays as well the female artist attempting to choose between literary languages and authorial relationships to her text; she is examining the connection between sexual and poetic uses of the female.[3] If in *Mary Barton* Gaskell was attempting to create new forms of fiction, in *Ruth* she is taking on existing literary conventions and examining them for what they do and do not allow a woman writer to say about female experience, and for the ways in which they appropriate and manipulate women as aesthetic objects and subjects of literary plotting.

As with *Mary Barton*, Gaskell could be sure of enraging much of her audience through her choice of subject matter alone: in telling the story of an unwed mother, speaking openly of female sexuality and of exploited young women, she was challenging accepted notions not just of female behaviour but of what belonged in decent fiction. In a period that saw increasing marketing of novels through lending libraries and increasing legislation of female sexuality, Gaskell made an essential connection between literary and economic uses of the female body – saw it as 'written on', a key cultural text.[4] But being so consciously literary a writer, she saw this cultural inscription as enabled by – made possible by as well as criticised by – literary treatments of women, specifically of female sexuality and female beauty. One cannot, of course, tell which came first for Gaskell: her concerns were always social, and there is abundant documentation for the events that drove her to write *Ruth*. But the specific literary heritage the novel invokes and criticises is the Romantic heritage she claimed as the inspiration for her earliest attempts at writing, and one whose treatment of women's sexual and textual status she must have considered even before beginning this novel.

The Romantic story at the novel's centre – the plot of the fallen woman; the pliant subject seduced yet once more, this time into posing for the lyric poet – was at the centre of key Victorian debates about the connections between art and morality, between beauty and society, debates about the representation of female sexuality. *Ruth* focuses on forms of perception, in literature, in nature, in religion, taking as its 'object' or its text female beauty, taking its place in turn as document, as icon, as commodity, turning that plot (female sexuality) into a recognisable story (the 'fallen woman'). But *Ruth*'s thematic focus on acts of perception extends to the novel's interest in acts of reading: the novel reveals and critiques its own position as a text of socialised (aestheticised) female subjectivity. It is in its moments of failure – its over-plottedness; its jolting from one discourse to another; its inability to imagine a satisfying ending – that it reveals both Gaskell's continued enmeshment in the literary strategies of Romantic lyricism, and its awareness of the difficulty of the Victorian (female) plot. It acts out those difficulties in its foregrounding of its own construction, and in the brutality of its ending: it is only by murdering the beautiful woman that it can imagine closure for the story of sexual and aesthetic seduction.

The tradition of the 'tragic poem' of humble life and specifically of the tragedy of the seduced daughter of nature is Wordsworthian; Gaskell's own literary apprenticeship was with Wordsworth, her earliest authorial experiments connected with those 'tragic poems', and the Victorian story of the creative artist was itself largely an inheritance from Romanticism. But Gaskell read the fallen woman poem as a story of *male* creativity, worked out through use of a female object, and thus as a story of difference, invested with literary significance. While the Romantic text often seems emptied out of social content, the woman silenced or rendered incomprehensible in order to displace her story into the poet's psychological reflections,[5] Gaskell saw the fallen woman as not merely an aesthetic object, but as socially determined *and* determining: the Romantic story is part of a larger way of reading women. This plot, as we shall see, was central to the Victorian re-working of culture, specifically in Rossetti and Ruskin, but has further links to the ways all cultural stories get inscribed: the fallen woman story, in short, was appealing as story, and Gaskell considers the way its plot and social plotting come together.

Gaskell's sense of herself as a writer – and of what it meant to write – were always connected to the Wordsworthian project,[6] to the 'beauty and poetry of many of the common things and daily events of life in its humblest aspects'. But what she found in Wordsworth when she tried to write the Wordsworthian story, to write herself into that story, was not women who write but women who are read: women, for Wordsworth, exist to conjure up poetry. If the commitment of her favourite 'The Cumberland Beggar', and of much of Wordsworth's early poetry, is to see experience as it is reflected in the poet's sensibility, the poem literally needs an object – not just to summon up poetic inspiration, but to stand as an emotional equivalent for what the poet needs to bring out of himself. The poem's object serves as a passive receptacle for the poet's reflection on his feeling: as Wordsworth writes when describing poems on 'the Naming of Places, as a Transition to the Poems relating to human life',

> This class of poems I suppose to consist chiefly of objects most interesting to the mind not by its personal feelings or a strong appeal to the instincts or natural affections, but to be interesting to a meditative and imaginative mind either from the moral importance of the pictures or from the employment they give to the understanding affected through the imagination and the higher faculties.[7]

Not only does the object lift the 'meditative and imaginative mind' above its 'personal feelings', it is also, for the essentially solitary Wordsworthian poet, a proof of his presence in the world. In a world of dichotomised subjects and objects, the poet needs a mediating figure.

The figure of the woman, particularly a seduced woman, does more than provide a subject for the poem: she represents aesthetic perception itself. But this figure is at once empty and over-full of meaning: the poet needs a victimised woman to represent both a blankness he can fill and the excess of his own emotion. Her silence justifies his writing about her, while his poetry fills up the space around her. So, in 'She Dwelt Among the Untrodden Ways', the speaker ends:

> She lived unknown, and few could know
> When Lucy ceased to be;
> But she is in her grave, and, oh,
> The difference to me!

The 'difference' to the poet is what the poem is about; if Wordsworth didn't see her, Lucy would have no story, for she exists outside writing – indeed, almost outside language. The silent but adored heroine is essential to Wordsworth, justifying the poetic enterprise (marking the difference) at the same time that the speaker holds up her life as itself 'poetry'. The relationship is symbiotic; neither poet nor subject exists without the other. What Gaskell questions in *Ruth* is the sexual politics behind the sexual poetics. The male poet immortalises the female 'poem' only by killing her off; her death displays his sensibility, but turns her into an object. There is no hint that her death might mean anything to her; the difference is exclusively the poet's to experience and describe.

The question *Ruth* poses is what the 'difference' is when a woman read and re-wrote that story. It is a peculiarly empowering story for male writers; Laura Mulvey has argued in her discussion of 'narrative cinema' that:

> Woman then stands in patriarchal culture as signifier for the male other, bound by a symbolic order in which man can live out his fantasies and obsessions through linguistic command by imposing them on the silent image of woman still tied to her place as bearer of meaning, not maker of meaning.[8]

Wordsworth is constantly writing – and constantly interrupting – that story of silence. But what Gaskell focuses on, and what *Ruth* singles out, is the way the male 'ordering' transforms those 'fantasies and obsessions' not merely through 'linguistic command' but through their re-formation into story.

The abandoned women poems all focus on the difficulty of reading the meaning of the woman: her story is hard to elicit; her appearance is hard to describe; her voice is difficult to hear. In each, the focus is on the simplicity of the heroine, the pastoral setting with which she is in harmony, the 'nature' which absorbs her loss, and of which she is also, somehow, an emblem. There are specific plot elements that link them to Gaskell's abandoned heroine: the women have been driven mad by faithless lovers, by lost husbands, by passion turned bitter; they have children who link them to their community; they have been mistreated by dead or neglectful parents. But in each, the difficulty focuses on the nature of the story to be told – or, more basically, the question of what the 'event' of the poem is. The 'Mad Mother' is an unreliable narrator; further, in her madness, the 'fire in her brain' has burned out all real traces of history. In 'The Thorn' we see a pedantic narrator staring through a telescope at a woman in a red cloak, trying to fill in her story and to give substance to her only lament, which is 'Oh misery! oh misery! oh woe is me! oh misery!' The poet or poet figure in these poems, we might argue, always has his telescope trained on a scarlet woman, but her hysteria somehow communicates itself (or is inscribed?) by the increasingly nervous narrator, who can never quite size up the object in front of him.

The extent to which the authority of the poet's voice remains problematically connected with the silencing of the female subject's voice for the Victorian poet is suggested by poems ranging from Patmore's *The Angel in the House* to Morris' 'Defense of Guenevere'; but the works in the 1840s which suggest most clearly the aesthetic tensions Gaskell's novel reflects are the lyrics of Browning and Tennyson.[9] Like Gaskell, the poets confront the narrative urgency of the seduced woman's story, accentuating, through that peculiar morbidity and sexual tension of early Victorian literature, the difficulty of both writing and silencing female desire. Browning's 'My Last Duchess' and Tennyson's 'Lady of Shalott' and 'Mariana' highlight many of the same issues that *Ruth* does, suggesting the ways in which the female 'text' becomes not just aestheticised but pictorialised for a Victorian writer. The silent women in these poems become both more perfect images of themselves and images of poetic creation, at the same time that they stand in for the objectification and commodification of art itself. Browning's vision of the simple heroine, a bit ridiculous herself, with 'a heart too soon made glad', suggests the dilemma Gaskell will take up in her novel: a culture which breeds women as objects will breed them, in the language of *David Copperfield*, 'altogether diminutive', and not terribly bright. It will train them, in short, only for their own status as objects – in this poem, train them to be thrown away. In the poem itself, description (depiction) is synonymous with death. But for the Duke, the perfection of description is possible only with the mediation of art; the picture must exist to generate the story, but without the painting of the picture and her innocent flirtation with the painter, there would in essence be no story. Without the commissioned work of art, there would be no 'smiles', no 'looks', no murder. She needs to be a painting, in short, only because he had needed another painting; women come and go, but the *painting* of women provides the only real permanence in this world.

Tennyson's 'Mariana' poems, 'The Lady of Shalott', and 'Oenone' all, despite their self-consciously literary heritage, bear traces of the ballad poems and specific echoes of Wordsworthian language: Oenone's statement that 'whereso'er I am by night and day,/ All earth and air seem only burning fire', echoes the fire burning in the mind of the mad mother; Mariana's repeated 'She only said, "My life is dreary,/ He cometh not", she said/ She said, "I am aweary, aweary,/ I would that I were dead!"' conjures up the 'oh misery! oh misery!/ oh woe is me! oh misery!' of the woman in 'The Thorn'. Like Browning's poems, Tennyson's seem to focus on passive women:

not the wandering, wild women of the *Ballads* but women drawn from literary or historical sources, frozen in their situations, always already part of an interpretive frame. But Tennyson's abandoned women have a fierce sexuality not found in the others: Mariana's obsessive desire, the Lady of Shallott's impassioned cry of 'the curse is come upon me' and her immediate response to Lancelot's helmet and helmet feather that 'burned like one burning flame together', Oenone's wish that 'my arms/ Were wound about thee, and my hot lips prest/ Close, close to thine in that quick-falling dew/ Of fruitful kisses', all speak of an intensity lacking or mediated in Wordsworth or Crabbe, but key to Gaskell's depiction of a woman's 'fall'. They have a narrative history lacking in the Wordsworth poems; they live in a world of sensual objects and human desires, and in a world of power relations.

We can begin to make precise the 'relations' within *Ruth* by looking at the particular revolution in aesthetics in England in the 1850s. In 1850, the year that Wordsworth died and that Gaskell's 'girl' sailed to Australia on a 'good ship' to begin her life again, the Pre-Raphaelite Brotherhood began publishing its journal *The Germ* – and the journal began with the lines: 'I love my lady; she is very fair'.[10] Throughout the 1850s, the story of female vulnerability is reworked into something typological: her beauty becomes emblematic not just of her seduction but of the artist's labour. As history re-enters her story, the social meanings of beauty (its cultural creation) become legible; her status as an object of exchange reflects the artist's alienation from his labour. With this increased attention to the social production of art comes the inclusion of the act of reading (the audience's involvement in the 'ritual of interpretation')[11] and a new attention to the moral uses of beauty, as both a sign of the virtue in the artist and a barometer of moral health in the society that created the work. Dante Gabriel Rossetti's 'Hand and Soul', the artistic manifesto he published in the same issue of *The Germ*,[12] clarifies these Victorian revisions of female beauty, focusing as it does on the conjunction of the artist's labour, the religion of painting, and the positioning of the female (uninterpretable) icon.

In Rossetti's fable, Chiaro, a Pisan painter, has fallen into a decline after the flush of his first fame. As he despairs, a beautiful woman 'clad to the hands and feet with a green and gray raiment', the embodiment of his 'soul', visits him in his room, and prompts him to paint his greatest work – only to sing him to his sleep, and watch him die. In the afterward to the fable, the portrait is seen by Rossetti's other double in the sketch, a 'young Englishman of the present day', who considers it 'my picture', but it remains an unfixed sign. The other painters who puzzle over it say it must mean nothing, and dismiss his interest as 'English mysticism'. The painting of the woman, which originally represented his own soul back to the painter, has come to represent the painter's 'labour', his 'heart' – through the skill of his 'hand' – made manifest to another painter: an odd kind of trafficking in women, this, the woman serving as conduit for male artists to find each other across the ages. Further, she becomes an interpretive crux for all onlookers, an artistic Babel, a meeting point of nations and writers. The woman, who was never more than a 'figure', becomes a figure of a figure; never alive to be 'killed into art' like a Browning heroine, she rather kills the artist in his quest for his own perfection – though, of course, his soul will presumably die with him. In this particular 'dream of fair women' there is no art without the female, but there is no real female either: this is men looking at the paintings of other men, paintings that exist only to embody their own souls.

But the image of the nameless, sweet, freshly-dressed girl is at the heart of *Ruth*, and at the heart of that most/least Wordsworthian of Victorian art critics from whom Gaskell learned aesthetics: John Ruskin.[13] The obsessive gazing at women – narrativising of women – that marks his later oeuvre, particularly the reflections on Saint Ursula, the inscription of Rose LaTouche's name and letters into his every work, the ravings on 'The Queen of Air', and the economics of 'Queen's Gardens', are the more obvious outpourings of some confusions of aesthetics and desire that we cannot account for adequately here, but at the heart of *Modern Painters II*, the Bible of the Pre-Raphaelites in the 1850s, we see repeated instances where objectifying the quiet woman stands as a mark of male aesthetic creation.[14] For Ruskin the image that reveals a whole story is most often an image of a woman.

In the long passage in *Modern Painters* on the perfection of Tintoretto, Ruskin resolves the problem of what to do with art through scenes of women, as if their blankness made them more easily vessels of truth, but at the same time he suggests the threat of female beauty itself. Tintoretto's 'Annunciation' and his 'Massacre of the Innocents' can be summed up by their use of female icons. In the former, the 'wild thought' of the artist is balanced by a 'pure vision' of the 'exceeding loveliness' of the meek, seated virgin, desolate amid the ruined city. And in the 'Massacre of the Innocents' among the 'hopeless, frenzied, furious abandonment of body and soul' of the other victims, one woman, again 'sitting quiet, – quite quiet – still as any stone, . . . look[ing] down steadfastly on her dead child', represents 'the only imaginative; that is, the only true, real, heartfelt representation of the being and actuality of the subject of existence'.[15] The stillness of women is the critic's place of faith for the 'truth' of art.

All this leaves Gaskell, as a reader of Ruskin and a fellow inheritor of the Romantic tradition of 'seeing' as 'poetry, prophecy, and religion all in one', with the problem of what happens when women begin to see. Women, in the tradition I have been sketching, exist not to observe but to be observed: as such, they are 'poem', 'type', and their emblematic status is transformed into narrative only through the (male) artist's imagination. For Rossetti and the Pre-Raphaelites, a woman's only story is her beauty made into narrative – that is, when she is seen by a man; for Ruskin, a woman's story, as it appears in art, is only an object against which narrator and reader negotiate an aesthetic understanding. Beauty, in both cases, is made moral. The thought that a woman's beauty might not be a moral, but only a physical fact, is not imaginable in either system. Gaskell, however, suggests the possibility that a woman's beauty is a fact not in an abstract moral or aesthetic situation, but in a very real context in a socially determined world.

Ruth's beauty is what makes her an object of interest in the novel. It is what causes her to have any story at all, and her own love of natural beauty and confusion of beauty with truth lead to her fall. The novel carefully places beauty – and the various interpretations placed on it – at its centre, taking the aesthetic debates I have been tracing and asking, not, how does beauty become moral, but, what are the specific costs of turning a woman into a story about beauty? Ruth herself is identified as a heroine precisely through her own love of beauty – an innate sensitivity to nature, an associative vision connecting memory and aesthetics, that marks her as the consummate Romantic: her simplicity and identification with nature make her sympathetic to us – but they are also what mark her as a victim. It is as a *Romantic* heroine that Ruth can be seduced – though it is as a Christian heroine that she will be redeemed.

Ruth as a novel is caught up in explaining how Ruth as a heroine fell – that is, it takes an innocent girl, follows her inscription into sexuality, re-inscribes her seduction as betrayal, allows her to recognise her 'sin', and then allows her to work out her own repentance. But the novel cannot tell its own central story: it cannot be 'about' sexuality, in that a Victorian novel could not write out a woman's free possession of her own sexual desire; indeed, Ruth is a heroine so naïve she does not recognise her own sexual desire, and spends much of the first half of the novel worrying about the 'pleasures' she feels. What the novel narrates instead, repeatedly, is stories of interpretation, highlighting scenes in which other people watch Ruth, and try to tell the story of her sad beauty. This is the connection between the aesthetic history we have been tracing and the aesthetic seduction the novel highlights: it is also the difficulty in reading the novel, for while it attempts to move 'inside' the fallen woman's story, to move from description to feeling, it also transforms its heroine in turn into an object lesson. The attempt to tell the story of the fallen seamstress becomes an attempt to redeem not just the woman, but narrative itself – to find a different way of telling the story – here, of telling the 'difference'.

Gaskell begins with elements reminiscent at once of the real Pasley's story and of the Wordsworthian trope: Ruth Hilton, an orphan apprenticed to a seamstress, meets her seducer, Mr Bellingham, when she goes to work at a local ball. He is immediately attracted to her simple, quiet beauty – and to her utter unselfconsciousness. Her passivity is that of a romantic heroine: she is nature's child, unable to dissemble, regarding her own beauty as a simple natural fact. Her own loveliness gives her:

> a sense of satisfaction for an instant, *as the sight of any other beautiful object would have done*, but she never thought of associating it with herself. She knew that she was beautiful; but *that seemed abstract*, and removed from herself. Her existence was in feeling and thinking, and loving.[16]

The 'feeling and thinking, and loving' heroine is exactly the Wordsworthian daughter of nature, but inherent in her 'abstraction' is what this love of beauty precludes: any understanding of power. Ruth is too simple, in fact, to know she is being seduced. For Bellingham, however, the attraction in the simplicity is her ignorance of power relations: 'It would be an exquisite delight to attract and tame her wildness', he thinks, 'just as he had often allured and tamed the timid fawn in his mother's park' (*Ruth*, p. 33).

Bellingham makes Ruth more than a fawn – she is a pet, a toy, a plaything. More, she makes of him a connoisseur, and her only pleasure is in making him happy.

> Her beauty was all that Mr Bellingham cared for, and it was supreme. It was all he recognized of her, and he was proud of it. She stood in her white dress against the tree which grew around; her face was flushed into a brilliancy of colour which resembled that of a rose in June; the great, heavy white flowers drooped on either side of her beautiful head, and if her brown hair was a little disordered, the very disorder seemed to add a grace. She pleased him more by looking so lovely than by all her tender endeavours to fall in with his varying humour. (p. 74)

There is a kind of aesthetic prostitution portrayed here: the sensations are both sexual and visual, allowing him to watch his own pleasure in watching. He owns and parades Ruth's beauty; it gains value by being his alone. To discuss her sexuality in this way is to put aesthetic perception itself into question. The same trafficking in women one saw in Rossetti's work can be seen here: from woman as a piece of art to woman as a sexual 'piece' is a short step.

The fallen women of Romantic verse remain 'timid fawns', natural forces, living outside moral censure and social restriction. But the socialised seduction plot requires moral judgement. Further, Ruth *is* socially restricted: economically dependent; socially immobile; devastatingly lonely until she meets her seducer. Her existence within power relations lays the Romantic myth open to question. But the real critique is of the way Ruth's innocence, the 'blankness' that makes her the perfect aesthetic object, makes her the perfect victim.[17] To make that critique, Gaskell must move from one plot to another: from the 'natural' plot, where Ruth's innocence is perfect, to the plot in which she is a fallen woman. The fall into the story of 'sin', the Christian story, has been seen by Gaskell critics as a flaw in the novel, jarring readers: the heroine who, in the Wordsworthian world, could not 'fall' except into guilt, must fall in order for the novel to focus on her redemption. If she was as innocent, as unrealistically naïve, as Gaskell made her out to be, why isn't she a victim? Why does she need to be redeemed? Why does the novel seem to shift terms on us?

It shifts terms, in essence, because it picks up the 'story' of the fallen woman at the moment when aesthetics become social determinism. Ruth, the heroine whose point of view framed our reading of the first volume of the novel, runs headlong into social censure: she has not remained nature's daughter, a Wordsworthian figure, but has become an object of ridicule, soon to be abandoned by her lover, soon to find herself pregnant and alone. The 'plot', as society reads it, is about to be enacted on her body. They will find the fallen woman where they expect her to be, and will read her in pre-determined ways. But this happens, and here the critique of the Romantic fallen woman becomes clearer, precisely because Ruth is the perfect aesthetic object: because she is entirely passive. She 'takes' Bellingham's reading of her – 'quiet. . . quite quiet' – because she is content to remain within nature. She is, as he calls her, the 'beautiful ignoramus', willing not to comment, to analyse, to reflect: she is capable, he tells her, of:

> sitting there watching this detestable weather with such a placid countenance; and for the last two hours you have said nothing more amusing or interesting than – 'Oh, how beautiful!' or, 'there's another cloud coming across Moel Wynn.' (p. 65)

After her abandonment, she goes from 'sitting there . . . with such a placid countenance' to fits of despair equal to those of Wordsworth's mad women, but never to the extreme of self-plotting. To be that 'mad mother' means to be 'read': Ruth's story always seems to be in the process of being written for her.

And this 'plottedness' is exactly what Gaskell wants a reader to notice: the jolt when Ruth's innocence is re-interpreted as sin, the shock of her first confrontation with a boy who thinks she is a prostitute, the jumbling of plot when she is rescued by a Dissenting minister and his earnest sister, all remind a reader of the way cultural plots shape our understanding of the world.[18] Ruth's experience is never primary to the narrative-interpretive-frames in which her life is placed. The conflicts in the village when people learn that – contrary to the evidence of her gentle, quiet habits – she is a 'fallen woman' suggest the social usefulness of such texts: if we can all spot a fallen woman, we never need to challenge our assumptions about moral behaviour. Not only did the Romantic text not tell the whole story of the seduction, eliding the power of the seducer, but it is not innocent of Ruth's fate: it plays a part in enabling those around her to further encode her.

This awareness of the social 'making' of the heroine is echoed in the tendency of the novel's plot to remind us of its own 'making', its

constructedness. Nowhere is this clearer than in the novel's conclusion. After turning Ruth into a devoted mother and talented
teacher, after having moved Ruth's seducer back into her life by
making him appear in her new-found home as a candidate for
Parliament, after showing Ruth's strength in rejecting his offer of
marriage, after testing Ruth by having her secret (her child's il-
legitimacy) revealed, having the town turn against her, only to have
her prove herself as a nurse – following all these vicissitudes of plot
(plot for plot's sake, it seems) Gaskell proceeds to kill her heroine
off. Ruth dies of typhus fever after nursing her seducer back to
health – a conclusion no reader can survive with equanimity.
Contemporary readers were indignant: Elizabeth Barrett Browning
wrote to Gaskell:

> I am grateful to you as a woman for having treated such a subject –
> was it quite impossible but that your Ruth should *die*? I had that
> thought of regret in closing the book – Oh, I must confess to it –
> pardon me for the tears' sake![19]

Charlotte Brontë wrote, after being given a sketch of the novel:

> Yet – hear my protest! Why should she die? Why are we to shut up
> the book weeping? My heart fails me already at the thought of the
> pang it will have to undergo. And yet you must follow the
> impulse of your own inspiration. If *that* commands the slaying of
> the victim no bystander has a right to put out his hand to stay the
> sacrificial knife, but I hold you a stern priestess in these matters.[20]

But that 'pang' the reader undergoes is more than the sentimental
tears one might expect from a painful conclusion to a melodramatic
novel: Gaskell's 'slaying of the victim', as Brontë calls it, forces the
reader to reflect on the ways subjects are sacrificed to the demands
of plot.

One can suggest the ways in which Gaskell meant our sense of
Ruth's 'making' as a fallen woman to parallel the dress-making her
heroine does in the beginning of the novel: the shaping of beauty
into something marketable, the transformation of sexuality into
form. But the question one is left with at the end of *Ruth* is of
Gaskell's own shaping of the story: for all that she is undoing the
fallen woman story, does she avoid turning her heroine into another
kind of 'object lesson', another example of the moral behind beauty,

the 'heartfelt representation' of the 'subject of existence'? Does she 'sacrifice' Ruth to her own vision of redemptive plot? Ruth does not function to display Gaskell's sensibility or 'difference' in the way the woman functions as Romantic icon, but Gaskell does not so easily avoid the confusion of aesthetics and morality which enthralled the Pre-Raphaelite Brotherhood. At times, Ruth seems exactly the kind of 'pure vision' which Ruskin thought women must represent to be placed in narrative art.

There are two correctives to this objectification of the feminine in *Ruth*: the first, and simpler, is that Ruth herself does learn to speak up, and increasingly in the novel comments on her own alienation from her symbolic place in the town. While her nursing career leads her to be spoken of as if she were a saint, one who 'will be in the light of God's countenance when you and I will be standing afar off' (p. 425),

> She herself did not feel changed. She and the distant hills of Eccleston that she saw from her chamber window, seemed the only things which were the same as when she first came to Eccleston. (*Ruth*, p. 392)

Unlike a Wordsworthian heroine, Ruth gets to talk back to those who mystify her; unlike Rossetti's 'soul', she is never just truth. She remains a real and suffering heroine, the specifics of whose struggle to find 'circumstances in which she might work out her self-redemption' move us. Unlike Lucy Gray, she never disappears into the silence of art, with rocks, trees, and other pure objects.

But the other way in which the novel escapes the absolute objectification of its heroine, the continuation of the Romantic problematic, is in its attention to problems of representation. The dissenting minister, Reverend Benson, calls out at one moment, 'oh! for a seraph's tongue, and a seraph's powers of representation'. But as he notes, 'there was no seraph at hand'. In this post-lapsarian world, there rarely is a representational seraph 'at hand', and Gaskell, in trying to write a novel which was not like other narratives of fallen women, questions the limits of representation itself. In her social opposition, she saw herself as taking on what she referred to as an 'unfit subject for fiction': the response to the novel left her feeling, she said, like 'Saint Sebastian . . . shot at with arrows'.[21] In attempting seraphic representation she becomes, like Ruth, a martyr of the text. There may yet be no perfect way to 'fit' the 'unfit' subject for fiction into narrative, but the harshness of Ruth's end, with its reminder of the arbitrariness of plot, and Gaskell's own foregrounding of fiction through the lies which characters are forced to invent to protect Ruth and the constant literary allusions through-out the text, remind us of the uncomfortableness of the fit. These reminders, like the trace memory of the original sixteen-year old girl, Pasley, in prison, are Gaskell's attempt to escape the plot for herself as novelist as well: to write the seduction straight. That she cannot, attests to the power of the narratives that shape the world before we reach it: how was she, as a novelist, even to see Pasley's story before narrative? And how could a 'representative' fiction, a fiction that sets out to transform its readers as well, remain in the prison of Pasley's 'real' story?

These tensions account for *Ruth*'s success and its failure: the difficulty of critiquing a narrative from within its framework cannot be over-estimated; nor did Gaskell entirely overcome it. She did ask new questions of the old Romantic myth, both of the way it shapes reality into art, and the ways in which it is responsible, as myth, for shaping our understanding of reality itself. But in the traces of the tension in the story, we can see the novelist attempting to find a voice of resistance against what she saw as a stunningly male tradition, and finding a new way to *see* as well as *narrate* that story. To begin to find your voice by commenting on the tropes and icons of others is at once the way of a literary apprentice, and the way of a woman intent on creating her own individual voice for herself by consciously rejecting what is offered her. Gaskell's sense of unease as she did so may account for some of the uncertainty of tone in the novel, but the somewhat ironic plea for the 'tongue of the seraph' suggests she knew all too well what she was up against, and was not unhappy with the challenge.

This questioning of inherited languages marks her movement from reader to writer – from daughter to self-created author. She remained a passionate reader of Wordsworth, Tennyson and Ruskin her whole life, but her relationship to male authority shifted: *Ruth* marks the moment of that shift. In this way, the heroine's story and the novelist's story do come together: neither escapes entirely the plottedness of the narrative already written before she comes to it, but Ruth as character and *Ruth* as literary production suggest new alternatives and new ways of reading (and writing) the old tale.

Notes

1. *The Letters of Mrs Gaskell* (hereafter *GL*), edited by J. A. V. Chapple and Arthur Pollard (Cambridge, Massachusetts: Harvard University Press, 1967) no. 61, 8 January 1850.

2. See variously Angus Easson, *Elizabeth Gaskell* (London: Routledge and Kegan Paul, 1979), who claims Gaskell 'knew she was tackling a subject likely to bring adverse, even painful criticism on herself, yet felt she was called to do something' (p. 110); and Gerald deWitt Sanders, *Elizabeth Gaskell* (New Haven: Yale University Press, 1929), who claims that the novel 'teems with Christian thought', that the heroine is a 'blameless and wholly lovable woman', and that 'so strong was convention that no writer before Mrs. Gaskell had dared utter such opinions in fiction as she uttered here' (p. 48).

3. Critics have generally been dismissive of Gaskell as in any way a consciously literary writer, and their insistence on her naïvety has led to a neglect of her use of literary sources and allusions. One exception to this is Michael D. Wheeler, 'The Sinner as Heroine: A Study of Mrs Gaskell's *Ruth* and the Bible', *Durham University Journal*, vol. 68 (NS 37), 1976, pp. 148–61.

4. In historical terms, it is interesting to note that Josephine Butler was inspired by *Ruth* to organise the resistance to the Contagious Diseases Acts, the social movement that united feminists and prostitutes in an attempt to re-imagine precisely these issues of the autonomy of the female body that concern us here. See further, Judith R. Walkowtiz, *Prostitution and Victorian Society: Women, Class and the State* (Cambridge: Cambridge University Press, 1982). For a recent treatment of the body as text, one which unfortunately largely ignores Victorian aesthetics, see Helena Michie, *The Flesh Made Word: Female Figures and Women's Bodies* (New York: Oxford University Press, 1987). My own discussion moves between aesthetics and power, drawing as well on the work of Michel Foucault on the textualising of the body.

5. For the clearest summary of this habit in Romantic criticism, see Jerome McGann, *The Romantic Ideology: A Critical Investigation* (Chicago: University of Chicago Press, 1983), especially his discussion of Wordsworth's 'The Ruined Cottage', pp. 82–92, where he discusses the 'erasures and displacements' involved in the poem.

6. See especially her letter to Mary Howitt, 18 August 1850 (*GL*, no. 12), where she claims she and her husband have been writing lectures on the 'Poets and Poetry of Humble Life', and '*trying* to write sketches among the poor, *rather* in the manner of Crabbe'. (Crabbe, of course, also wrote a poem about an abandoned woman named Ruth.) In this letter, she quotes 'The Cumberland Beggar' at some length, ending with the line, 'That we have all of us a human heart', a key idea for *Mary Barton* and for her subsequent fiction. The year 1850 was, of course, one in which to think of Wordsworth – the year of his death; the year of the publication of *The Prelude*. Talk of Wordsworth, as Arnold and others note, was everywhere. For an interesting discussion of this phenomenon, as well as of some of the connections

between Wordsworth and Tennyson, as well as Wordsworth and *The Germ*, see Carl Dawson, *Victorian Noon: English Literature in 1850* (Baltimore: The Johns Hopkins University Press, 1979), particularly the chapter on *In Memoriam*. Dawson reports that Wordsworth's commercial success was higher in the 1850s than the 1830s, despite his fall in critical reputation. 'When Moxon issued *The Prelude*, he printed two thousand copies, a sizable edition even for an established poet. He needed a second edition by 1851' (p. 37).

7. *The Letters of William and Dorothy Wordsworth, The Middle Years, Part I, 1806–1811*, edited by Ernest de Selincourt, 2nd edn, revised by Mary Moorman (Oxford: Clarendon Press, 1969) p. 335. I owe this reference, and a greater understanding of the difficulties of this problem, to Peter J. Manning, 'Placing Poor Susan: Wordsworth and the New Historicism', *Studies in Romanticism*, vol. 25 (Fall 1986). For a slightly different argument, one in which Wordsworth more easily 'reasserts and solidifies the priority of male needs and desires', (a reading which I would argue presumes a more solid status as subject than Wordsworth ever acquired) see Marlon B. Ross, 'Naturalizing Gender: Woman's Place in Wordsworth's Ideological Landscape', *ELH*, vol. 53 (1986) pp. 391–410. One might amend Ross' attempt to gender Wordsworthian readings with Alan Liu's account of Wordsworthian denial: 'Wordsworthian "nature" is precisely such an imaginary antagonist [as Napoleon's diversionary force in the Simplon Pass] against which the self battles in feint, in a ploy to divert attention from the real battle to be joined between *history* and self.' ('Wordsworth: The History in "Imagination"', *ELH*, vol. 51 (1984) pp. 505–45). The 'subjectivity' Ross claims women are denied, is not readily available to male subjects (or poets) either.

8. Laura Mulvey, 'Visual Pleasure and Narrative Cinema', in Philip Rosen (ed.) *Narrative, Apparatus, Ideology* (New York: Columbia University Press, 1986) p. 199. On this necessary silencing of women, see Nancy J. Vickers, who argues in an essay on the fragmented female body, that 'bodies fetishized by a poetic voice logically do not have a voice of their own; the world of making words, of making texts, is not theirs'. 'Diana Described: Scattered Woman and Scattered Rhyme', in Elizabeth Abel (ed.) *Writing and Sexual Difference* (Chicago: University of Chicago Press, 1982) p. 107.

9. Gaskell rarely mentions Browning, though she seems to have liked Elizabeth Barrett Browning. In a letter of 1859 she asked Eliza Fox, 'Will you give my very kindest regards to her, and my kind regards to him. (I liked her better than him; perhaps for the reason that might be that he fell asleep while I was talking to him)' (*GL*, no. 421, 21 March 1859). Tennyson, on the other hand, was probably her favourite poet: on the 1850 tour of the Lakes when she met Mrs Wordsworth, her chief regret was in not meeting Tennyson: when James Kay-Shuttleworth revoked his promise of a visit, she said she had to 'bit[e] my lip' (*GL*, no. 79, [27] August 1850).

10. *The Germ: A Pre-Raphaelite Little Magazine*, edited by Robert Stahr Hosmon (Coral Gables: University of Miami Press, 1970) p. 1.

11.   I have borrowed this term from Richard Stein's *The Ritual of Interpret-ation* (Cambridge, Massachusetts, Harvard University Press, 1975), which is the best discussion of Ruskin, Rossetti, and the trans-formation from Romantic problems of individual perception to Victorian problems of shared vision.

12.   *The Germ*, pp. 23–33 (see n. 10).

13.   Gaskell was a great admirer of Ruskin's, and she and her daughter Meta were reading *The Seven Lamps of Architecture* in these years. (Her daughter went on to study art with Ruskin.) Interestingly, Gaskell went to school with Ruskin's wife, Euphemia Gray, and once noted, somewhat viciously, that she 'really is very close to a charming character; if she had had the small pox she would have been so' (*GL*, no. 195, 17 May 1854). Gaskell seemed, too, to sense the deeper dilemmas of Ruskin's relationships with women, saying that 'I can not bear to think of the dreadful hypocrisy if the man who wrote those books is a bad man'. But in terms of *Ruth*, one might note her recounting of how Effie, during her marriage, used to 'come down to *breakfast* with natural flowers in her hair, which he also objected to but she continued the practice' (*GL*, no. 211, 11 to 14 October 1854).

14.   Hilary Fraser, in her useful and interesting discussion of Ruskin and the distinction between '"Vital Beauty" and "Typical Beauty"' in *Beauty and Belief: Aesthetics and religion in Victorian literature* (Cambridge: Cambridge University Press, 1986) especially pp. 107–36, discusses Ruskin's 'characteristic mistrust of subjectivism and . . . effort to move the imaginative focus away from self-contemplation towards an autonomous object'. She argues that in his discussion of the Pathetic Fallacy, Ruskin 'suggests that the inability to distinguish between metaphor and fact, between reality and views of it, the confusion of the internal with the real landscape, far from indicating man's access to nature, implies his alienation from nature' (p. 128). Despite this, his work veers between 'subjective' and 'objective', lyric description and 'pedantic' detail. It was his own 'subjectivity', or, at least, the 'egotism' that he claimed had marked Romantic writing, that Ruskin never confronted in his work.

15.   John Ruskin, *Modern Painters, Volume II*, (New York: John Willey and Sons, 1899) p. 181.

16.   Elizabeth Gaskell, *Ruth*, (Oxford: Oxford University Press, 1985) p. 73; emphasis mine. All subsequent references included in text are to this edition.

17.   George Watt, in *The Fallen Woman in Nineteenth Century Fiction* (Totowa, New Jersey: Barnes and Noble, 1984), has suggested some of the ways in which fallen women are actually idealised versions of angelic women in Victorian fiction, but does not identify this with aesthetics.

18.   At this point, my debt to recent work in narratology must be clear, and I can only make more explicit the implicit assumptions of the chapter. One can use the traditional terms 'plot', 'story' and 'dis-course' to account for the dissonances in the narrative, but I do not intend my discussion to be limited to the traditional structural uses of

these terms. While one can learn from the haunting of one term by another, in the constant syntactic echoes of structuralist theory, this incessant, unrelenting similarity suggests a more closed text than I feel *Ruth* finally *is* for a reader. The structuralist terms most useful here might be those of Roland Barthes in *S/Z* (New York: Hill and Wang, 1974; French edition, 1970), and I have always in my mind his play with the 'writerly' text, in which the 'tutor text' is constantly 'broken'. But I prefer Pierre Macherey's sense of the making of the text to this kind of critical game/engagement. In his *A Theory of Literary Production* (Routledge and Kegan Paul, 1978) he emphasises repeatedly the importance of reading the work 'against the grain of its intended reading': more, he argues that 'the questioning of the fiction [is] accomplished by the fiction itself' (pp. 230; 222).

There seems little space for social readings in traditional narrative theory, and my goal here is to recapture formalist concerns for the socially committed critic. For these reasons, my sense of narrative is closer to what Peter Brooks describes in *Reading for the Plot* (New York: Alfred A. Knopf, 1984) as 'the play of desire in time that makes us turn pages and strive towards narrative ends' (p. xiii). In his discussion of 'prostitution, serialization, and narrative', with its connection between the 'thematics of the desired, potentially possessable body, and on the other toward a readerly experience of consuming . . . bound to take on commercial forms' (p. 143), he suggests more, I think, of what narratology has to offer readers. Brooks defines his work as psychoanalysis of narrative, an 'erotics of art', but when he suggests that the text's 'potentialities are transformed by the proliferation of narratives it provokes', (p. 166) we are as close to the politicised as the psychoanalysed text.

Following his example we might note that while Gaskell was careful not to make Ruth a prostitute – she is a scaled-down test case, as it were – we can locate in her the same narrative energies Brooks locates in the figure of the prostitute: we can, in short, realise the power of this novel to shock by the narrative trope Gaskell invokes, and the powers of desire the novel focuses. Only by placing the (formalist) structuralist terms back in the twin contexts of our desirous and socially placed reading, can we understand the contradictions at the centre of narrative.

19.   Quoted in Winifred Gerin, *Elizabeth Gaskell* (Oxford: Oxford University Press, 1976) p. 140. Terry Castle, in *Clarissa's Ciphers*, discusses a similar tension in the initial response to *Clarissa*, and particularly Richardson's dismay at the tendency of female readers particularly to 'yearn for a "happy" ending'. She quotes a letter in which he claimed 'I intend another Sort of Happiness (founded on the Xn. System) for my Heroine, than that which was to depend upon the Will and Pleasure, and uncertain Reformation and good Behaviour of a vile Libertine. . . . But I find, Sir, by many Letters sent me, and by many Opinions givven me, that some of the greater Vulgar, as well as all the less, had rather it had had what they call, an Happy Ending.' Castle goes on to claim that Richardson 'patronizingly ascribes to his female

readers precisely that sort of flighty bad judgment and sexual *faiblesse* that his heroine's fictional persecutors belabor her with – and his remarks carry an unpleasant burden of unacknowledged, almost Lovelacean misogyny. . . . It does not occur to him, obviously, that a female reader – even a moderately pious one – might not necessarily take an unalloyed pleasure in seeing one of her sex made over into a decomposing emblem of Christian womanhood, or respond wholly favorably to that equation between sexual violation and death which he seems unconsciously to have accepted as a given.' Terry Castle, *Clarissa's Ciphers* (Ithaca, NY: Cornell University Press, 1982) pp. 172–3. Note again that Gaskell's angriest readers (at least on this point) are women – and that Gaskell seems to shy away from seeing in her murdering of Ruth the need to impose 'authority' on her text, much as Richardson did in his revisions of *Clarissa*. Castle's reading suggests that Gaskell, as well, may have wanted to close down the interpretive play of *Ruth*.

20.   Quoted in Gerin, p. 132.
21.   *GL*, no. 150, ?Early February 1853. The novel was burned, widely denounced, and forbidden in many households. While Gaskell was aghast at the treatment, interestingly enough she did not want her own daughters reading *Ruth* without parental supervision. I wish to acknowledge here my own best readers: Barbara Charlesworth Gelpi, Garrett Stewart, Donna Landry and James F. English).

10

'Death-In-Love': Rossetti and the Victorian Journey Back to Dante

Robert Zweig

Dante's rapture after being greeted by Beatrice in the *Vita Nuova* is so great that he retires and dreams about Love, who utters half understood words. The journey to his new life, following the vicissitudes of passion mediated by the intellect, leads Dante, the journeyer, to a new understanding of love and directs Dante, the poet, to a new aesthetic synthesis. Dante's passion finds its course, its ultimate direction, at the end of the *Vita Nuova* where he 'envisions a new perception born of grieving love' – where 'It sees a lady round whom splendours move / In homage'; but '. . . the pilgrim spirit stands at gaze. It sees her such, that when it tells me this / Which it hath seen, I understand it not, / It hath a speech so fine.' (*Vita Nuova*, p. 618)[1] Dante determines to write no more until such time as he can 'discourse more worthily' (p. 618) of Beatrice. This paradoxical challenge, to bring words into confrontation with the ineffable, resulted in the supreme aesthetic achievements of medieval Europe, the *Commedia*.

Rossetti, who in the 1840s began translating the *Vita Nuova* and the troubador poets,[2] many of whom were Dante's antecedents or contemporaries, wrote his own 'New Life'. While this has often been recognised, important qualifications must be made in asserting Dante's influence. Many critics have stressed similarities and differences with the *Vita Nuova*, the *Commedia* and Rossetti's achievement. But Rossetti was writing in his own, different manner, exploring such themes as love and death in a poetry consistent with a poetics of his own time. Charles Singleton has observed that Dante merged two 'dominant' and 'antagonistic traditions' in the *Vita Nuova*; the troubador tradition (whose dominant themes are – in

Guinizelli for example – the love and veneration of woman; the effect of that love on the lover) and the Christian tradition (love of God).

> The antagonism of the two may be put in its simplest formulation by saying that within troubador ideology there is no place for an object of love higher than the lady; whereas in the Christian, not only can there be no object of love higher than God but all other loves must show subordination to love of Him. (Singleton, p. 63)[3]

The achievement of Dante's 'vision' of Beatrice was therefore an accomplishment deeply rooted in Dante's own 'world'. Thus, comparison with Dante is useful, but there are important departures from direct comparison which must be taken. Unable to exploit a philosophical pattern as dogmatic, determined and complex as Dante's, Rossetti, probing much of Dante's thought, explored in a philosophical and sensual poetry an understanding of love, death and immortality. Much of Rossetti's achievement, particularly *The House of Life*, is a kind of *Vita Nuova*, a questioning of perspectives by which to unite material desire and spiritual salvation. If *The House of Life* is a failed intellectualisation about matter and spirit, or even an understanding of what it means to wed matter and spirit, its groping with sexuality and death has a basis in a series of interwoven debates about Dante's life and achievement, and the resurrection of passion through the resistance to fulfilment so characteristic of the troubadors. While many Victorian critics looked to Dante as a kind of guide and called for a kind of poetry with Dante's seriousness, they nevertheless were aware of the possibilities and restraints that a truly contemporary poetry must have.

The medievalised landscape which comprises *The House of Life* and so many other Rossetti poems has a context in Victorian thought which recent criticism has not fully explicated; and there is wide disagreement about the scope of Dante's influence. Because of thematic similarities and parallels in imagery between Rossetti's poems and the *Vita Nuova* and *Commedia*,[4] many critics have judged Rossetti's poetry by the standards applied to Dante, although Rossetti had no pretensions of approaching the ambitions that are set forth at the end of the *Vita Nuova*. Rees, for example, in *The Poetry of Dante Gabriel Rossetti*, devotes a chapter to acknowledging Rossetti's debt to Dante, but although she finds an allegiance in temperament between the two artists, there are irreconcilable differences in world views which cannot be bridged.

> An intellectual scheme, certainly, is missing but a framework does exist and it consists of these poems of Dante's so deeply infused in his whole nature. It is to them that all Rossetti's various approaches to the mysteries of life should be referred. Christian symbols occur in his poetry not simply because of the piety of his mother and sisters but because Dante uses them and gives them the full weight of grave conviction. For Rossetti, therefore, they carry poetic conviction since his imaginative need for the spiritual has been accustomed to be satisfied by them. Idealisation of love derives its seriousness in the poetry from the intellectual and spiritual authority which Dante gives it. (Rees, p. 138)

For Rees, Rossetti has a Dantean sensibility and a need for a 'symbolic entry' into the spiritual world but, in lacking a metaphysics, he cannot approach Dante's achievement.

> The polar opposites of Rossetti's experience, siren and pure love, mystic vision and sensual appetite, ecstasy and sense of sin, can all be traced to the impact of Dante and Dante's world upon his imagination. But though his imagination was coloured and moulded by that powerful influence, Rossetti in his time and country could not begin to accept the intellectual premises on which Dante's poetic structures are founded. (Rees, p. 139)

Rees finds unifying principle in Rossetti's poetry by an increasing movement towards an 'inner consciousness where natural forms respond to the pressures and moods of the imagination' (p. 74). Rossetti's explorations about love and death were certainly less ambitious than Dante's, but, as has not often been pointed out, were quite different. From the beginning of the *Commedia*, Dante's course of action, his didactic–moral intention, is clearly announced. His mission to 'tell' what happened overcomes his fear and disorientation which even in recollection is resurrected.

> Midway the journey of this life I was 'ware
> That I had strayed into a dark forest,
> And the right path appeared not anywhere
> Ah, tongue cannot describe how it oppressed,

> This wood, so harsh, dismal and wild, that fear
> At thought of it strikes now into my breast.
> So bitter it is, death is scarce bitterer.
> But, for the good it was my hap to find,
> I speak of the other things that I saw there.
>
> (*Inferno*, ll.I, 1–9)

Dante's journey has ended and has been understood, has been mapped and structured when he begins his journey and his story. Whatever philosophical understanding Dante, the poet of the *Commedia*, has about morality, death and the meaning of his love for Beatrice, pre-exists the 'telling' of the story. But Dante, the journeyer through hell, purgatory and heaven, Dante, the character of the *Commedia*, experiences the environment contemporaneous with the narration of events. He questions his guide Virgil about what he is seeing, is surprised at who is in hell and faints at what he sees. The heart and the mind tug in different directions, one struggling to comprehend God's justice, the other reacting humanly to suffering and ecstasy. The *Vita Nuova* also announces its roots in memory and recollection. The memory is likened to a book whose words will be put down and 'be' the *Vita Nuova*.

> In that part of the book of my memory before the which is little that can be read, there is a rubric, saying, 'Here beginneth the New Life'. Under such rubric I find written many things; and among them the words which I purpose to copy into this little book; if not all of them, at the least their substance. (*Vita Nuova*, p. 547)

Dante's journey in the *Commedia* brings to him a gradual understanding of God's ways and parallels a life's struggle to comprehend or approach a divine plan. But from the moment Dante enters hell, the world is morally ordered and understood beyond the mind of Dante, the character. God has judged human action and motive and assigned them to their proper places. Thus, the world Dante journeys through is a spatialised and temporalised map of God's rationale; a world arranged by a comprehensive metaphysics. The world of the *Vita Nuova* exists prior to this understanding, organised by memory and a pre-rational sensibility. It is a story of how Dante struggled to arrive at that 'other' world, of how his earthly passions were focused on that 'higher' aim. It is in this sense, in this exploration of the worldly, in the possibilities that are offered through love, the fear of death, and an intellectual understanding of death that *The House of Life* is like the *Vita Nuova*. But there are important differences, differences which accommodate a world of scepticism and the challenges posed by science to 'poetic' under-standing. Although much of the *Vita Nuova* is in verse, there are prose passages which give it its narrative flow, which link the verse to the 'real' events to which they refer. The prose is necessary for explaining the rational progression and sublimation of earthly passion into an understanding of God as love. Rossetti's poetry, particularly *The House of Life*, shows little progression in this sense. As the introductory sonnet implies, the form allows for intense moments to be explored and aestheticised.

> A sonnet is a moment's monument,
> Memorial from the Soul's eternity
> To one dead deathless hour. Look that it be,
> Whether for lustral rite or dire portent,
> Of it's own arduous fulness reverent:
> Carve it in ivory or in ebony,
> As Day or Night may rule; and let Time see
> Its flowering crest impearled and orient.
>   ('The Sonnet', ll. 1–8)

Unlike Dante's clearly stated direction, and his systematic explora-tion of love, Rossetti encounters love and death from various perspectives; he finds in earthly love the possibility of fulfilment, although he is often frustrated in his attempts. He also explores the possibility that love for a woman can be sublimated to satisfy spiritual yearnings. Death is feared, but also offers possibilities of fulfilment.

In two of Rossetti's most sensuous sonnets, 'The Kiss' and 'Nuptial Sleep', desire is fulfilled and love is an end in itself, but while they borrow religious imagery, it does not hold any meta-physical authority. Rather its evocation expresses an ecstasy about sex which is understandable only in the language of the spirit. 'The Kiss' ends in a celebration of sensual delight.

> I was a child beneath her touch, – a man
> When Breast to breast we clung, even I and she, –
> A spirit when her spirit looked through me, –

A god when all our life – breath met to fan
Our life-blood, till love's emulous ardours ran,
Fire within fire, desire in deity.

(ll. 9–14)

In 'Nuptial Sleep', a poem at the centre of the 'Fleshly' controversy
and 'omitted by Rossetti from the completed *House of Life* in 1881'
(Rossetti, p. 74), Rossetti pictures two lovers, who while sleeping
after sex, dream while 'Slowly their souls swam up again, . . .'
(l. 11). When the lover wakes he is incredulous that his beloved is
there and is 'real'. This celebration of the world and love with the
wonder at reality is also pictured in 'Her Gifts', where the lover
admonishes himself to 'Breathe low her name' (l. 14), presumably,
because in naming, in tying her to reality, she is diminished.
Rossetti constantly 'moves' in and out of reality, often confusing the
distinction between earth and heaven, between heavenly aspirations to be found through earthly pleasures and sensuous pleasures
to be found in heaven. The intense gratification of a moment opens a
'window' to a world beyond itself, and the eternity of heaven offers
a refuge where passion finds fulfilment. The 'Blessed Damozel', a
seductress 'fixed' in heaven, yearns for earthly pleasure; and earthly
lovers find eternity through passion: 'But lo! what wedded souls
now hand in hand / Together tread at last the immortal strand / With
eyes where burning memory lights love home?' ('Stillborn Love',
ll. 9–11) Rossetti explores various stances towards earthly love and
there is often dissatisfaction with the limits life; frustrated in the
'here and now' of reality, Rossetti, sometimes, nevertheless, finds it
the source of extreme pleasure. In 'Her Heaven', one of the three
poems comprising 'True Woman' (sonnets LVI, LVII, and LVIII)
love forestalls the onslaught of time; a woman's love offers a glimpse
of heaven:

If to grow old in heaven is to grow young
(As the seer saw and said,) then blest were he
With youth for evermore, whose heaven should be
True Woman, she whom these weak notes have sung.

(ll. 1–4)

. . . The sunrise blooms and withers on the hill
Like any hillflower; and the noblest troth
Dies here to dust. Yet shall Heaven's promise clothe

Even yet those lovers who have cherished still
This test for love: – in every kiss sealed fast
To feel the first kiss and forbode the last.

(ll. 9–14)

What greater glorification of life can there be than to find in a surrender to it the possibilities of escaping its limitations?

Rossetti's responses to love form an elusive tapestry in which love, death, immortality and heaven are in shifting relationships to each other. Florence Boos, in a careful analysis of the imagery throughout *The House of Life* and other poems, points to the importance of the figure of 'Love' for Rossetti, finding his attitude towards sexuality inconsistent; she identifies guilt as the prevailing obsession of the poems.

> 'Love' in Rossetti, as in almost all nineteenth-century poets, is a metaphor for all that is best and most concentrated in life – memory, sensuousness, idealism, the aesthetic and the intense. . . . An ambiguity pervades the sequence, [*The House of Life*] as a result of Rossetti's unclarified and perhaps inconsistent attitude toward sexual love. In his narratives and ballads sexuality is more frequently and overtly associated with moral guilt, although considered inevitable. 'The House of Life', by contrast, has virtually no moral context; whether the love it celebrates is socially appropriate or 'caused' is not explained. (Boos, p. 88)

Nicolette Gray contends that Rossetti did not have an understanding of the medieval-Dantean conception of love. By pointing to Rossetti's 'mis-translation' of *The Vita Nuova*, Gray shows that Rossetti's knowledge of medieval philosophy was weak, and that he did not 'know love from God'. (Gray, p. 39). What Rossetti was most interested in was Dante's image:

> Rossetti did not altogether follow Dante either in his idea of the nature of Love itself or in his idea of the relation between love, the Beloved, and God– . . . But Rossetti was not really interested to know, these were Dante's intricate and fantastic analogies; what interested him passionately and influenced him profoundly was Dante's image. (Gray, p. 38)

In discussing Rossetti's poetry of love, Steve Ellis states that

'. . . Rossetti has no philosophy: The woman is purely and simply an end in herself' (Ellis, p. 126). Certainly Rossetti's attitude is ambiguous, elusive, and enquiring but to confuse metaphysics with philosophy does not account for the seriousness of Rossetti's poetry and a philosophy which many Victorians were probing; a concern with the immediacy of experience and symbolic pattern for poetry, one that could accommodate a poetics appropriate for the time, one in which reference to Dante was an important element.

The most sustained explanation of Rossetti in the context of nineteenth-century thinking about Dante is Steve Ellis's discussion of Rossetti and the *Vita Nuova*. Tracing the reception of Dante from Shelley to Eliot, Ellis notes that '. . . an extremely important change in the nature of the interest in Dante starts to emerge in the 1830s and becomes apparent in the next two decades. It may be summed up in one word: Beatrice' (Ellis, p. 103). The Victorians 'took' to Beatrice for several reasons; they '. . . had no difficulty in equating her with the heroines of contemporary romance' (p. 105); and '. . . they could associate the "angiola giovanissima" (youthful angel) of the *Vita Nuova* with . . . Patmore's "Angel in the House"' (p. 106). Rossetti's own interest in Beatrice and Dante never emerged into an appreciation of the *Commedia*, or even into a full fascination with the *Vita Nuova*. 'The drama of the *Vita Nuova*, love, separation, hope of reunion stimulated Rossetti's imagination' (p. 126). Not willing to exploit the symbolic potential of the Beatrice of the *Commedia*, woman for Rossetti is not a 'vehicle' of a 'divine force' but rather replaces it. Thus, Rossetti's own poetry is a weakened form of Dante; the '. . . ideas and passions [of Dante have been] whittled down into something Rossetti himself could cope with' (p. 111). While these reflections are useful in determining differences and similarities between Rossetti and a powerful stimulus to his work, one must account for the refractions that an influence through time must take; for the models of aesthetic possibilities available. Just as Ellis points out that Eliot's understanding of his own [Eliot's] belated 'appreciation' of Beatrice was 'held up' by conflicting responses to 'The Blessed Damozel', so too was Rossetti's reaction to Dante mediated by the intensifying nineteenth-century interest in Dante and the possibilities he offered for a new poetry.

The nineteenth-century debate about Dante was a part of Victorian critical thinking by the time Rossetti was working on his poems and his translation of the *Vita Nuova*. Victorian critics accorded Dante an acclaim and stature unprecedented in English literary history. To the most eminent Victorian critics, Dante was both exemplary poetic artist and touchstone against which the intellectual and aesthetic concerns most commonly identified with the spirit of Victorian thought are viewed. Before the nineteenth century there were no complete translations of the *Vita Nuova* or the *Commedia*. Although there was almost total neglect of Dante in the seventeenth century, by the early nineteenth century there was involved critical interest in Dante and clear manifestations of influence on Romantic poets. One of the major achievements of the Romantic interest in Dante was Henry Francis Cary's translation of the *Commedia* which appeared in instalments between 1805 and 1814. With its biographical notes, it brought to focus issues revolving around Dante's art and its relationship to his life. Between Cary's translation and the end of the century there were eighteen full translations of the *Commedia* along with sixteen of only the 'Inferno'. Dante was a major figure for most Victorian critics. Macaulay, Carlyle, Arnold and Pater all have important essays on Dante and discussions of the *Vita Nuova*, the *Commedia*, Beatrice, and Dante and medievalism appear throughout their work. This intense interest has a bearing on understanding *The House of Life* and on nineteenth-century concerns which formed part of the ethos of Rossetti's time. Many Victorian critics attempted to free poetry from dogmatism, attempted a 'disinterested' posture. In doing so, they asserted poetry's autonomy as a way of 'knowing', freed it from the 'epistemological superiority' of science. Macaulay had set the tone of much thinking about aesthetics when he observed in 'Southy's Colloquies' that the power of poetry and advances in civilisation are inversely proportional. Rossetti's plan of following various 'moods' rather than the achievement of vision (as Boos puts it) is one strategy of confronting a non-determinate world, a world whose values cannot be metaphysically pinned down. The poet, following his mood, enters a fragmented world where love and death lead to different places.

Despite their attempts at 'disinterestedness', critics were unwilling to see an art fully autonomous from moral and spiritual concerns. Pater, for instance, while flirting with the idea of substituting other than substantive criteria as a basis for evaluating art, returns to Dante as an exemplar of great art because of the seriousness of his subject. Dante's achievement had a double-sided claim to eminence in nineteenth-century aesthetic thinking. He was a supreme artist in form as well as theme, combining moral and aesthetic concerns which neither detached art from intellectual preoccupations, nor led to didactic or moralistic poetry.

While Rossetti's poems borrow religious symbols and a rich religious vocabulary, they express only a vague and inconsistent yearning for religious 'feeling'; religious dogma has no hold on Rossetti. As Ellis points out, very few sonnets (LXVI, LXXII and LXXVI) treat the 'biblical God'. Heaven is an idea responding to a very real human need, but it is abstracted from its Christian context. Immortality is an idea rich with possibilities, but death is also feared as the end of existence. These different attitudes towards death, like Rossetti's attitudes toward love are confusing only because they cannot be fixed to a systematic tradition.

In 'Love and Hope' a lover asks his beloved not to question whether '. . . when we are dead, / Our hearts shall wake to know Love's golden head / . . . Or but discern, through night's unfeatured scope, Scorn-fired at length the illusive eyes of Hope' (ll. 10–11, 13–14). Even in a time of love and union with the beloved, Rossetti questions and conceives a greater fulfilment in death than is possible on earth. The poem moves from a description of a troubled time in the past: but 'Those years, those tears are dead, . . . (l. 7); to a time of union and love: '. . . for we are here / Cling heart to heart; . . .' (ll. 8–9); and then points to the future and death. The lover's consciousness cannot rest, cannot find solace in the moment; its 'flight' through time touches remorse, desire and hope. They mingle to indicate the complexity of emotions which may simultaneously be entertained in one ego. The contrast with a past time of unfulfilled love is traditional, yet the admonishment of the lover to 'not' think of the future, disguises, in a conventional rhetoric, an impatience and awareness of unfulfilment in the present. 'Love' and 'Hope' are both blessed; yet they are distinct emotions holding different claims for the lovers. Death might bestow one 'or' the other; thus, in death the drama of life is played out again, offering the emotions and possibilities of reality. By placing no demands on 'this hour' (l. 9) to know of the future, the lovers acknowledge the authority of temporality, are conscious that they are 'time-bound', that time holds the answers to the uncertainties in the minds of the lovers. These complex emotions show a mind not at rest, even in love. 'Through Death to Love' and 'Death into Love' are differing views of the power and terror of death; and of its relation to love. In 'Through Death to Love' the speaker senses the encroachment of death on life: 'Our hearts discern wild images of Death, / Shadows and shoals that edge eternity' (ll. 7–8). But 'One Power' soars above this indirect and unsubstantial confrontation with death. An angel whose 'lord is Love' appears to signal the power of love to overcome the image of death's intrusion into the mind, (pictured metaphorically as the landscape). 'Death-In-Love' is an ambitious poem, picturing the 'oneness' of love and death.

> There came an image in Life's retinue
> That had Love's wings and bore his ganfalon:
> Fair was the web, and nobly wrought thereon,
> O soul-sequestered face, thy form and hue!
> Bewildering sounds, such as Spring wakens to,
> Shock in its folds; and through my heart its power
> Sped trackless as the immemorable hour
> When birth's dark portal groaned and all was new.
>
> But a veiled woman followed, and she caught
> The banner round its staff, to furl and cling, —
> Then plucked a feather from the bearer's wing,
> And held it to his lips that stirred it not,
> And said to me, 'Behold, there is no breath:
> I and this Love are one, and I am Death.'
>
> (XLVIII)

Here Love and Death are both the beholders of secrets, hiding themselves from the speaker's understanding. The words of Love cannot be understood and the face of Death cannot be seen. What the speaker comes to realise is the relation of love and death. Death overcomes love; it is the cessation of love as it is known in life; but it also merges with love to find unity in eternity. Death 'sneaks up' on love, withholding its [death's] identity, until it becomes articulate, 'unveiling' itself. The awareness of the possibilities and fears that death arouses often looms about the lovers of *The House of Life*. Their passion does not overcome an uneasy yearning and questioning.

In the four 'Willowood' poems (sonnets XLIX, L, LI, LII) at the 'centre' of *The House of Life*, the yearning of a lover and the death of a beloved form a bond of desire heightened by memory. A lover is aroused when Love, who has been sitting beside him by a well, plays his lute and makes '. . . audible / The certain secret thing he had to tell' (XLIX, ll. 3–4). As love 'ripples' the waters of the well, the lover '. . . stooped, her own lips rising there / Bubbled with brim-ming kiss at my [his] mouth' (ll. 13–14). The reunion with a dead lover, the crossing-over from life to death is a common Rossetti theme; but here the moment of extreme passion is mixed with unhappy memories of past days. Unable to immerse themselves in joy, the lovers cannot find solace and rest in the moment.

> And I was made aware of a dumb throng
> That stood aloof, one form by every tree,
> All mournful forms, for each was I or she,
> The shades of those our days that had not tongue.
>   (L, ll. 5–8)

The lovers separate and her 'face fell back drowned, . . .' (LII, l. 6). Finally, the lover is comforted by Love. The 'dreamlike' state of the 'Willowood' poems enacts both the state of mind of lovers who suffer loss of the beloved object and the constant paths into the future that the mind travels, even when immersed in passion. Death always 'lingers' at the edges of life. Passion heightens the fear of mortality, but it also penetrates into the possibilities of death; it opens a window on to eternity.

But although Rossetti's poetry is a questioning of ideas, much has been made of the autobiographical impulse in the *House of Life*. Rossetti's own life has been the source of much speculation about the motivations and circumstances for much of his poetry. Rees observes that Rossetti's 'life and career invite description in terms of duality' (Rees, p. 17) and that 'The theme of duality . . . leads to more interesting discoveries than the mere recognition of separate sets of competing claims' (p. 17). Rossetti's brother Michael, in paraphrasing the poetry, often related specific incidents to the composition of much poetry; and Baum does not hesitate to relate even speculative analysis about the relationship between Rossetti's life and the composition of *The House of Life* in his annotated volume of the poetry. But although this autobiographical interest has persisted to the present day, and may have been given impetus by the spirited debate about Dante's own life and work,[5] the reading which most adequately manifests Rossetti's 'Victorianness' is to approach the *The House of Life* as it reflects a questioning of universal themes; an understanding of love and death in a symbolic pattern appropriate for its time.

The capacity to find symbolic expression appropriate for creativity was a subject of intense critical debate in the nineteenth century, one which often included Dante. In 'Milton' (1825), – a touchstone of early Victorian sensibility – building on a tradition that extended back to Peacock and Hume, Macaulay deprecated the relative importance of poetry in relation to science. Structured in part on a contrast between Dante and Milton, Macaulay reflected about many of Dante's most relevant elements to later critics; he called attention to Dante's detailed imagery and was clear to distinguish between aesthetic and personal estimates of the two artists. In considering Dante's achievement, Macaulay emphasised a stark difference between Dante's time and his own, and focused on a subject of fascination to Rossetti: the possibility of exploring the 'inner' world of the mind.

> No person can have attended to the Divine Comedy without observing how little impression the forms of the external world appear to have made on the mind of Dante. His temper and his situation had led him to fix his observation almost exclusively on human nature. . . . He leaves to others the earth, the ocean, and the sky. His business is with man.

> The feeling of the present age has taken a direction diametrically opposite. The magnificence of the physical world, and its influence upon the human mind, have been the favorite themes of our most eminent poets. (Macaulay, vol. VIII, pp. 77–8)

But, Macaulay's 'insular' view of literary development and 'anti-art' aesthetic were soon to be challenged, ironically, by many critics who saw in Dante's work the very possibility of guiding new aesthetic conceptions and establishing poetry as an important and legitimate spiritual pursuit.

It is Arthur Hallam who gives the early nineteenth century its most sustained effort at making Dante relevant to 'contemporary' poets. An often overlooked critic of Dante, Hallam's interest extended beyond the critical and speculative. At the time of his death in 1833 Hallam was at work on an English translation of the *Vita Nuova*, which would have been the first. His major emphasis, however, was on formulating an aesthetic for 'modern times' with Dante as exemplar. Reacting against the implied threat that science posed to literature as a form of knowledge, Hallam championed the notion that poetry could be a moral 'guide' and relevant to those of his generation.

Hallam's lecture–essay, 'Oration, on the Influence of Italian

Works of Imagination on the Same Class of Compositions in England' (1831) is an important statement on the value of Italian literature to England; an early document of comparative literature, it attacks the chauvinism and assumed insularity of English literature. In tracing the movement of Italian literature, Dante is perceived as the culmination of a progressive and expansive environment, coalescing, in his work, the major intellectual tendencies of the medieval mind. In the *Commedia*, Italian poetry achieved the union of a religious and an aesthetic ideal under similar historical circumstances present in Hallam's England. That ideal is a 'spiritual Christianity'; not a dogmatic set of beliefs, it refers to the basic human values implied in the Christian moral code. It was a coalescence of the possibilities offered by the love of woman along with Christianity which supplied Dante with his substance, with the necessary symbolic structure for making the *Commedia* a monumental structure, distinguishable from his other work.

> But it was not in scattered sonnets that the whole magnificence of that idea could be manifested, which represents love as at once the base and pyramidal point of the entire universe, and teaches us to regard the earthly union of souls, not as a thing accidental, transitory, and dependent on the condition of human society, but with far higher import, as the best and the appointed symbol of our relations with God, and through them of his own ineffable essence. In the Divine Comedy, this idea received its full completeness of form. (Hallam, pp. 224–5)

The retrospective glance at Italian literature, particularly as it culminated in Dante, is a valid source of inspiration for 'contemporary' poets; an inspiration that might be exploited because the historical moment is opportune.

> I have endeavoured to point out some of the wonderful and beautiful consequences of this marriage of religion with literature; and I have been the more anxious to do this, as it has appeared to me by no means impossible, that the recurrence of analogous circumstances may produce, at no vast distance of time, a recurrence of similar effects. (Hallam, pp. 233–4)

While a call for a 'moral' poetry rooted in Christian ideals may not have appealed to many Victorian poets, including Rossetti, the importance of the essay lies in this direct and unprecedented appeal to Dante; in its justification of a retrospective look at medievalism which could not be termed 'escapist'.

Perhaps it is Walter Pater who most succinctly evaluates Rossetti's achievement and its relation to Dante. In 'Dante Gabriel Rossetti' he perceives that Dante's coherent, Christian world view is necessarily incongruent with the claims of sensuality and the possibilities of vision in Rossetti's own time; but Dante and Rossetti also share a similar way of apprehending the world:

> Practically, the church of the Middle Ages by its aesthetic wor-
> ship, its sacramentalism, its real faith in the resurrection of the
> flesh, had set itself against that Manichean opposition of spirit
> and matter, and its results in men's ways of taking life; and in this,
> Dante is the central representative of the spirit. To him, in the
> vehement and impassioned heat of his conceptions, the material
> and the spiritual are fused and blent: if the spiritual attains the
> definite visibility of a crystal, what is material loses its earthiness
> and impurity. And here again, by force of instinct, Rossetti is one
> with him. (Pater, pp. 213–14)

The Victorian 'road' back to Dante was a conscious immersion in contexts which were part of a series of debates about the preservation and high status of poetry; about the balance between artistic integrity and a basis of spiritual sustenance in a world in which scepticism in many forms was determining the possibility of dogmatic and doctrinal prescriptions as a basis of authority. Rossetti's poetry is part of this fascination and 'historical usurpation' of Dante into his own time. Although he 'looked back' to produce his own 'New Life', he never found refuge in Dante's world. His representations of love and death in new syntheses mirror the mind of a poet firmly rooted in his own time.

Notes

1. References to the *Vita Nuova* are from Rossetti's own translation, see *The Portable Dante*, edited by Paolo Milano (New York: Viking Press, 1947).
2. Rossetti's translations were published in 1861 under the title, *The Early Italian Poets*. A volume with a different arrangement was published in 1874, entitled, *Dante and his Circle*.

3. References in the text are to titles given in the Bibliography following these notes.
4. Florence Boos, in *The Poetry of Dante G. Rossetti*, explores 'Dantean' imagery throughout Rossetti's career.
5. See Thomas Carlyle's chapter, 'The Hero as Poet', in *On Heroes, Hero-Worship and the Heroic in History*, Vol. V of *Works* (London, 1896; New York: AMS Press, 1969), and Matthew Arnold's 'Dante and Beatrice' in *Lectures and Essays in Criticism*, Vol. III of *The Complete Prose Works of Matthew Arnold*, edited by R. H. Super (Ann Arbor: University of Michigan Press, 1974) for Victorian discussions of the relationship betwen Dante's life and art.

Bibliography

Boos, Florence Saunders, *The Poetry of Dante G. Rossetti* (The Hague and Paris: Mouton, 1976).

Dante, *The Portable Dante*, edited by Paolo Milano (New York: Viking Press, 1947).

Ellis, Steve, *Dante and English Poetry: Shelley to T. S. Eliot* (Cambridge: Cambridge University Press, 1985).

Gray, Nicolette, *Rossetti, Dante, and Ourselves* (London: Faber and Faber, 1947).

Hallam, Arthur, *The Writings of Arthur Hallam*, edited by Motter Vail (New York: Modern Language Association of America, 1943).

Macaulay, Thomas Babbington, *The Complete Works of Lord Macaulay*, edited by Lady Trevelyan (New York and London: The Knickerbocker Press, n.d.).

Pater, Walter, *Appreciations* (London: Macmillan, 1922).

Rees, Joan, *The Poetry of Dante Gabriel Rossetti: Modes of Self Expression* (Cambridge: Cambridge University Press, 1981).

Rossetti, Dante Gabriel, *The House of Life: A Sonnet Sequence*, edited by Paull Franklin Baum (Cambridge, Massachusetts: Harvard University Press, 1928).

Singleton, Charles S., *An Essay on the 'Vita Nuova'*, 2nd edn (Cambridge, Massachusetts: Harvard University Press, 1958).

11

ath and Sex from Tennyson's Early Poetry to *In Memoriam*

Sylvia Manning

Some of the poetry Tennyson wrote before the death of Arthur Hallam is intrinsically interesting; the entire corpus is interesting as it contextualises the poetry written in late 1833 and after. I propose to map the appearances of death and sex in the early work not to be inclusive, but rather to point out the prominent codes, conventions, and gender associations in Tennyson's representation of two fundamentals of life not yet very real to him, with a view to representational changes that will emerge in *In Memoriam* when real experience supervenes.

Tennyson's early representations of death and sex are literary representations of literary experience. His only encounter with death prior to September 1833 was in the death of his father on 16 March 1831, a loss in which bereavement and a sense of deprivation were not likely the dominant feelings.[1] As to sex, biographers agree that all evidence suggests, at this age, a knowledge wholly literary. Yet these *topoi* exhibit by 1833 certain features that are well formed, particularly in their associations with each other. Thus when reality confronted Tennyson in the form of Hallam's death, it disrupted not merely a (none too firm) religious faith but also a repertory of expression. That repertory and its complications and reversals in *In Memoriam* are the subject of this essay.

I

Representations of death in the early poetry fall largely into four types. One group consists of poems that express a Keatsian longing

194

for death as a reach beyond the physical confines of life or merely as an end to weariness. Although the second-rate sensitive mind may supposedly confess a wish for 'a common faith' that will 'hold a common scorn of death', in the more typical 'Song [A spirit haunts the year's last hours]', also published in 1830, the speaker immerses himself in the air 'An hour before death':

> My very heart faints and my whole soul grieves
> At the moist rich smell of the rotting leaves,
> And the breath
> Of the fading edges of box beneath,
> And the year's last roses.
>
> (ll.16–20)[2]

The most extended expression of this longing – stasis almost mesmeric – is 'The Lotos-Eaters', which had its essential shape by the first publication in 1832. An earnest narrator does doubtful battle against such lassitude in the 1833 version of 'The Two Voices', known as 'Thoughts of a Suicide'. And in 'If I were loved, as I desire to be', a sonnet presumably addressed to Hallam, Tennyson indulges in the sestet a vision of death as an overwhelming rush of auditory and visual sensation:

> 'Twere joy, not fear, claspt hand-in-hand with thee,
> To wait for death—mute—careless of all ills,
> Apart upon a mountain, though the surge
> Of some new deluge from a thousand hills
> Flung leagues of roaring foam into the gorge
> Below us, as far on as eye could see.

In another group of poems, with images generally drawn less from scientific and more from biblical sources, Tennyson presents death in conventional Christian frameworks, as consolatory relief from life ('My life is full of weary days'; 'A Dirge'; 'The Dying Man to his Friend'; 'To J.S.'), as Judgment ('Remorse'; 'Why should we weep for those who die?'), or as the decay of mere flesh (the extended image of the body as the soul's coffin in 'Perdidi Diem'). A protracted exercise in the last of these modes is the very early 'The Coach of Death' (written probably between the ages of 14 and 16), in which the young Tennyson parades with gusto a caravan of skull-and-crossbones images:

> The skin hung lax on his long thin hands;
>   No jolly host was he;
> For his shanks were shrunken to willow wands
>   And his name was Atrophy!

>   (ll. 33–6)

Third, there are the visions of destruction that portray death in the conventional gore of armageddon or historical war epic. Curiously, the militaristic poems that concern the present – the purer jingoes – tend not to mention death, even as glorious sacrifice or ultimate heroism. In the battle poems death is the effect of male power, with meaning not much different from that of razed buildings, understood in numbers but not in individual experience.

Finally, in several poems, notably 'Mariana', 'Mariana in the South', and 'Oenone', Tennyson associates death with abandoned women. Deprived of their lovers, these women long for death, and the centrality of that longing to the poem is indicated by its inscription as refrain: 'I am aweary, aweary, / I would that I were dead!'; 'To live forgotten, and love forlorn'; 'O mother Ida, many-fountained Ida, / Dear mother Ida, harken ere I die'. I shall return to these poems below.

Tennyson's representations of sex during this period, roughly from the ages of 14 to 24, show, as one might expect, a progress of maturation. The earliest work, 'The Devil and the Lady', is remarkable for its puerile sniggering. The play, derivative in tone and manner, depends upon a notion of female lasciviousness held not only by the two central male characters, Magus and the Devil, but as well by Magus's wife Amoret, who embodies this quality. In a typical passage in Act I, scene v, the Devil hastens Amoret to bed:

> Get thee to bed—yet stay—but one word more—
> Let there be no somnambulations,
> No colloquy of soft-tongued whisperings
> Like the low hum of the delighted bee
> I' the calyx of a lily—no kerchief-waving!
> No footfalls i' the still night! Lie quietly
> Without the movement of one naughty muscle,
> Still as a kernel in its stone, and lifeless
> As the dull yolk within its parent shell,
> Ere yet the *punctum saliens* vivify it.
> I know ye are perverse, and ever wish,

Maugre my wholesome admonitions,
To run obliquely like the bishop at chess,
But I'll cry 'check' to ye, I warrant ye
I'll prove a 'stalemate' to ye.

(ll. 148–62)

Amoret replies, half aside, 'In all conscience / My mate is stale enough'.

Happily, adolescence is time-limited, for Tennyson as for the rest of us, and by the end of this period we find an adult acceptance of passion, enunciated in a way that perhaps surprises us and that seems to have taken Tennyson's friends somewhat by surprise as well. 'Life of the Life within my blood', apparently a fragment of a 'Ballad of Sir Lancelot', is supposedly spoken by Lancelot; nonetheless, in sending it to W. B. Donne in June 1833, J. M. Kemble wrote: '. . . for the sake of my future clerical views and Alfred's and Sir L.'s character, I must request that it be kept as quiet as possible.' It is only twelve lines long:

Life of the Life within my blood,
   Light of the Light within mine eyes,
The May begins to breathe and bud,
   And softly blow the balmy skies;

Draw nigh me; stay not to be wooed,
   It is not glorious to be wise.
Come feed my lip with costly food,
   My ear with low replies;

Bathe with me in the fiery flood,
   And mingle kisses, tears, and sighs,
Life of the Life within my blood,
   Light of the Light within mine eyes.

An intermediary stage is represented in 'Recollections of the Arabian Nights', published in 1830. Like 'Life of the Life within my blood', the poem begins with a Shelleyan echo, this time a suggestion of voyage back to the centre, the origin:

When the breeze of a joyful dawn blew free
In the silken sail of infancy,

The tide of time flowed back with me,
The forward-flowing tide of time;
(ll.1–4)

Travelling night and day in his 'shallop', the speaker floats down a river, through a canal, and on to a lake surrounded by exotic glories of nature and art. Anchored, he sleeps on land, then walks through gardens to the pavilion. He steals forward and gazes:

. . . on the Persian girl alone,
Serene and argent-lidded eyes
Amorous, and lashes like to rays
Of darkness, and a brow of pearl
Tressed with redolent ebony,
In many a dark delicious curl,
Flowing beneath her rose-hued zone;
(ll.134–40)

The sense of secrecy and the forbidden enhances the eroticism and builds tension for the expected arrival of the girl's rightful lord in the remaining stanza. And indeed he comes – but with 'his deep eye laughter-stirred / With merriment of kingly pride, / Sole star of all that place and time' (ll.150–2). The good Haroun Alraschid takes no affront at the young gazer, and the poem ends abruptly, somewhere between relief and anti-climax.

In the conventional male-spoken love lyrics, sexuality is effaced: love remains wholly spiritual and flirtation a matter of glances and naïve kisses. Love in these poems is certainly heterosexual, but minimally sexual. Tennyson's 'light Lisette', 'wanton Rosalind' (two of them), 'sweet pale Margaret', 'spiritual Adeline', 'Claribel', 'Isabel' of 'perfect wifehood and pure lowlihead', and even overly bold 'Kate', all devolve into the type elaborated in Alice and Rose, who appear in their titles not by their own names, as do the others, but by the domestic, patriarchal designations 'The Miller's Daughter' and 'The Gardener's Daughter'. The representation of the latter, Rose, depends heavily on Tennyson's prelapsarian view of the natural world. She is deeply entwined with the rose and other beauties of nature. The point of the 'plot' is to prove how fully distinct from art is her effect on the speaker. Love is inspired by beauty and association with nature and it leads to a marriage of lifelong devotion.

Sexuality is implicit in the abandoned-female poems, and there are muffled hints of sexual transgression in 'The May Queen' and of sexual libertinism in 'Anacaona'. The most explicit sexuality comes in the paired poems 'The Merman' and 'The Mermaid'. Safely under the sea and safely non-human, the mermen and mermaids have a fine and guilt-free time. The mermaid exults that her beauty captivates even the 'great sea-snake' with his 'large calm eyes', the merman looks forward to living 'merrily, merrily' because 'Soft are the moss-beds under the sea'. Not surprisingly, the most explicitly sexual human figure, Cleopatra in 'A Dream of Fair Women', is also associated with the sea:

> 'The ever-shifting currents of the blood
>   According to my humour ebb and flow.
>   . . .
>
> 'The man, my lover, with whom I rode sublime
>   On Fortune's neck: we sat as God by God:
> The Nilus would have risen before his time
>   And flooded at our nod.
>   (ll.133–4, 141–4)

The poems of moment for the purposes of this essay are those in which sexuality and death intersect. Because I am concerned with poems in which women, sexuality and death are related less through causalities of plot and more ontologically, I exclude from this discussion 'The Lover's Tale' and the balladic 'The Sisters', both narratives of revenge killings; 'Oriana', also balladic, sung by the knight who has killed his beloved by mistake (or bad aim); 'Mithridates Presenting Berenice with the Cup of Poison', in which sexuality is a *donne* of the situation (Berenice is his concubine) but has little presence in the poem; and 'Eleanore', which in the last section (viii) employs the trope of death as orgasm at the climax of its otherwise typically early-Tennysonian praise of Eleanore ('Yet tell my name again to me, / I *would* be dying evermore, / So dying ever, Eleanore').

II

The two Marianas and Oenone long for death. Oenone's refrain ('hearken ere I die') may seem merely to anticipate, rather than long, but Tennyson is explicit: in language close to Mariana's, she complains 'I am all aweary of my life' (l.32), and she pleads with death, 'let me die' (l.240). The repetition itself mounts to longing. 'Mariana in the South', with greater variation in the refrain, effects a significant transformation from 'To live forgotten, and love forlorn' to 'To live forgotten, and die forlorn', which suggests equivalence between 'love' and 'die'. (It is 'love' in stanzas 1 and 2, 'die' in stanzas 5 and 6, and 'love' again in stanzas 7 and 8 – but in the latter two the promise of death has come, in the 'image' of stanza 7 and in her premonition in stanza 8 that '"The night comes on that knows not morn."')

These women are not suicidal. They do not have death in their power just as they do not have sex. They speak of death in tonalities shaped by sexual desire, until the two objects of longing – the male and death – become fused. Sex and death, courted in rapid interchange, are deeply implicated in each other, and insofar as men exist in these poems only as absences or as the indifferent, sexuality and death constitute a thoroughly female subject.

The less well-known poem 'Fatima' presents the same essential situation in a form not only condensed (forty-two lines, exactly half the length of 'Mariana' and a quarter of 'Oenone') but correspondingly heightened in sexuality. Fatima's expression, in action and language, is fiercer ('I rolled among the tender flowers: / I crushed them on my breast, my mouth', ll.10–11) and her desire is explicitly sexual ('O Love, O fire! once he drew / With one long kiss my whole soul through / My lips, as sunlight drinketh dew', ll.19–21). And in the final stanza, even the equation of sex and death is made explicit:

> My whole soul waiting silently,
> All naked in a sultry sky,
> Droops blinded with his shining eye:
> I will possess him or will die.
>   I will grow round him on his place,
>   Grow, live, die looking on his face,
>   Die, dying clasped in his embrace.
>   (ll.36–42)

The literal meaning of the latter half of the stanza is opaque, unless one imagines some fairly baroque innuendo for line 40 and the usual pun on 'die' in lines 41 and 42. The 'or' in line 39, however, supports one's sense that in this poem dying does not take on a metaphoric

function, as it does in 'Eleanore' (though both poems are indebted to
Sappho's 'Fragment 2'),[3] but retains its discreteness as an alternative to sexual satisfaction. The assertion appears to seize death as a
substitute for fulfilment, or as fulfilment, the intense experience to
satisfy the intense desire. The poem is abrupt in language and
rhythm as in development.

The rhyme and metre, nonetheless, are the same as those of 'The
Lady of Shalott', minus the latter's refrain after the fourth and final
lines of the stanza. But the Lady of Shalott is critically different from
the abandoned females. Though she too does not have sex in her
power, she does have death. If the poem is left unobscured by
allegorical interpretations, the centrality of sex and death to the
Lady's deprivations becomes clear. The first indication of lack in her
mirrored world comes at line 60:

> And sometimes through the mirror blue
> The knights come riding two and two:
> She hath no loyal knight and true,
>   The Lady of Shalott.
>
> (ll.60–3)

In the following stanza come the funeral and the young lovers lately
wed, which lead to the conclusion of Part II, '"I am half sick of
shadows," said / The Lady of Shalott' (ll.71–2). In Part III the
handsome Sir Lancelot arrives, four stanzas describe his masculine
beauty, and in the fifth, 'She looked down to Camelot'. Seized by
sexual desire, she hastens to her death.

That this death is apotheosis is perhaps clearer when one sets it
beside 'The Dying Swan', an earlier poem. The swan's death song is
a song of magnificent triumph:

> The wild swan's death-hymn took the soul
> Of that waste place with joy
> Hidden in sorrow: at first to the ear
> The warble was low, and full and clear;
> And floating about the under-sky,
> Prevailing in weakness, the coronach stole
> Sometimes afar, and sometimes anear;
> But anon her awful jubilant voice,
> With a music strange and manifold,
> Flowed forth on a carol free and bold;

> As when a mighty people rejoice
> With shawms, and with cymbals, and harps of gold,
> And the tumult of their acclaim is rolled
> Through the open gates of the city afar,
> To the shepherd who watcheth the evening star.
> (ll.21–35)

All the features of the landscape are 'flooded over with eddying song'. In the familiar 1842 version of the poem, the Lady of Shalott is described to create the visual image of a swan:

> Lying, robed in snowy white
> That loosely flew to left and right—
> The leaves upon her falling light—
> Through the noises of the night
>   She floated down to Camelot:
>   (ll.136–40)

In 1832 these lines were less imagistic but more explicit:

> As when to sailors while they roam,
> By creeks and outfalls far from home,
> Rising and dropping with the foam,
> From dying swans wild warblings come,
>   Blown shoreward; so to Camelot

And 'singing her last song' in line 143 was 'chanting her deathsong', closer to the swan's 'death-hymn' (l.21, quoted above).

The essential characteristics of the swan's song are abbreviated in the Lady's:

> Heard a carol, mournful, holy,
> Chanted loudly, chanted boldly,
> Till her blood was frozen slowly,
> And her eyes were darkened wholly,
>   Turned to towered Camelot.
>   (ll.145–9)

The death is fulfilment, completion, climax. In the revised ending of 1842, Sir Lancelot only half understands it: 'But Lancelot mused a little space; / He said, "She has a lovely face; / God in his mercy lend her grace"'' (ll. 168–70). If Lancelot is a figure for sexuality, his failure to apprehend suggests that the beauty of this death is somehow beyond sexuality.

In 'The May Queen' the connection between death and sex is obscured, compared to the poems discussed thus far. In the first section of the poem (lines 1–44) the speaker is a somewhat careless and self-regarding young beauty, marked by the refrain 'For I'm to be Queen o' the May, mother, I'm to be Queen o' the May'. She is proud of her bright black eyes and indifferent to her lover Robin:

> They say he's dying all for love, but that can never
>   be:
> They say his heart is breaking, mother—what is that to
>   me?
> There's many a bolder lad 'ill woo me any summer day,
> And I'm to be Queen o' the May, mother, I'm to be Queen
>   o' the May.
>
> (ll. 21–4)

This note of sexual triumph is entirely superseded in the second section, 'New Year's Eve', in which we find her reformed and dying. She refers to the May day, but there is no syntax between the two sections, no explanation of any relationship between the May day festivity and her oncoming death, between her confident cruelty then and her sweet repentance now, though there are some hints:

> I have been wild and wayward, but you'll forgive me
>   now;
> You'll kiss me, my own mother, and forgive me ere I go;
>
> (ll. 33–4)

The third section, 'Conclusion', added in 1842, increases the confusion. We discover that in fact she did not die as she expected, but now, the following Spring, expects again to die momentarily. The difference is that whereas before she was repentant but regretful, now she is eager 'To lie within the light of God, as I lie upon your breast' (l. 59). Assuming that Tennyson's intentions in 1842 were not to change the drift of the poem, it is still not clear whether any sort of irony is intended in the commentary that the third section constitutes upon the second: surely there is an implication of hypochondria, and that she will not die this time either? Or is there? Nothing in the tone permits such criticism. Her sobriety, seriousness and trite religiosity in the latter two sections contrast oddly with the first section, and the contrast is heightened by the absence of transition. What is the connection between being Queen of the May and dying? Come-uppance for hauteur? Transgression and punishment? We are given only juxtaposition and the inference suggested by convention. On the one hand, what the poem tells us is that she slighted Robin; on the other, the only sense we can make of the sequence is to infer sexual sin, perhaps with someone unnamed, whoever she slighted Robin for. Even this is problematic, though, since she says in the last section that she 'might have been his wife' (l.47) – not likely if she betrayed him. We are left with only a mysterious illness.

Tennyson concludes 'Anacaona' with a similar mystery. The 'dark Indian maiden', 'golden flower of Hayti', welcomes the Spaniards. We are told in the last stanza that she 'led them down the pleasant places' (l.74) and then, abruptly, that she was never again seen wandering happily by the sea or in the wood. For this poem, however, we have the source to confirm our uneasy intuition: she was later killed by the men. Casual Caribbean sensuality is followed by death.

In 'Lilian' punishment for sexuality takes another turn. The poem has an un-Tennysonian lightness:

> Airy, fairy Lilian,
> Flitting, fairy Lilian,
> When I ask her if she loves me,
> Claps her tiny hands above me,
> Laughing all she can;
> (ll.1–5)

Lilian teases, flirts and holds back. The speaker wearies, and then abruptly threatens:

> If prayers will not hush thee,
> Airy Lilian,
> Like a rose-leaf I will crush thee,
> Fairy Lilian.
> (ll.27–30)

It is a male threat of extinguishing power. Again, this time humorously, death is a come-uppance for sexual self-assurance.

What we see in all these poems is that Tennyson's sexually deprived women long to die and, except for the Lady of Shalott, live to moan. The sexually confident are punished by death. In 'A Dream of Fair Women' the two types are brought together. Tennyson's 'dream' follows his reading of Chaucer's *The Legend of Good Women*, a peculiarly vivid experience. Asleep, he seems to wander through a glorious wood lit by 'the maiden splendours of the morning star' (l.55) and filled with familiar flowers and leaves. The smell of violets brings back the times he remembers 'to have been / Joyful and free from blame' (l.80). In this setting of virginal freshness, he encounters five women.

The first is Helen of Troy, whose beauty freezes his speech 'with shame and with surprise' (l.89). But Helen speaks briefly and tersely, seeing herself as a cause of calamity. She is sorrowful, bitterly repentant, and almost bewildered. The next is Iphigenia, angry and filled with resentment. Her consciousness of 'stern black-bearded kings with wolfish eyes' (l.111) watching her death suggests a sexual dimension to the rite. Then Cleopatra calls: richly sexual, she is eager to look upon the speaker because '"Tis long since I have seen a man"' (l.131). She, the only character Tennyson takes from Chaucer, speaks at length. When she stops he hardly knows, so dazzled is he by her beauty and passion, until he hears Jephtha's daughter, carolling her deep inner peace. In contrast to Iphigenia, Jephtha's daughter is grateful for the privilege of having redeemed her father's vow through her self-sacrifice. Finally, we have a brief appearance of Rosamond de Clifford, bewailing her poisoning at the hands of Queen Eleanor (wife to Henry II, of whom Rosamond was a mistress). Cleopatra mocks her weakness, and the poet wakes. He lists the women of whose presence waking has deprived him: Margaret Roper, who cherished her father's severed head, Joan of Arc, and Eleanor, the wife of Edward I, who sucked the poison from her husband's wound.

The configuration of this line-up is noteworthy: the woman whose legendary beauty spelled destruction, now miserable and repentant, followed by the woman who epitomises female sexual prowess, she framed by a pair of sacrificial daughters and followed by a string of ever more briefly presented punished or sacrificial women (Rosamund is punished; Margaret Roper, Joan of Arc, and Eleanor are sacrificial). The women who are killed – especially Iphigenia and Jephtha's daughter, who also are presented at the greatest length – are the subjugated. With Cleopatra at their centre, they constitute a set of signs that seem to realise more fully the hints of 'The May Queen', 'Anacaona', and 'Lilian'.

III

In these poems Tennyson presents a range of female figures in whom sex and their own deaths are conjoined. The narratives may show death as wooed, glorious, pathetic, or punitive; what remains constant is the connection, and a strange beauty.

In the lyrics of *In Memoriam* the conjunction emerges in a different form. The only women in this poem are the characterless sisters familiar in the domestic idylls, but there is another, very powerful female present: Nature, shrieking and bloody. In this poem, unlike, for instance, 'The Gardener's Daughter', the natural condition is the condition of life in a purely physical world, a world in which death is final. Section 35 brings together the poem's obsession with geological change:

> The moanings of the homeless sea,
>   The sound of streams that swift or slow
>   Draw down the Aeonian hills, and sow
> The dust of continents to be;

and its rawest sexuality:

> . . . Love had not been,
> Or been in narrowest working shut,
>
> Mere fellowship of sluggish moods,
>   Or in his coarsest Satyr-shape
>   Had bruised the herb and crushed the grape,
> And basked and battened in the woods.

Cleopatra in 'A Dream of Fair Women' boasted, 'I governed men by change, and so I swayed / All moods' (ll.130–1); Nature in *In Memoriam* cries, 'I bring to life, I bring to death' (section 56). Like Helen, Nature brings only calamity. The connection between love and the natural beauty of flowers (central to 'The Gardener's Daughter' and ornamental – perhaps influenced by the *Legend*'s Prologue – in 'A Dream of Fair Women') is severed. Heterosexuality is brutal generation.

One is less likely to notice that Nature not only destroys but wreaks that destruction on herself. That is, what is destroyed is also nature, uncapitalised. It is the species of Nature that die. Nature thus subsumes not merely the powerfully sexual female destroyers, but the females who are sacrificed and the females whose deprivation leaves them longing for death. She is all aspects of death in a world in which 'The spirit does but mean the breath' (section 56).

In the slough of despair, it seems to Tennyson's speaker that Hallam has suffered Nature's death, not God's – that is, death beyond which there is no life, no meaning. Gone is the Christian acceptance of 'A Dirge' or 'The Dying Man to his Friend'. Gone too is the intoxication with death in 'The Lady of Shalott' and 'The Dying Swan'. Finding himself abandoned, the mourner repeatedly conceives himself as female. One may read these images not as signs of a 'real' homosexuality but as continuity in the trope of the mourner, a sort of archaism from the earlier poetry: the earlier subjects may survive in the similes because Tennyson has a richly developed language for female abandonment, but no voice for male deprivation. Moreover, for the imagined females death was the comforter, whereas for the mourner of *In Memoriam* it is the enemy. Death as the breaker of masculine bonds has no romantic quality. In this mature work, the victim is beloved and male, and death is a female, sexual force.

At the risk of overstatement, let me clarify the point. For Mariana, Oenone, Fatima, death is an unattained consolation for sexual deprivation. For the Lady of Shalott, Jephtha's daughter, Joan of Arc, it is fulfilment. For Anacaona, Lilian, Iphigenia, it is part of the mystery of female sexuality. In all this poetry, imagined death is represented in a coding that associates it with sex and confines it to women. Death is not given gender or otherwise personified, but it is frequently sought. For the May Queen to welcome her own death is not part of her illness but a sign of her redemption from frivolity, perhaps from something more. In contrast, real death comes to Tennyson in 1833 in connection with a man. In the lyrics that inscribe the struggle with that death, Tennyson frequently personifies death. While his faith wavers, he represents death as unremitted evil, threatening all value. And at the height of struggle, he perceives it as the agent of a larger, eminently powerful, female force committed to an endless and pointless alternation of generation and destruction. The representation of the death of Arthur Hallam turns out to be very different from the representation of the imagined deaths, but predicted by its associations.[4] The wrenching of a subject from female to male experience and expression is accompanied by a dramatic reversal: from the remarkably empathic presentation of female suffering and female longing for death Tennyson moves to the conflation of femaleness, sexuality, and death-dealing in a figure of brutality and blood. This reversal is anticipated in the antipathetic turns against sexually confident or successful women in the early poetry. Tennyson wants not only a voice for masculine grief and helplessness, but a gender-neutral image of death.

A likeness of imagery offers an instance of how he achieves such expression. This passage from 'Mariana' is generally recognised as phallic:

> But when the moon was very low,
>   And wild winds bound within their cell,
>   The shadow of the poplar fell
> Upon her bed, across her brow.
>
> (ll.53–6)

Section 67 of *In Memoriam* begins:

> When on my bed the moonlight falls,
>   I know that in thy place of rest
>   By that broad water of the west,
> There comes a glory on the walls;

The likeness is the moonlight on the bed. The differences are in effect. For Mariana, the light shows emptiness or absence: Mariana bemoans her nights as well as her days. For the poet of *In Memoriam*, the moonlight connects him, albeit inconclusively, with the lost beloved; it forges a tentative link across the boundary of death. The poet then sleeps, 'closing eaves of wearied eyes'; Mariana continues in her sleepless exhaustion, 'I am aweary, aweary'. Mariana's moonlight betokens the isolation of withheld sexuality; the poet's moonlight casts a glow of liminally sexual intimacy upon an involuntarily broken relationship.

The full expense of rage is marked by another lyric in which moonlight plays a major role, but also a lyric in which female sexuality is finally seen as blessed procreativity: the epithalamium for Cecilia. The titling and placement of this lyric as epilogue, however, are not trivial; it stands outside the experience, marking an achievement through but not in it. That death is never wholly released from sexuality may at least in part explain the strikingly, perhaps stridently, masculine opening of the other epilogue, placed in the poem as 'Prologue': 'Strong Son of God, immortal Love'. Love at full expanse, not 'in narrowest working shut', is also Love as male divinity, whose generation from the Law pointedly by-passes female sexuality.

The human figures of *In Memoriam* are protected from sexuality because the sexual element hitherto associated with death has been aggregated to Nature, the death-dealing foe. In the later poetry, notably the *Idylls of the King*, the destructive, sexual, female force is again embodied in women. Guinevere, Ettare, Vivien – these figures retain the transformations of the thirties and forties that are expressed in the personified Nature of *In Memoriam*. They bring to death, and their joining of death with sexuality is evil, their beauty specious. The figure of the swan returns, but this figure is male and the swan is black:

> So said he, and the barge with oar and sail
> Moved from the brink, like some full-breasted swan
> That, fluting a wild carol ere her death,
> Ruffles her pure cold plume, and takes the flood
> With swarthy webs.
>> ('The Passing of Arthur', ll.433–37)

Arthur is pure and his death is heavily overlain with Christian signification. Three shadowy and vaguely allegorical Queens replace the destructive, sexual women who have contributed to the downfall of the men's Round Table. Those women too have vanished, and Bedivere is left standing utterly alone, much like the poet in *In Memoriam*. The poem may promise 'the new sun . . . bringing the new year' (l.469), but Bedivere remains unconsoled, groaning, 'The King is gone' (l.443). Nonetheless, this abandoned figure does not ask to die.

In the early poems, Tennyson may have adopted his female voices to render feelings seemingly unsuited to male voices. That is, whereas the cultural assumptions make immediate sense of 'Mariana' or 'Oenone', masculine expressions of similar despair are in greater danger of sounding mawkish. Tennyson's male death-desirers tend to be explained, as it were, by a special circumstance:

Tithonus's cruel senescence, or the mariners' lotus-drug. Further-more, the eagerly dying or eager to die female is a literary trope of high frequency in the period. One need only think of Dickens. But for Dickens, the real death was also the death of a perfect and pure young woman. For Tennyson, in contrast, real death came counter to the literary codes he had elaborated.

He had represented imagined death amply in his early, frequently melancholic, poetry. In that repertory, women wail and women are punished for sexual passion. For *In Memoriam*, new roles are re-quired: Death, by its association with Nature, still retains a female sexuality, but the victim of death is a man, and the elegiac survivor is a man. To represent real death – to invent a form for masculine grief – would take seventeen years of re-vision. We see the force of the earlier codes in the repeated metaphors that render the speaker female, despite their awkward fit with the narrative. But we also see in the parallel between 'Mariana' and section 67, an instance of how successfully Tennyson manages the needed self-revision. Our understanding of this particular instance suggests the extent to which the originality and audacity of *In Memoriam*, and hence its power, may arise from gender-reversal, reversal of conventions that were not just the young Tennyson's, but cultural.

Notes

1. See Christopher Ricks' discussion of 'To J. S.', in *Tennyson* (New York: Macmillan, 1972) pp. 28–9. Or compare the passionless propriety of Tennyson's letter of 15 March 1831, to his uncle Charles, in *The Letters of Alfred Lord Tennyson*, edited by Cecil Y. Lang and Edgar F. Shannon, Jr. (Cambridge, Massachusetts: Harvard University Press, 1981) vol. 1, p. 53.
2. All quotations are taken from *The Poems of Tennyson*, edited by Christopher Ricks (London: Longman, 1969).
3. Noted by Ricks, in *Poems*, p. 382.
4. Gerhard Joseph notices that after Hallam's death the deserted lovers change from women to men and female protagonists become rare. Gerhard Joseph, *Tennysonian Love: The Strange Diagonal* (Minneapolis: University of Minnesota Press, 1969) p. 72.

12

The Double Death of Eurydice: A Discussion of Browning and Mythology

Robert Steiner

But give them me, the mouth, the eyes, the brow!
Let them once more absorb me! One look now
    Will lap me round for ever, not to pass
Out of its light, though darkness lie beyond:
Hold me but safe again within the bond
    Of one immortal look! All woe that was,
Forgotten, and all terror that may be,
Defied, – no past is mine, no future: look at me![1]

The scene of myth is public, in this case the underworld, a site identifying desire with rhetoric and rhetoric with death. Timeless, stateless, permanently abject, this new scene for the hero is the border of his magic and of his relations with the gods. The same passion that drove him underground will insure his failure, a failure that must insure the success of the myth in which, knowingly and unknowingly, he plays a part. The underworld is quiet and solemn, as befits the meeting of lovers, informed by mystery that the hero only identifies with death and violation. Orpheus must be stunned by Eurydice's words: surely she would not undo the future they might yet have? Does Eurydice have her own set of laws for the encounter? Where in Orpheus there is only sexual loss, in his wife there is a clear demand for the blissful moment which she, in her timelessness, understands as perpetuating their passion. Her state makes literal the lovers' desire for eternity; ironically, romantic union has its perfect rhetoric in the underworld. To explore the borders of this public scene, we must consider the inversions it makes possible. Lovers' language, what the Greeks call *krevata murmurata* (bed murmurings), which elsewhere and in time would itself work like the hero's magic, demands the perversion of magic, inaugurating the metamorphoses of will and passion.

Eurydice celebrates what Orpheus can only suffer, so that while the hero has expected silence around them in the face of his music, the music means for her an occasion *to speak*. While her husband can only look with awe (*paptánein*), Eurydice is no stranger here, avowing the sexual possessiveness her husband must displace in order to retrieve her. Rather than suspending the true nature of their relationship in order to secure a domestic future, Eurydice fixes it for all time, demanding violation of the law and by so doing clarifying what had always been their preference for the passionate and heretical over quotidian existence. So she would be *possessed* by his gaze (*therkésketo*) for a singular mythic moment rather than enact the commonsensical drama of returning to life as his possession according to the gods. The *teatrum mundi* is no place for her, nor for their love, but rather the site of their desire and loss, the scene after all of her death because of his forgetfulness.

As a prelude to reading Browning we must understand his reading of the myth as heretical, as a violation written in grief for a public occasion (the exhibition of Frederic Leighton's canvas in London on the Orpheus 'theme') in which he commits misprision against the text that has, in tradition, signified Orpheus' impetuousness at the cost of Eurydice's life. There is much to be said for the conservative view of the myth's function as a discovery of Fate on the part of the hero, but such a view treats Orpheus' bereft return to the world as a coda when in fact it is the commentary on the underworld journey, in effect the interpretation that makes the drama chiastic and offers the myth up to discourse. Orpheus may enter the underworld as a property owner but he returns to the light as *text*, no longer the guilty grieving husband but a mythic function bearing with him what the quotidian life could never offer: duration. The knowledge is sacred; the self-consciousness of it profane.

To the extent that the fate of Orpheus reiterates the fate of Dionysus, whom in variant versions Orpheus betrays or loyally serves, it also reiterates that of the enemies of Dionysus. The transparent knowledge Orpheus carries from the underworld is the immutability of the circle of Fate, a message of the inexorable cycle of life that includes eternal repetition (death). The heresies of Orpheus, in both the *teatrum mundi* and the netherworld, are reflected by Eurydice's death and repetition of death, explained by her attachment to the laws of nature, whereas her husband is bound solely to the concept Apollo–Dionysus, signifying both the source of his power and the inevitability of his fall. The tradition surrounding and defining Orpheus' fate is characterised by historical circumstances, that is to say the appropriation of heresy and underworld journeys on behalf of the profane nature of Eros, the subversive tendencies inherent in doubling, repetition, mirroring, and auto-destruction. The unwritten text of Orpheus engenders a gap in the myth, seeking a paradoxical unutterable border to the mythic circle. Lineaments of potential destruction operate at the back of the myth, from its etymology to its historical treatment, but traditionally its form has remained unquestionable, its historical meaning inherently positivist.[2]

From its inception among the Pythagoreans the credo that *all things flow* was hung in cipher around the necks of the dead. A monition against forgetfulness, the credo sustained the truth of Orpheus that, in the face of the eternal Wheel, death becomes immortality by virtue of memory. In order that the dead remember not to drink from the Lethe, the living inscribed it on them, a script originating with interpretations of the floating head of the dead hero. Within the Pythagorean reading the two primary functions of Apollo are complementary: music and healing reciprocate each other. By insuring that each would remain an aspect of Orphic meaning, the Pythagoreans appropriated the myth as a model of the ratio between mystery and the sensual. In doing so they engendered a fundamental dysfunction on the part of the myth because music (mystery) retains its mathematical origin while healing (sensuality) directly conflicts, founded for instance in such acts as Orpheus overwhelming the song of the Sirens so that the Argo can sail undaunted. The *harmonia* the Pythagoreans achieved was produced by a concept of memory that was conservative by nature, that viewed exceptions to the law (out-singing the Sirens) as reiterations of it, following the sacrificial order of Orpheus' various heresies.

The Dactyls of Elis were magical fingers whose incantatory power was promulgated by Orpheus wherever he travelled. As tools of his power, the fingers were correlates of his capacity to 'unknow' the world, to bracket experience in favour of perfect intuition. His littlest finger was considered oracular, and in Phrygia he taught that the middle, or fool's finger, was the 'U', the vowel of sexuality. This could be pointed in derision and insult, so that by the time of the Scholiasts it was termed *digitus impudicus* and *digitus obscenus*.

Considered therefore the digital equivalent of the *fascinum*, or evil eye, dactyl *obscenus*, the impudent sign of Orpheus' heresy, signified the loss of a wife's affection, the defeat of Eros and the obversion of the Heraklean phallic thumb. Yet this sign of Orpheus' hopelessness as a husband suggested he merely returned to life bereft, ignoring the pagan truth that he entered the underworld already bereft, already impudent as a singer among the silents. His music causes the definition of Erebus to be forgotten: Erebus weeps, the Wheel of Ixion's torment ceases to move, and throughout the underworld a lament pacifies eternal functions. The song of Orpheus' despair and impudence makes the netherworld regret itself, forget its identity so that the hero may speak as arrogantly as his intuition commands: 'Weave over Eurydice's life, run through too soon', (Ovid, *Metamorphoses*, X). The quest born of despair, and which will end in despair, brings flux into the circle as the Orphic voice creates a discontinuity in the *mythos* of life and death. It is however the fate of Orpheus, according to tradition, that he fail at discontinuity, no sooner entering the scene of his wife's torment than *doubling* it. By trusting the intuition that his singing signifies, by trusting in the power of the gods who gave him that intuition, Orpheus brackets experience. Despite the fact that he has been given the power to enchant the underworld he is himself enchanted in order to exert it. Without the paradox that Orpheus will suffer circular fate even as the eternal circle will cease, the mythic logos would itself suffer a discontinuity it could not afford. As tradition must have it, Orpheus kills Eurydice twice by twice forgetting his heroic limits.

From its inception as a borrowable myth, the heresy of Orpheus restated its originary explanation of the circle of fate by condemning the forgetfulness without which it would not have existed, leaving intact the credo, the ratio of symbols and the perpetual wheel they serve. The perfectness of the construction, formed around error and arrogance, remained unassailable because of its repetition of natural signs, devices and iconography. To the extent that the heresies could be viewed as committed *against nature* as well as gods, the suppression of all radical readings was assured. However Orpheus might be interpreted, his alienation could be seen to double without ever negating itself. The profoundest abjection on the part of the hero could only be reinforced by his consciousness of it. All passion, all yearning, all loss accounted for by nature, by the *teatrum mundi*, must be read as *speculum mundi*, in the context that, by representing the representation of his sorrow, Orpheus' song is perpetually relegated to be a sign of the sign. It is here, of course, that Orpheus traces a path leading to the reading of the myth as symbolic of the artist rather than the husband. The symbolic dimensions of his tale excise all but the meaning of the severed head. Orpheus descends out of vanity, the same vanity that will have him defy even the ruse his most 'unconscious' self can devise.[3] With his dismemberment the vanity is purged once and for all, the prosaic nature of the myth transmuted into the symbolism of legend and the philosophy of Orphism into aesthetics. Bodiless, Orpheus is eloquence itself, the vinculum of the flowing river and the tree that renews itself on the bank. After Orpheus, art is latent in nature.

The animation of nature discourages myth, though in most variants natural laws can only be appropriated within the conscious play of imagination, in the self-possession of artifice. But in Egypt the severed head gave birth to a radical revision as the connectives between myth and the unfolding of experience became negative. In Alexandria the authority of Orpheus vindicated the history of the Jews. The *Testament* prophesies the fall from Law, though not in the name of Musaeus (Moses) but in that of Orpheus because his 'prophecies' had already been confirmed by history. The value of the Orphic to the literature of the Hellenics and medieval apostates derives from their history of oppression. Orpheus the Apocalypt models his *Testament* after Homer in order to speak of Moses' assumption so that the pagan past is the metaphoric system of the illuminated Jewish history. The 'double-folded Law' of which Apocalypt speaks is the 'ancient tradition' revealed by the monitions on the broken tablets of Moses. Orpheus recants, warns and prophecies in the same breath: 'All things are brought to pass'. The law that all things flow has become a law of prophetic history. The cult of the psychopomp is a latent function of the Orphic heresy, inscribed by the 'in my advent is my entheos' to be found in the theurgic art on the walls of Christian catacombs.

Flowing seaward from the Hebrus into a world more expansive than the misogynist myth, the head of Orpheus establishes a metaphor of the stones his song can move and of the imagination his dismemberment has set free. The Alexandrians memorialise his etymology to signify his motion: the name derives from *ereph*, which means *to conceal*, and this likens him to Erebus itself, but conceal has its synonym in *kaluptos*, the root for *Apokalupsis*. No longer a function of Apollo, the de-realised Orpheus writes radical history based on a reading of the myth in which his singing is a mystification of the gods rather than by the gods of him, a crime for which not even death is sufficient punishment. As the eternal animation of nature in the face of death, Orpheus dismembered is both present and not, stealing from the underworld the knowledge of static form (art) and by siting imagination in the mundane world (Orpheus becomes the 'alder by the river' and 'the willow') revealing the gods and their laws to be at most unconscious fictions.

His identity fully absorbed in the terms of his debasement, Orpheus the Apocalypt can speak of historical necessity. He writes epigrammatically for the *Testament*, critiques of the technique that placed him there, though no longer within the dominant logos, no longer reciting to the gods. As the advent of history Orpheus evokes the reflexive nature of the power of *script*, not in mediation with the past but the power of the script *to be*. The writing of the tale as future knowledge has displaced the avuncular myth. This at the same time that the dominant tradition, in the form of Ovid, speaks of Orpheus' decisive moment as when he cannot still the moment or transform the intent of the Cicones by his music: 'Whose voice, for the first time, moved no one'. The *concealed* heresy of Orpheus lies in his unconsciousness of the power he holds, his alienation from history which the myth enforces by its paradoxical origins in Apollo–Dionysus, origins that leave Orpheus straddling between reflection and event, between representation and the thing itself. It is by viewing this scene of myth as itself the concrete experience of oppression that the Alexandrians delimit the borders of the logos. For Orpheus, as for Homer, there are not only two kinds of memory but two kinds of forgetfulness. The first is induced – by music, whether it is Orpheus' or the Sirens' – a forgetting that is essentially a possession of the gods. The second is a loss of consciousness that feeds uncritically upon desire – in this the lotus is eaten, the water of the Lethe drunk, the ruse that harrows hell ignored. The Apocalypt distinguishes between these, as no variant of the Orpheus myth does. The distinction is significant, drawing into focus the most dangerous heresy of all: the recovery of Eros requires that a desirable object reside in hell.[4]

The excavations at Nineveh, Thebes and Babylon prompted Browning to consider a post-Romantic classicism that would explicate mystery and appropriate signs such as the Uroborus, which surrounded the Orphic icon on Christian amulets. But he would not tremble between two worlds, would not structure as did the Pythagoreans for example, nor fix on the sort of disharmony rooted in the backward critical glance of Plato. For Browning the classical form would constitute a mask, not a resurrected myth. He would leave the pathological need to vivify myth to his speakers, nowhere so variously and persistently as in *Dramatis Personae*, where, through Abt Vogler, Rabbi Ben Ezra, Caliban and Eurydice, he sacrifices the immediate needs of the self in order to reflect the historical tradition that has developed around natural law as mythic function. Appropriating music, circularity, silence and sight thematically from their classical scene, he approaches tradition as a *taboo*, denying the self-preserving aspect to subjectivity in each case. Reflexivity displaces reflection as the immanent teleology of consciousness, so that loss and transformation complement historical passage, categories of need that cannot be considered without interiorising the discoveries of objects and languages sedimented in ancient sites. States of loss have their proofs in found objects, and abstractions of desire suddenly have expressive forms, recovered icons. Browning uses the speakers of *Personae* to write the Ur-history of tradition in which objects of desire, lifted from their graves, surface as knowledge not of a dominant logos, not of the myths which their creation served, but of the underground Eros whose history had only been written from the mythic point of view, whose destructive authority could only rise previously as the incomplete, erroneous or inauthentic image. This concrete newness that gives the lie to the mystifications of the past drives away the possessiveness associated with the absent object of desire, negating the *mineness* that tradition viewed as subjective pathos of the kind which doomed Orpheus and Eurydice as husband and wife. Where the erotic had always been absorbed by reason, Eros could only appear as unformable flux, the untrue poignant moment, the discontinuity of a yearning for *kairos* which Orpheus, for example, enacts but which, in Browning's brief lyric, Eurydice makes permanent, miming the absorption that only the logos knows. The unwritten Ur-history then of a *harmonia*, possible by tradition mediated with excavated objects, points the departure for Browning. The ocular mote of personal anxiety is retained by Browning's speakers, not by the written. They do not know that what they name has not been lost, that it can be located, though underground. They do not know that the negation and destruction they identify with Eros, and which has defined their immanent subjectivity, is retained in the Ur-historic trace of the *harmonia*, what the Orphics characterised as music of the spheres. Whether we consider these spheres as Platonic notions or as the

krater through which Orpheus returned to the world of Apollo–
Dionysus, their emblems in the form of ritual bowls were being
unearthed daily in Browning's lifetime.

Dedicated to Eros ('only the heart, the seat of thought, did they
(the Maenads) leave', (*Proklos, fragment 210*)), the Orphic tradition
remained marginal, secret and eminently metamorphic in that its
writings were essentially interlinear fragmented commentaries
against the presiding Logos. From the fullest treatment in the
Argonautica of Appolonius, in which Orpheus is Jason's first chosen
crew member, the subterranean tradition's loathing of sudden death
engendered critiques of sacrifice that undermined the capacity of
Orphism itself to overthrow the dominant models. To survive even
marginally, Orphism, like Eros itself, went underground. Viewing
itself as a civilising cult between the lines of a brutal rhetoric,
Orphism (and the aesthetic born within and around it) prized script
over speech: in the purest ancient rite Orphics *tattooed* one another.
Within the isolation known by the double meaning of *sema* (sign and
tomb, marking the spot), the living body (*themos*) was bound to a
corpse (*soma*, born of *sema*). Thus the unwritten history of Orphism
can be characterised as a mysterium of writing in the name of a unity
to come, whose only organon is composed of fragments authored by
various writers over several centuries, each of whom invoked the
'voice' of Orpheus as his authority. The pseudepigraphy that kept
the tradition alive was a sequence of 'forgeries' extending from
Pythagoras himself through the Jewish authors of the *Testament* and
into the mystical Christian writings of the early Middle Ages. As
early as Aristotle the effect of such writing was evident; in the
Metaphysics he attacks those *theologoi* who confuse the time of
creation, placing potential ahead of actual and so preferring the
incomplete and open-ended to the reasoned totality.[5] From its
'origin' then, the Orphic was a *future writing*, drawing to it those
who would 'cease from the circle and have respite from evil', *Proklos,
fragment 229*. The Orpheus who provides that eponymous authority
is, of course, dismembered, absent of gods and their languages, an
Apocalypt.

Browning's lyric takes account of its century's archaelogical
achievements by separating Eros from myth. More to the point, we
witness the fateful gaze as a result of an imperative speech by a
future goddess straight from the heart of the mythic dark. If we read
the poem as an example of obsession we find that the language at
once overcomes and generates both the Other and the absence of

the Other. If all variants of Orphic narrative are submerged in mythic presence as nineteenth-century thought understood it, it is still a moment of *absence* that the Browning lyric celebrates. The enormous body of poetry Browning centred upon the good 'infinite moment' and gazing can, of course, be attributed to the aesthetic of Orphism, but once the appropriation of mythic functions is over-turned, as 'Eurydice to Orpheus' overturns it, we find something more profound occurring than the use of a naïve model. There is here a treatment that radicalises the use of the myth, perhaps radicalising Browning's own understanding of 'look' and 'moment', implicating his verse in a pagan tradition that equated killing the loved one with cannibalism. The gaze, in Browning's briefest poem, will devour Eurydice, 'absorb' her, not as she dies but *by* the act of killing her in what is at least a perversely esemplastic experience since perception and creation are one and the same.

The cannibalism in the Orphic tradition is not muted by Browning, nor is it intellectualised. The scene in the underworld repeats the domestic life Orpheus and Eurydice led above – the hero turned away, entranced by his music, his wife yearning for him in the face of her demise. The division between them that killed her once, kills her again, and the source of their strife is, as always, the laws of the gods and the lovers' desires. The Greek for this murder and can-nibalism is *phonos*. When Eurydice speaks she does not commit suicide, she exhorts her husband to murder, but this obsessive Browning theme is here a defeat of mythic barbarism and a victory for Eros. Here the rhetoric of death and dismemberment engenders the future history of eroticism. Because Eurydice catalyses the repetition, Orpheus is no longer dutiful when he transgresses, as the myth has traditionally been read, but a function of negation. That is, Eurydice's eloquence does not serve Fate in this instance except to announce Fate's obsolescence. The effect of the Orphic mirroring among all elements is to render oblivion oblivious and to categorise the underworld as a *fantasy*. Eurydice's double death is necessary for the liberation of Orpheus from the myth which, as Apollo's manifestation, he created. In Browning's poem the radical position of eloquence signifies an end to the spectacle of *dutiful* heresy by displacing Orpheus as forgetful heretic. The position and relation of subject to object are wilfully *misunderstood*; Orpheus turns because he is addressed, addressed because he is seen. Eurydice teaches that the price of presence is eternal sameness.

From the viewpoint that myth is a set of metaphoric relations refusing to acknowledge itself as such, Browning reads into the Orpheus tradition and is read by it: the *mythic* encounter *per se* no longer takes place; instead, it is unwoven. For Eurydice to be gazed upon by Orpheus – a gaze that makes his eye the *fascinum* – not only annihilates her as the object of his search and desire, but as a speaking subject. Her speech ends speech, and the end of her speech brings Orpheus' magic to an end. As a moment of mythical borrowing, unusual for Browning who preferred to fictionalise historical figures already infected by the Orphic aesthetic, the poem, despite its brevity and occasional site in the Victorian canon, signifies both a gap and a commentary. It is a gap in the momentum of *Dramatis Personae*, a volume that finds little to celebrate or salvage in the discourse of desire, for here we can see the masking made textuality, the convexity of rhetoric itself made convex. The 'infinite moment' suffers a momentary guilt, which accounts more for the poem's invisibility among Browning critics than does its brevity. And by its critique of the rhetoric of desire the poem threatens to contravene our understanding of Browning's treatment of erotic life, especially in its attachment to death.

From these viewpoints the poem is subversive, a radical forgetting not only because Eurydice is 'safe' within the 'bond' of Orpheus' gaze but because she *says* so. The sado-masochism of the poem likewise condenses Browning's horror of the conjunction between art and nature. Orpheus gains his historical meaning by losing his mythic one; in this sense Eurydice reduces him at the same time that she liberates him. It is as if Orpheus stood on the brink of truth only to be told that if it exists, truth is debasement. If Orpheus seeks to regain his presumed identity in Eurydice, he discovers that using the power that earned him that identity can only now lose it one last time. Let us say he begets himself out of hell, becoming the antithesis of his former self by virtue of his wife's projection. This may be Shelleyan in several respects (Shelley's 'Orpheus' did not appear until 1862, two years prior to Browning's poem) but it has neither the purposefulness nor ambition of Romantic self-destruction. More to the point the reversal at the heart of the poem is a clear rejection of the theurgic nature the myth propagates. What we may read as Eurydice's celebration on behalf of her husband's true fate may also be the pure ego of the spurned lover wanting no truck with her husband's effort to assuage his guilt; while she declares against forgetting and terror in favour of defiance she does so because for her there is neither past nor future, while for him there will be nothing but future, future containing the past. With his gaze straight ahead and his voice a lament, Orpheus' immortality is theologically as well as aesthetically schizoid. This is because his profane properties will not be mythic though they were born there. What replaces the mythic forgetfulness that makes Orpheus dramatic will be the loss of origins. It may be that this is the only condition in which Browning can make use of the figure – as a mediation between modes of repression and the representations of them, a sign of the sign.

It is possible to read the Browning poem within a radical tradition of discontinuity and appropriation without at the last viewing it as inherently ambiguous. If we understand that Eurydice is not usurping her husband's role by calling him to it, yet displacing not only the problematic nature of the myth but its apparent origin in a transcendent intentionality, we are faced with answering the question, what is usurped by her speech? To answer that we refer first to the readings already suggested and, most importantly, to the poem's own site within the tradition. That is, we are forced to recognise the significance of the spaces surrounding this poem, namely what, according to the myth, precedes and follows the moment Browning has fixed. The poem removes us from its context to the extent that we, in fact, cannot actually read the work certain of the absent text. As an instant of inverted performance the poem offers no signature outside of itself by which we might measure the discontinuous meaning it would extend to the totality of the myth. The circle is not merely breached by the poem, it is erased either with the confidence of using a naïve tradition – in this sense all that is missing is, by not naming it, alluded to – or with a puzzling urge to awaken us to the mystery of what is absent, namely a frame.

It is not enough to say the poem is all climax, neither because of its diction nor the reversal that the moment enacts. We must therefore consider the poem as framed by what is not surrounding it or, to speak positively, as framed by significant spaces above and below. This becomes more problematical when we learn that the poem was first published as prose for the Leighton exhibition catalogue and only sonnetised for the publication of *Dramatis Personae*. What was first linear, therefore descriptive for the occasion, later became its opposite in all respects, at once framed by the painting, by the catalogue, then by the volume of 1864 (the same year of its composition), after which it effectively vanished from all considerations of Browning's work. Whatever its authenticity with regard to the myth or the painting, its integrity was immediately compromised, its centrality outside discussion. Composed for an occasion, it is marginal because it accompanied the 'original' canvas that supposedly offered Browning the idea of the reversal. The poem is indeed parasitical, not only of Frederic Leighton and of the Orpheus 'theme' but in fact of the occasion of *Dramatis Personae* itself, less a poem in the volume than a space between poems. It is considered an interlude, one of those minor reading experiences we refer to as a breathing space. In this sense it encourages an informed myopia, a willed misunderstanding caused by the nature of framing as tradition knows it and as the poem comments upon it.

The encounter in the underworld transforms Orpheus' concrete possessiveness into abstract loss, reiterating by the gaze trope the nature of voyeurism: desire resides in distance. Browning's recentred subject makes voyeurism a prominent characteristic of the myth. Eurydice speaks in the lacuna between Orpheus' blindness and his sight, fixing not only the timeless, stateless nature of their passion but the incompleteness of the lovers as a text. By seeing Eurydice, Orpheus sees himself because his gaze is not only a matter of killing her twice but of twice committing heresy. The scene of voyeurism then reveals Orpheus to be self-conscious, Eurydice to be conscious, the underworld itself the site known as unconscious. The *trompe-l'oeil* effect lies in the fact that Orpheus' gaze changes everything but only to the eye; in reality everything remains the same. It is the coming to consciousness of sameness that Eurydice's speech occasions, and it is the self-consciousness of the process that changes everything. In part this self-consciousness teaches that Eurydice lured him by her voice, as the Sirens did sailors whom Orpheus protected, and that he valued the *representation* of his wife more than the existence of her. That is to say, the scene of Browning's poem is itself that of the *beholder and the painting*. The lyric enacts the complex relations between representation and gaze. Once he has looked at his wife Orpheus no longer sees a speaking subject but a memory of one; his gaze makes the real vanish before him.

To the extent that the gaze of Orpheus is a writing implement it graphs a phenomenology of loss which can be seen historically in the uses of the figure from betraying and bereft husband through the astrologue of the Pythagoreans to the apocalyptic voice of immutable future. Orpheus identifies the space of possibilities by himself being a frame of both past and future which Browning's poem indicates by abstracting the so-called climactic fatal gesture from the myth. Like his desire his authority is limitless, beyond the law in which it is born. The tradition informed by Orpheus is one of always desiring-to-be and by desiring always being, for others if not for himself. The Browning scene of Orpheus is multiply misconstrued, rife with wish that transforms subjectivity into agency, a construction spaced between meaning and being, in the veil of Self and Other, a neither and a nor. Does this mean that the gaze is perpetual, both in the myth and outside of it? Are we speaking of a frozen moment in the manner of the Leighton painting which depicts the instant before the hero turns, when he is struggling to remain faithful to his god? The Lacanian answer would be yes, because the gaze is a castrating agent, immediately erasing whatever intersubjective relations the urge to gaze might have desired, leaving the scene a purely primordial one. In this reading we are confronted not only by a painting representing the moment before a fateful gaze, thereby deriving its effect by what does not in fact occur on the canvas, but by a poem that would fill in what the painting omits even as it offers up absence to contemplation.

The painting and the poem differ significantly in that while Eurydice 'yearns' in the former she is not addressing Orpheus, nor is there anything to suggest within her desire (for him? for life? for a return to the underworld?) that she is about to speak. The drama of the Leighton canvas is both intimate and internal, fixing the struggle of the moment in the opposition between private desires and mythic demands. Eurydice desperately wants something; Orpheus, wanting something (else?), is intent on leading his wife out of the netherworld without looking at her, as the unnatural position of his body shows. In the painting, as in the poem, it is Eurydice who gazes upon Orpheus, and with a yearning reminiscent of Odysseus' when he *looked with longing* (*therkésthai*) from Calypso's rock in the direction of Ithaca. Is this the pre-objective primordial gaze which Bruno Snell speaks of as found nowhere in Greek literature after Homer? Wistful, travelling in the mind, the look sees nothing and reveals Being rather than sighting. The look of Eurydice does not rest on anything in the painting, is therefore entirely different from her husband's gaze, which indeed is meaningful in its sighting function in much the same way that *ofthalmoisi* expresses the Gorgon's glance, as the signal of an event, the transformation of subject into object because of a transcendental law. In the painting, unlike the poem, there is light at the tunnel's end, indicating still another lost form of looking, *lefso*, which is associated with gleaming and whiteness, with Apollo in the *Illiad*. This seeing of the light to which husband and wife are headed can be cited as a reason for Orpheus turning his head – the brightness blinds him so that he sees Eurydice only incidentally, as the result of reflex.

Such a reading unmakes the gaze as the source of Eurydice's second death, returning her fate to the inadvertent function of sight itself. With regard to the myth then, in practical terms there would be no distinction between gaze and sight because the heresy lies in the presence of a particular object in the visual field. No matter how arcane a verb we find to pinpoint the event, in substance Orpheus' violation demands a predicate so that what he actually enacts is closest to the essential function of *theoren, to look on* or behold. He is always-already-trapped by the verb because in beholding he creates what there is to behold, not Eurydice *per se* but *her disappearance*. He does not contemplate his wife so much as witness her sudden absence, thereby reiterating the relationship of the painting's beholder to a spectator of the unpainted total drama. In this sense his momentary fate is to be a spectator. In the projection of motives that Browning's poem offers, the indefinition of 'look' creates the incompleteness, the space the poem's reductiveness alludes to. This is an exceptionally economic sado-masochism, an exchange of roles at the same time that the scene is a brief blur of presence and absence. While it may appear as though, in this instance, the power inherent in the language of desire serves to overturn the repression of sexual possession, the latter remains committed to death. The theme is always already resolved regardless of the reading of details – one reason why the details have become the tradition – by the death drive that the look, inadvertent, intended or fated, realises. The uncertainty about the look forces us to gaze upon the gaze, then to gaze upon the gaze of Eurydice which prefigures the all-important absent gaze of Orpheus, the soon-to-be deadly gaze which neither the painting nor the poem gives us precisely because once it occurs there is nothing dramatic to be seen.

While for Leighton the future gesture beckons in the intransitive look of Eurydice, for Browning the truncated monologue points the way. What Leighton understates is hysterical in Browning; in the one Eurydice is victimised, in the other she collaborates. In Browning we find sexual desire displaced, with Eurydice's speech framed so that the very diagram of the myth discloses passion's separation from it. The ambiguous 'Give them me' that opens the poem misleads us by being an offer of self-sacrifice tht must conclude with a demand for action on Orpheus' part. Eurydice's control effaces the speaker herself as object of desire and undermines Orpheus' quest as the climax of meaning. The etymological passage of Orpheus from a primitive to a modern stage degrades the physical origins of the myth so that the ruse of consciousness in the underworld will be revealed as the aim of consciousness as well. Eurydice's plea, once heard, will end pleading, just as the sight of Eurydice literally means not seeing her. The myth is exchanged for a metaphor of its degradation; the silence *after* the fatal gaze unmasks the meaning of the silence before Orpheus entered the underworld. The apparent object that Eurydice provided proves to be the unconscious desire of Orpheus to be the image of the Other. Eurydice disappears to bring an end to desire, and by so doing makes myth obsolete.

Notes

1. Robert Browning, *Dramatis Personae* (1864) in *Complete Poems of Robert Browning* (Cambridge: 1895).
2. Among the earliest to consider Orpheus historically are Isocrates, Horace and Quintilian. The implications of anti-positivist readings toward the concept of logos can be found in M. I. Finley, *The Use and Abuse of History* (New York: Viking, 1975) pp. 1–45. More to the point of tradition are John Block Friedman, *Orpheus in the Middle Ages* (Cambridge: Harvard University Press, 1970) and Jean Seznec, *Survival of the Pagan Gods* (Princeton: Princeton University Press, 1953).
3. By the sixteenth century, the debate over the status of Eurydice was a heated one. The economy of the myth emphasised the spectacle of the underworld journey, the heresy and bloody fate, not only overwhelming the sexual origins and phallic imagery, but virtually eliminating Eurydice as an element. The notion of Orpheus as a civilising figure, argued in Robert Holcot's *In Librum Sapientiae* (Basel, 1586), stood in direct contradiction to the misogynist of John Lydgate's *Fall of Princes* (c. 1450). See Friedman, pp. 169–71, 237n.41, 231n.42.
4. This heretical interpretation first appears in Notker Labeo's High German translation of Boethius' *Consolation*, but resolves Orpheus' 'chiding' of the gods within doctrine by condemning his original urge as lust, (cf. Friedman, pp. 102–4).
5. For number will not, either as mover or as form, produce a *continuum*. But again there cannot be any *contrary* that is also essentially a productive or moving principle; or it would be possible not to be.' (*Metaphysics*, XII, Ch. 10). The attack on mathematical first principles, 'that things exist by the imitation of numbers', identifies Democritus' theory with Pythagoreanism: 'the real is differentiated only by rhythm, inter-connection and turning (*clinamen*), (*Metaphysics*, I,

Ch. 4). Aristotle's critique further links Pythagorean thought to the virtual indistinction between Being and Non-Being: '. . . being no more is than non-being, because solid is no more than empty', (*Metaphysics*, I, Ch. 4). The characterisation implies, of course, that the Orphic credo of 'flow' is essentially a credo of contrary flux rather than reason. Heaven as a musical scale, for example, permits endless repetitions but no development. See Aristotle, *Metaphysics*, Clarendon Aristotle Series, edited by J. L. Ackrill (Oxford: Clarendon Press, 1963).

13

The Power of Excommunication: Sex and the Feminine Text in *Wuthering Heights*

Regina Barreca

Nelly Dean [sat] sewing and singing a song, which was always interrupted from within, by harsh words of scorn and intolerance, uttered in far from musical accents.

'Aw'd rayther, by th'haulf, hev'em swearing i'my lugs frough morn tuh neeght, nur hearken yeh, hahsiver!' said the tenant of the kitchen, in answer to an unheard speech of Nelly's. 'It's a blazing shaime, ut Aw cannut oppen t'Blessed Book, bud yah set up them glories tuh Sattan, un'all t' flaysome wickedness ut iver wer born intuh t'warld! . . . O, Lord, judge 'em, fur they's norther law nor justice among wer rullers!'

'No! or we should be sitting in flaming fagots, I suppose,' retorted the singer. 'But wisht, old man, and read your Bible like a Christian, and never mind me. This is "Fairy Annie's Wedding" – a bonny tune – it goes to a dance.'[1]

'Read your Bible like a Christian and never mind me', is Nelly Dean's reply to Joseph's 'interruption from within'. Nelly will continue to sing. In doing so, she continues to create an alternative, feminine text which forms a parallel to Joseph's punitive, stuttered threats. Nelly's song, like the other texts created by the female characters of *Wuthering Heights*, indicates an appropriation of the power of language which women then use as an instrument of control against the dominant order. They appropriate the power of inscription. They invert the paradigmatic system in which women are absorbed and oppressed by the unavoidably patriarchal nature of language. In other words, it is the female characters of *Wuthering Heights* who create and shape all the language play of the text. Women in Bronte's novel take control of language, in much the same way as they take control of sex – and for the same reasons. They claim the authority of the 'author' – the initiator and the inscriber; they usurp the male prerogative. They create a system of feminine 'excommunication', whereby they appropriate discourse and desire, surrounding the patriarchal text, so to speak and render it ineffective, if not obsolete.

'Excommunication' here has a number of implications: 'ex' indicates the heretical, unacceptable nature of the action, its expulsion by standing order; 'ex' also indicates the idea of formerly belonging to the standing order, but now remaining out of or above the boundaries of that order. I would like to suggest picturing the female characters of *Wuthering Heights* as forming a circle – or frame – outside of but completely around the male characters and, by association, the patriarchal society presented in the text. The system of feminine discourse in this book is expelled from, existing outside of, but more powerful than the traditional script: the female characters are the only ones who have the ability, desire and will to speak, write and sing. Joseph, muttering overseer of the dominant ideology, has his text overwritten by Nelly's song, in much the same way that Catherine writes all over the blanks of her New Testament, creating a much newer, much more personal testament than the one she had been given. Filling up the empty spaces of the one with her own words, she literalises the conventional phrase: 'Catherine Earnshaw, her book'.

It is important to note the strategies women use to control narrative in the text. Wuthering Heights is a place where women possess the means of 'illumination' and the means of access to language, where: 'the females were already astir: Zillah urging the flames up the chimney with a colossal bellows, and Mrs Heathcliff, kneeling on the hearth, reading a book by the aid of a blaze' (pp. 36–7). Gilbert and Gubar see Nelly acting 'throughout the novel as a censorious agent of patriarchy' (Gilbert and Gubar, p. 292) and Kavanagh spends much of his time enlarging on this idea. He argues that Nelly is the primary instrument by which patriarchal law and lineage are kept intact. Using Jane Gallop's theories on the phallic Mother to support his claim, Kavanagh argues that: 'for the woman, the control of language and writing provides a kind of counter-phallic power which surreptitiously . . . channels libidinal energies through social ambitions. . .' (Kavanagh, p. 20), but will identify writing solely with the processes of sublimation. He links Catherine with the 'effete Lockwood' in using 'literacy and sublimation as indicators of a class difference . . .' in opposition to Heathcliff whom Kavanagh names the most 'radically disruptive' character (p. 20).

However, an argument can be made that in *Wuthering Heights*, the power to write and speak are evidence of women's power, not women's subjection. The female characters are the subjects, not the objects, of the discourse. They challenge the male characters by creating texts that exist in opposition to the prevailing ideology. They make use of the books they are given, 'though not altogether for a legitimate purpose', as Lockwood notes (Bronte, p. 24) since the 'treasure' of the texts for the female characters are the blanks, the absences, where they can inscribe themselves and therefore alter the texts they have been given. The most important language distinctions in *Wuthering Heights* are not based on class but on gender.

In *Desire and Domestic Fiction*, Nancy Armstrong argues that certain scenes out of Wuthering Heights are 'definitely outside of culture' (Armstrong, p. 180). She can in fact find no grounds for the traditional assumption that the Brontes 'found writing a repressive mechanism' (p. 189). Adapting Armstrong's argument for the purposes of this discussion, it can be seen that Emily Bronte's own 'excommunication' from traditional discourse is the source of her power with language:

> Their marginal relationship to the tradition of letters gave the Brontes access to an entirely different body of knowledge that by its very nature disrupted the life of the parlor. (Armstrong, p. 190)

Armstrong continues that 'the Brontes had to dismantle' the language of social behaviour (p. 192) in order to tell a 'tale told by a woman . . . a history of sexuality' (p. 197). The prevailing language of *Wuthering Heights* is, paradoxically, not the language of the law but the 'not altogether . . . legitimate' language of the letter, the song and the story.

Women are always inscribing themselves in Emily Bronte's text. Catherine is characterised by her persistent and disruptive commentary: 'her tongue was always going – singing, laughing and plaguing everybody . . . a wild, wick slip she was . . .' (Bronte, p. 51). When the curate gives her passages from the scriptures to learn as punishment, Catherine immediately and instinctively turns this punishment to her own advantage since the texts are simple for her to absorb: '. . . punishment grew a mere thing to laugh at. The curate might set as many chapters as he pleased for Catherine to get by heart . . .' (p. 57). (Catherine does not, in fact, seem to share the idea that Gilbert and Gubar attribute to Emily Bronte: '. . . education for Emily Bronte is almost always fearful, even agonizing . . .' (Gilbert and Gubar, p. 275). Catherine's daughter is tellingly des-cribed as 'a second edition of the mother', (Bronte, p. 188) and Cathy effectively inherits her mother's possession of the text. It should come as no surprise that 'ere the tiny thing could stammer a word' Cathy wields 'a despot's sceptre in her father's heart' (p. 226). She has 'curiosity and a quick intellect' (p. 232) and a desire to use language for her own end; she sends letters to Linton for her own pleasure: 'playthings and trinkets . . . transmuted into bits of folded paper' (p. 274). Cathy defies Hareton who tries to steal her books by announcing that 'I've most of them written on my brain and printed in my heart and you cannot deprive me of those' (p. 364). Cathy is territorial when it comes to her possession of language. She threatens Joseph by telling him that 'his library should pay for hers' (p. 383) should he tamper with her books. And Cathy tells stories to the ultimate story-teller, Nelly. Nelly is often reduced to 'the censorious agent of patriarchy' (Gilbert and Gubar, p. 292) even though she is acknowledged as having 'a keen literary consciousness' (p. 291). But Nelly's relationship to the spoken and written word should not be summarily dismissed. Nelly has herself 'read more than you would fancy . . . You could not open a book in this library that I have not looked into, and got something out of also . . .' (Bronte, p. 78), bringing herself to the texts, and 'getting out' of them what she desires. Most importantly, Nelly has in her possession the un-written, contraband history of folk-lore, songs and ballads. Cathy can 'charm' Linton with this feminine inheritance of songs – 'your songs, Ellen' (p. 302), and so control a situation.

Even the less obviously rebellious female characters create texts. Isabella's letters are vivid documents that serve as revisions of the romances she had been taught to read and not to question. It can be argued that Isabella married Heathcliff, as Gilbert and Gubar note, because she 'has been taught to believe in coercive literary con-ventions' (Gilbert and Gubar, p. 288). Yet when Isabella learns to question, however, she begins to narrate her own story in a letter to Nelly and so re-inscribes and dislodges the inherited convention. She learns to use the power of language against Heathcliff, who resorts to the use of violence against Isabella. Also using language to fight is Zillah, the servant who, 'not daring to attack her master . . . turned her vocal artillery against' him (Bronte, p. 21). The passing on of an otherly-inherited language subverts the male text; an inheritance of 'old songs . . . nursery lore' (p. 280) drowns out the old testaments by writing across their curriculum, so to speak. Women, having been given only the blanks, fill those blanks with – quite literally – a vengeance:

> Catherine's library was select, and its state of dilapidation proved it to have been well used, though not altogether for a legitimate purpose; scarcely one chapter had escaped a pen-and-ink commentary – at least, the appearance of one – covering every morsel of blank that the printer had left. (Bronte, p. 24)

The male characters, in contrast, can barely articulate their simplest thoughts. Although Lockwood, as the nominal narrator, is inevitably associated with the discourse that would link Bronte's novel itself with the production of patriarchal and repressive texts, he in fact can only hand over Nelly's story. Nelly recognises the fact that Lockwood will inevitably misread her 'you'll judge as well as I can, all these things; at least, you'll think you will, and that's the same' (p. 227). As a narrator, he is sadly in need of invention; he is publisher rather than writer. He is a conduit for the true narrative constructed by women, rather than, as Eagleton implies, the powerful voice that can at times 'clearly . . . confiscate' not only Nelly's discourse, but Emily Bronte's own voice (Eagleton, p. 118). At the beginning of Chapter X, for example, Lockwood is capable of reducing Nelly's story to the following: 'I can recollect [the story's] chief incidents, as far as she had gone. Yes, I remember her hero had run off, and never been heard of for three years: and the heroine was married' (Bronte, p. 112). Lockwood must rely on the fact that 'looks have language' since he cannot bring himself to declare his affections in words to the unnamed woman to whom he is attracted (p. 7). Men cannot speak their desire in *Wuthering Heights*: they can barely acknowledge it.

Heathcliff appears entirely separated from language, having, as Stevie Davies notes, 'no mother country and no mother tongue' (Davies, p. 118). Heathcliff enters the Earnshaw household repeating over and over again 'some gibberish that nobody could understand' (Bronte, p. 44) and he grows up little minding 'what tale was told' as long as he 'had what he wanted' (p. 49). Heathcliff, 'deprived . . . of the instructions of the curate' (p. 56), cannot keep pace with Catherine's learning: 'He struggled long to keep up an equality with Catherine in her studies and yielded with poignant though silent regret; but he yielded completely . . .' (p. 84). Catherine is impatient with his silence, and lets him know that 'It is no company at all, when people know nothing and say nothing' (p. 86). Even as an adult, Heathcliff is given to garbled, guttural responses; Isabella can only 'guess' that he utters certain words because 'his voice was hardly intelligible' (p. 223).

Perhaps the most telling incident involving Heathcliff and language occurs when Heathcliff 'is impatient and proposes' that he and Catherine 'should appropriate the dairy woman's cloak, and have a scamper on the moors. . .' (p. 26). It is not coincidence that Heathcliff proposes this, as Catherine's diary indicates, right after she 'reached this book, and a pot of ink from a shelf, and pushed the house-door ajar to give me light, and I have got the time on with writing for twenty minutes; but my companion is impatient . . .' (p. 26). While Kavanagh believes this scene shows that Heathcliff pulls 'Catherine away from her own book . . . pulling her from sublimation . . . to her own sexuality' (Kavanagh, p. 19), I believe we can more accurately read this scene as providing an outline of Heathcliff's fear and frustration at Catherine's desire and ability to write. This scene represents Heathcliff's struggle to have Catherine 'appropriate' a proper feminine garment to replace her inappropriate appropriation of the masculine text.

It is true that, in contrast to Heathcliff, Edgar Linton is often associated with books. Yet Edgar remains separated from the texts he owns; unlike Nelly, who steals his language and makes it her own, the owner of the library simply 'shuts himself up among books that he never opened'. He is emblematic of the commodification of literature that identifies libraries as evidence of conspicuous consumption rather than evidence of imagination or intelligence. Like Lockwood, he is the nominal owner, rather than the creator or 'true' possessor of texts. Edgar will not write; he refuses to correspond with Isabella despite his sister's earnest plea, or Nelly's request (Bronte, p. 147). Edgar, like Joseph, is purveyor of inert texts, of little use to Catherine who has a far more active relationship with language than her husband.

Unlike his father Hindley, who is at least understandable, Hareton Earnshaw speaks to Isabella 'in a jargon' she 'did not comprehend' (p. 167), and he can barely comprehend Cathy's language when he first meets her: '. . . comprehending precious little of the fluent succession of remarks and questions which her tongue never ceased pouring forth' (p. 237). Hareton is 'too awkward to speak' (p. 238) and he must be told to 'say your words slowly and keep your hands out of your pockets' (p. 266). Hareton has no ability to read 'damnable writing', while of course Cathy can not only read it but also wants to know 'why it's there' (p. 268). Hareton is finally taught to read by Cathy, who trains him to sound words properly the way you might teach a dog to beg: by offering him attention when he comes close to completing the act effectively. She teaches him the letters of his own name. Could it not be argued, in fact, that Hareton's inability to name himself through writing is in direct contrast to the elder Catherine, who named herself over and over again by writing various surnames in the wood of the windowsill? In any event, young Cathy is keeping close watch over her language. Cathy does not want Hareton to 'appropriate what is mine, and make it ridiculous . . . with his vile mistakes and mispronunciations' (p. 365). She claims language, 'damnable writing', as her own.

Linton Heathcliff, it is true, does write, but Nelly, with her finely critical response, reads and dismisses Linton's prose as 'very worthless trash' by 'decomposing' it in a detailed textual analysis, declaring that his letters to Cathy are: 'odd compounds of ardor and flatness; commencing in strong feeling and concluding in the affected, wordy way . . .' (p. 275). Linton complains to Cathy that 'it tired me dreadfully, writing those long letters. . .' (p. 288) in much the same way as he says, 'No—don't kiss me. It takes my breath . . .' (p. 288). For Linton, the kisses and composition desired by Cathy are equally fearful and unappealing. He equates feminine inscription with feminine sexuality and fears both. In fact, he fears, as well he might, that Cathy has the power to kiss him – or write him – to death.

Joseph is the primary instrument behind the 'fouling of language' that annoys Cathy. He is the self-proclaimed agent of patriarchal discourse which, of course, pretends to be a totalising and just system. He is fiercely didactic and unrelentingly unintelligible: a combination that suggests that the dominant ideology is hardly to be respected. Joseph believes in the Bible, in sermons and in the laws of inheritance. He is terrified of women. They represent the refusal of his dogma; they are inherently dangerous. They can, as

Catherine did, tear 'th'back off "The Hemut uh Salvation'" (p. 26).
Yet it is her language, written and spoken, that is impeccable; he is
barely intelligible. In the first chapter, Joseph accuses Cathy of
witchcraft; she laughing agrees that she is indeed a sorceress.
Calling him 'a scandalous old hypocrite', the first action she uses to
verify his verdict is to reach for a book:

> 'Stop, look here, Joseph,' she continued, taking a long, dark book
> from a shelf. 'I'll show you how far I've progressed in the Black
> Art – I shall soon be competent to make a clear house of it. The red
> cow didn't die by chance; and your rheumatism can hardly be
> reckoned among providential visitations!'
>   'Oh, wicked, wicked!' gasped the elder, 'may the Lord deliver
> us from evil!'
>   'No, reprobate! you are a castaway – be off, or I'll hurt you
> seriously! I'll have you all modelled in wax and clay; and the first
> who passes the limits I fix, shall – I'll not say what he shall be done
> to – but, you'll see! Go, I'm looking at you! The little witch put a
> mock malignity into her beautiful eyes, and Joseph, trembling
> with sincere horror, hurried out praying and ejaculating 'wicked'
> as he went. (p. 18)

In a carefully constructed inversion of the patriarchal code, Cathy
sets the limits beyond which Joseph cannot go; she laughs at his
'ejaculation' of curses. She joyfully accepts excommunication from
his domain and sets up her own.

She looks him in the eye and steals his definition of her, embracing rather than refusing his condemnation, and so usurping his
power to name and thereby confine her. Looking him in the eye
doubles her act of defiance; Armstrong notes, in obvious reference
to Lacan, that the female characters of *Wuthering Heights* profoundly
disturb the male characters by returning their gaze, and 'so violate
the aesthetically grounded notion of desire as they become the signs
of the active female self' (Armstrong, p. 196). Cathy's response to
Joseph echoes a gesture made by her mother, Catherine, years
before: when chastised by Joseph for not seeing that there are 'good
books enough if ye'll read 'em' (Bronte, p. 26), Catherine immediately
goes to her own book and writes. Women reach for pots of ink and
paper when men threaten them. The ghostly figure of the child
Catherine pushes her books on to Lockwood even though he had
'hurriedly piled the books in a pyramid against' her. He might

believe he is protected by these volumes, but he is mistaken: 'the pile of books moved as if thrust forward' (p. 31). Catherine controls the texts.

Men reach for weapons or clench their hands into a fist rather than around a pen. Heathcliff hits Cathy so hard in Chapter XIV that, in a bloody echo of the ghostly Catherine in Lockwood's dream, Cathy goes to the window, her 'mouth filling with blood' (p. 341). In another act of violence meant to silence her or drive her to submission, Hareton hits Cathy, 'a manual check given to her saucy tongue' that Lockwood hears 'not altogether disapprovingly' (p. 366) because 'the little wretch had done her utmost to hurt her cousin's . . . feelings, and a physical argument was the only mode he had of balancing the account . . .' (p. 366). Yet Cathy still manages to hurl a retort at Hareton; he has not, in fact, silenced her. She has not surrendered.

In a similar act of defiance of the 'law', Nelly refuses to surrender to Hindley. She employs language to control the situation even when her mouth is being violated in a manner that cannot but suggest a sexual violation:

> 'You'd rather be damned!' he said, 'and so you shall – No law in England can hinder a man from keeping his house decent, and mine's abominable! open your mouth.'
>
> He held the knife in his hand, and pushed its point between my teeth: but, for my part, I was never much afraid of his vagaries. I spat out, and affirmed it tasted detestably – I would not take it on any account. (p. 92)

Hindley's weapons, like the one he shows Isabella (p. 170), are quite useless, unless they are used against him.

By inscribing the action, the women in the text can exert control and contain action, resetting boundaries through narration of the event. Rather than reduce Bronte's novel to offering only 'the subordination of the rebellion within the ideological order' (Kavanagh, p. 91), rather than forever locking women into silence by damning all their inscription as mimicry, we should look at the way words free rather than bind women. Writing and reading are not symbolic of repression in the context of this novel; like Catherine's 'faded hieroglyphics', they encode a decipherable text of resistance (p. 24). In *Wuthering Heights*, reading and writing are forms of engendered 'excommunication' that defy the sanctity of the atrophied social, religious and domestic order. Women's narrative in this text is not concerned with good books; it is concerned with control and with the will to possess the page – insofar as the page represents power.

In what Kavanagh calls the 'standard statement on the book image in *Wuthering Heights*', (p. 106), Robert C. McKibben writes that the 'book is used to sustain a shallow view of the world, a view rendered false by its omissions . . .' (McKibben, p. 163) and sees the book as the representation of the difference between the Heights and the Grange. According to McKibben's essay, Catherine's downfall is caused by 'the overestimated power of her will' (p. 168), and her daughter's superior 'accomplishment' is not in 'the glorification of the will, but within . . . the modification of the will' (p. 168). Because Cathy can modify her will, 'Hareton in his turn endows her existence with a purpose' (p. 168). He can endow her existence with a purpose, it seems, only after he has destroyed the 'prose and verse' she has called 'consecrated' (Bronte, p. 365). Out of Hareton's burning of Cathy's books McKibben makes heaven: 'the fire has returned things to themselves, to the paradise of normalcy: Cathy and Hareton are ready to resume their rightful places . . .' (McKibben, p. 168). He claims that 'Emily Bronte's conception of the effectiveness of the book and its rightful use' was 'a world of eternal summer where the individual is reconciled to himself and to reality' (p. 169). This seems, to me, to be a key problem in McKibben's argument. It ignores completely the idea of language as power, even given that McKibben does not consider any gender-related issues in his discussion except where he apparently indicates that only a man can endow a woman's life with meaning.

It seems reasonable to claim, in contrast to these earlier observations, that the image of the book in Bronte's novel is not one of the passive recycling of a dominant curriculum, or of feminine resignation to the standing order. The engendered acts of reading and writing that structure Bronte's novel are aligned both with the feminine excommunication of story-telling and singing, and indicative of the power of language to rupture and dislodge the dominant discourse, as embodied by Joseph, Edgar and other male figures in the text. 'When women claim authorship', argue the editors of *The (M)other Tongue* in the introduction to that volume, they subvert the paradigm wherein 'women may be spoken of, spoken through, but may not bespeak themselves' and they raise questions concerning 'priority and the stories by which it is maintained and conferred' (Garner *et al.*, p. 24).

And finally, these acts of feminine inscription are linked to another important inversion of the patriarchal code that forms the excommunicated structure of Bronte's novel: it is the female characters who initiate and control sexual activity. Armstrong, in fact, comments on the 'curiously tenacious belief that writing and desire are ontologically different and ideologically opposed' that forms the basis for much Bronte criticism (Armstrong, p. 189). It is interesting to note that a number of critics do not see sexuality as an important narrative force. A. O. J. Cockshut, for example, claims that Catherine's love for Heathcliff 'is not sexual, and does not conflict with her love for her husband . . .' (Cockshut, p. 108) and Arnold Kettle argues that theirs is 'not primarily a sexual relationship' (Kettle, p. 31). But to trace the primary relationships between men and women in *Wuthering Heights* is to trace an outline of women's desire.

Women's desire in *Wuthering Heights* is explicit and catalytic. Women speak their desire and act on it. Catherine can articulate quite clearly her attraction to Linton as well as to Heathcliff; some critics seem remarkably surprised by the very idea that she can desire two men simultaneously. Albert Guerard, in a preface to *Wuthering Heights*, suggests that 'the oddity is that Cathy expects to "have them both", finds this expectation entirely "natural", and is enraged because neither Heathcliff nor Edgar will consent to such a menage-à-trois' (Guerard, p. 66). I find that Armstrong once again supplies the most convincing observations in this matter when she writes that 'the new territories of the self that the Brontes sought to represent were the unseen desires of women' (Armstrong, p. 192).

In the explicitly sexual encounter between Catherine and Heathcliff (and I find it impossible to see their relationship as founded on anything apart from sexual desire) 'he bestowed more kisses than he ever gave in his life before . . . but then my mistress kissed him first . . .' (Bronte, p. 194). In an interesting comment on what can be regarded as a scene central to the idea of excommunication in *Wuthering Heights*, Davies notes that this 'meeting is the conscious violation of a taboo, a sacrament celebrated through the communion of two spirits in vehement contradiction of the church service which is going on simultaneously' (Davies, p. 112). In one of her final actions, Catherine 'springs' at Heathcliff so that he might hold her (Bronte, p. 199). It is Cathy who expresses her desire to 'hold' Heathcliff 'until we were both dead' (p. 195), with physical desire overriding any spiritual context for that remark. It is her ghost that seems to seek him even after death to make good her desire to lie beside him. She seems to kill Heathcliff by her hauntings; she kills him the way Linton is afraid Cathy will kill him. Heathcliff twice attempts to dig up Catherine's corpse and he wishes to be united with her physically in death (pp. 349–50). When he sees her body, he finds that Catherine has not 'decomposed' at all.[2]

Isabella also pursues Heathcliff; Heathcliff explains his relationship with Isabella to Catherine in the following terms: 'I have a right to kiss her, if she chooses . . .', acknowledging Isabella's power to choose (p. 137). After they are married, it is Isabella who demands the key to their bedroom from Joseph, who seems surprised to hear that she intends to sleep with his master: '"Oh! It's Maister Hathecliff's yah're wenting?" he cried, as if making a new discovery . . .' (p. 174). Heathcliff refuses to acknowledge that, as Isabella claims, it is her room now: 'He swore it was not nor ever should be mine . . .' (p. 176). Heathcliff apparently refuses to submit to her desires in what John Hewish has called 'a sadistic denial of conjugal rights' (Hewish, p. 151). Obviously, since Isabella becomes pregnant very soon after her marriage, Heathcliff does submit at some point.

As we have seen, young Cathy pursues Linton with letters and books. He, on their wedding night, 'screams for vexation that he can't sleep' (Bronte, p. 339) and calls his father in to quieten his wife. Heathcliff does this by threatening to strangle her. Linton reclines on the settee and sulks, after his marriage to Cathy, occupied by 'sucking a stick of sugar-candy' (p. 338).

After Linton dies, Cathy initiates the relationship with Hareton, declaring 'Come, you shall take notice of me . . .' (p. 379). Despite the fact that he has thrown her books into the fire, having been frustrated in his attempts to win her approval and in doing so only managing to have 'produced the contrary result' (p. 366) to his wishes, Cathy is relentless in her pursuit of Hareton. She acts out her own scene of temptation by offering texts that are strewn suggestively throughout the house, their open pages seducing the illiterate boy almost against his will: '[w]hen Hareton was there, she generally paused in an interesting part, and left the book lying about – that she did repeatedly' (p. 377). They are seen together, finally, with Cathy attempting to teach Hareton how to pronounce 'contrary' (p. 371). At one point, in trying to win Hareton over, Cathy 'impressed on his cheek a gentle kiss' and then directly wraps 'a handsome book neatly in white paper' (p. 381) to give to Hareton as a gift.

Cathy and her books must battle with Joseph and his texts – Bible and bank-notes – for the 'possession' of Hareton. That books are the final analogue for feminine desire and triumph, as outlined in the following exchange, exemplifies the place of the female text and the power of excommunication in *Wuthering Heights*:

> [Joseph], poor man, was perfectly aghast at the spectacle of Catherine seated on the same bench with Hareton Earnshaw, leaning her hand on his shoulder; and confounded at his favourite's endurance of her proximity . . . His emotion was only revealed by the immense sighs he drew, as he solemnly spread his large Bible on the table, and overlaid it with dirty bank-notes from his pocket-book, the produce of the day's transactions. . .
>
> 'Tak these in tuh t'maister, lad,' he said, 'un'bide theare . . . This hoile's norther mensful nor seemly fur us . . .'
>
> 'Come Catherine,' [Nelly] said . . .
>
> 'Hareton, I'll leave this book upon the chimney-piece, and I'll bring some more to-morrow.'
>
> 'Ony books ut yah leave, Aw sall tak intuh th'hahse,' said Joseph, 'un' it'ull be mitch is yah fine 'em agean; soa, yah muh plase yourseln!'
>
> Cathy threatened that his library should pay for hers; and smiling as she passed Hareton, went singing upstairs. . . (pp. 384–5)

If the system of patriarchal discourse is upheld by the likes of Joseph, then it is obvious that this system fails to remain dominant in *Wuthering Heights*. The voices of Nelly and Cathy sing over Joseph's muttered threats. If patriarchal discourse exists in part through an ability to prevent the illegitimate, feminine use and creation of texts, then patriarchal discourse in *Wuthering Heights* is over-written/written-over and undermined by the strength and energy of feminine 'excommunication'.

Notes

1. Extracts from Wuthering Heights are all taken from the edition given in the Bibliography at the end of these notes. I would like to thank the following colleagues and friends for their comments and suggestions on the idea for this paper: Carol MacKay, Jane Marcus and Mary Ann Caws.

2.   *Wuthering Heights* is a book where sex and death are often allied; Gilbert and Gubar argue that '[f]unerals are weddings, weddings funerals' (p. 259). There are so many death/birth scenes in the book that it is difficult to see these comings and goings as coincidental. The births and deaths, weddings and funerals form equations: Heathcliff arrives; Mrs Earnshaw dies. Hindley marries Frances; Mr Earnshaw dies. Hareton Earnshaw is born; Frances Earnshaw dies. Catherine goes to the Grange; Mr and Mrs Linton die. Cathy is born; Catherine dies. Linton Heathcliff born; Hindley Earnshaw dies. Cathy meets Hareton; Isabella dies. Cathy and Linton marry; Edgar dies. Cathy befriends Hareton; Heathcliff unable to eat. Heathcliff dies; Cathy and Hareton will marry. While these events cannot inevitably be charted on a cause/effect basis, they do follow closely enough on the heels of one another to give us pause. It is important, then, to see which characters control sexuality in this novel.

Bibliography

Armstrong, Nancy, *Desire and Domestic Fiction* (New York: Oxford University Press, 1987).

Bronte, Emily, *Wuthering Heights*, edited by Hilda Marsden and Ian Jack (Oxford: Oxford University Press, 1976).

Cockshut, A. O. J., *Man and Woman: A Study of Love and the Novel 1740–1940* (New York: Oxford University Press, 1978).

Davies, Stevie, *Emily Bronte: The Artist as a Free Woman* (Manchester: Carcanet Press, 1983).

Eagleton, Terry, *Myths of Power: A Marxist Study of the Brontes* (London: Macmillan, 1975).

Guerard, Albert, preface to Thomas A. Vogler (ed.) *Twentieth Century Interpretations of Wuthering Heights* (Englewood Cliffs, New Jersey: Prentice Hall, 1968).

Garner, Shirley Nelson, Kahane, Claire and Sprengnether, Madelon (eds) *The (M)other Tongue* (Ithaca and London: Cornell University Press, 1985).

Gilbert, Sandra and Gubar, Susan, *The Madwoman in the Attic* (New Haven and London: Yale University Press, 1979).

Hewish, John, *Emily Bronte: A Critical and Biographical Study* (London: Macmillan, 1969).

Kavanagh, James H., *Emily Bronte* (New York: Basil Blackwell, 1985).

Kettle, Arnold, 'Wuthering Heights', in Thomas A. Vogler (ed.) *Twentieth Century Interpretations of Wuthering Heights* (Englewood Cliffs, New Jersey: Prentice Hall, 1968).

McKibben, Robert C., 'The Image of the Book in "Wuthering Heights"', *Nineteenth-Century Fiction*, vol. 15, no. 2, (September 1960) pp. 159–69.

14

Dialogue with the Dead: the Deceased Beloved as Muse

Elisabeth Bronfen

Woman is not a poet: She is either Muse or she is nothing. (Robert Graves, *The White Goddess*)

Death is the actual inspiring Genius or the Muse of Philosophy. (Schopenhauer)

I A FATAL EXAGGERATION

In Berlin, on the night of 29 December 1834, Charlotte Stieglitz (aged 28) sent her husband Heinrich to a concert in order to be alone while committing an incredible act. After having washed, dressed in a clean white nightgown and placed a white cap on her head, she went to bed and there stabbed herself directly in the heart with a dagger she had bought as a bride.[1] In her farewell note, Charlotte suggested that her suicide be understood as an act of self-sacrifice meant to inflict such pain and sense of loss on her manic-depressive husband that he would break free from his psychic lethargy. In this way she hoped to liberate his petrified poetic powers. His wife's violent death would enable him to regain what he had lost – his self and his poetic genius.

Although Charlotte's death failed to inspire a new phase of poetic creativity in her husband, it did make her into a public Muse. Triggering a 'vicarious' pain, her suicide provoked a plethora of interpretations from her contemporaries. Some saw her sacrifice as an act of 'true feminine genius', bridging the gap between flesh and spirit, others as an attempt to renew not only her husband's stifled energies but in fact the suppressed or thwarted energies of an entire generation of Germans suffering under the constraints of Biedermeier society. On the other hand, opponents of the writings of the *Jungdeutsche* who idealised her death saw her suicide as an emblem of the dangers of free morals. Far more striking than the ideological intentions inherent in the texts written about her, however, is the fact that Charlotte, who had never had any public role during her lifetime, came by her suicide to leave such an impressive mark in the public realm. One has the impression that in its Biedermeier garments, her dead body became the site for the interpretive inscriptions of her survivors – inscriptions that say more about those interpreting than the object being interpreted.

Susanne Ledanff suggests that what makes Charlotte's story so compelling is that she took the bombastic metaphors of self-obliterating love, heroism, self-sacrifice, and liberation of the soul from the body seriously, rather than treating them as quotations from previous cultural texts; that is, she made the fatal mistake of applying literary conventions to her own personal history. Yet even more disquieting, and for a critic also more fascinating, is the strange mixture of seduction by a false pathos of romantic and pietistic delusions and the calculation of effect inherent in her act, the doubling of deluded victim and consciously responsible actress. For she exposes the conventions of feminine self-sacrifice at exactly the same moment that she fatally enacts them. Far from being innocent or naïve, her suicide is pregnant with literary citations; in fact it is a cliché – suggestive of both Werther's and Caroline von Guenderode's suicides[2] after failed romances, of the iconography of sacrificial brides and martyrs dressed in white, for whom death is a mystic marriage and an erotic unity with God, as well as that of women dying in childbirth. At the same time her act perverts the image of the selflessly devoted housewife by introducing violence into the idyllic bedroom, by adding self-assertion to self-submission. Her act of self-sacrifice is so disquieting because it is both an imitation of cultural clichés, hovering between irony and kitsch, and a self-conscious effort to make herself into an object of discourse.

Due to the exaggerated manner in which she performed her suicide, however, this act also lays bare several implications of the traditional notion of creative power as an external gift bestowed upon a chosen artist by his Muse. For one, her act suggests that death transforms the body of a woman into the source of poetic inspiration precisely because it creates and gives corporality to a loss or absence. Since her gift to the poet is the removal of her body, what occurs is the exchange of one loss for another, the implication being that her presence has displaced his poetic genius. This equation reveals the central dichotomy of the Muse–artist relation: the poet must choose between a corporally present woman and the Muse, a choice of the former precluding the latter.[3] That is to say, what must occur is the transformation of a direct erotic investment of the beloved woman into a mitigated one (of the same woman who is now absent, or of another woman who never was present). The distance thus created by loss, the shift from presence to absence, opens up the space for poetic creation. In this respect the relation between Muse and artist is, of course, only an augmentation of the prerequisite of symbolisation in general. As Jacques Derrida explains, 'What opens meaning and language is writing as the disappearance of natural presence'.[4] Yet although any form of absence would suffice, the death of the beloved is its perfect embodiment, it seems, because it secures the distance and the loss forever. In an uncanny manner Stieglitz seems to collapse Graves's definition of woman's relation to art: by making her self 'nothing' she makes herself into the ultimate incorporation of the Muse.

At the same time Charlotte's suicide, and the rhetoric surrounding it, point to the interconnection between artistic renewal as a form of giving birth and death. She and Heinrich both call her act a Caesarean which saves the child while destroying the mother. Through her death she hopes to mother the genius of her husband while at the same time endowing him with the faculty of giving birth. For his poetry, written 'in memory of' the deceased, by invoking and making present her who is absent, will be a rhetorical animation of the dead beloved.[5] The disturbing twist Charlotte's suicide gives to the relationship between artist and Muse is the suggestion that poetic renewal – that is, the birth of the poet – necessarily entails someone else's death. Extreme as her form of self-textualisation might be, it is nevertheless only an exaggeration of the changed conception of the Muse that informs nineteenth-century imagination. In order to discuss the inversion that occurs here it is necessary, however, to recall the original function ascribed to the Muse.

While it is not clear whether in classical Greek culture the Muse had an objective divine reality or was merely a projection, a familiar and convenient metaphor for the creative process, her invocation points to a conception of the poet's gift as being dependent on an appeal to a higher power other than itself. Divine inspiration was the designation given to that element in poetry which exceeded craftmanship and the exchange between poet and Muse implied a moment of loss of self and possession by an Other. The Muse was thought to speak through the poet, making him the medium of her speech. She was mother to the poet in the sense that she literally inspired by singing her material to him – that is, she animated his poetic ability by breathing her song into him. As Plato in the famous passage in *Phaedrus* explains, the Muse was the source of divine possession or madness, stimulating the lyric poet's untrodden soul to rapt passionate expression; 'glorifying the countless mighty deeds of ancient times for the instruction of posterity'.[6] On the other hand, for a poet not to acknowledge the holy breath of the Muses as quintessential to poetic creation and to depend on his skill alone was to result in poetic failure and public oblivion. The self-sufficient poet and his work would, in Plato's words be 'brought to nought by the poetry of madness . . . their place . . . nowhere to be found'. For a mythic version of the Muse's intolerance for rivalry one could cite the story of Thamyris, as found in Homer. Because he boasted that he could surpass them in a competition, the muses maimed him, taking away his 'voice of wonder' and thus making him a 'singer without memory'.[7]

Ecstatically devoted to the Muse, the poet's utterances were also meant to glorify her, thus suggesting the occurrence of a two-way exchange. For the Muse's gift to the poet allows him to give birth to a text celebrating her. That is, she inspires or animates his poetic power so that he may, by virtue of his invocation, in turn reanimate the Muse. As a figure of inspiration, she is directly addressed, and thus serves a threefold function in this poetic dialogue. She is simultaneously maieutic producer, object of reference, and privileged addressee of the poet's speech. In addition she is always incompletely accessible, always beyond reach. For the rhetoric of invocation, always one of apostrophe, requires her absence while at the same time making the lack of presence, the distance of the addressee, its privileged theme and causing her, as the object reanimated by the poet's speech, to take on the status of presence-in-absence (life-in-death), a kind of double presence.[8] What is important to stress, however, is that the Muses were the daughters of Zeus and Mnemosyne – goddess of memory. Thus the apostrophe not only served to render the bodily absent addressee present, but also through her to make present an absent past knowledge or alterior truth. The Muses not only initiated the poet into passionate expression, as Hesiod's archetypal relation of his poetic experience at the foot of Mount Helican suggests, but also served as the source of knowledge outside the poet's realm of experience.[9] Poets invoked the Muses to make present what they were not present to see, needed them to remember, including that which was never part of their own personal history. Put another way, by addressing the absent Muse, the poet attempted to overcome his absence at previous historical events, his lack of complete knowledge.

In the course of the centuries, the vitality the Muse was said to possess paled, as Steele Commager puts it, into an abstraction, so that one could characterise her 'biography as the history of a fading metaphor'.[10] What in Classical Greece was a conviction became in Augustan Rome a conceit. By assigning to the Muses a merely decorative status or seeing them reincarnated in specific human beings, as Propertius does when he declares his mistress Cynthia's folly to serve as source and subject of his poetry, the poet, as Commager argues, 'no longer feels himself the creature of some higher power, but assumes that his own creative potency is sufficient'.[11] That is to say, in the same rhetorical move that gives a concrete body to the Muse, secularises her so to speak, she is denied that divine power which would be other and more encompassing than the poet's. As such she becomes a figure for the poet's peculiarly own poetic powers, mothering genius that is innate rather than inspired; a metaphor for the poet as 'possessing a special ability rather than as possessed by it' with the apostrophe addressing 'his own peculiar genius'.[12] In the late middle ages Dante takes up again the tradition of invocation, and he too transfers the role of the Muse to a real woman, Beatrice, who, by virtue of his idealisation and her early death, is corporally never accessible. The change from the Muse as metaphor for a divine inspirational source to that of metaphor for the poet's singular gift, is also visible in Petrarchan love poetry. As Silverman points out, the fixed distance between lover and Muse, which functions as a precondition for poetic production, has the effect of transforming the lady into a divine signifier, 'pointing beyond herself to God',[13] thus asking the reader to concentrate not on the woman but on that toward which she leads. The Muse is thus not only reduced to a rhetorical figure, but to the allegorical pretext for a signifier other than herself.

II   REANIMATING A FADING METAPHOR

What is remarkable about the Romantic inversion of the poet–Muse relation is the fact that the status of Muse is transferred again onto a corporally existent beloved, only now she is dying or already dead. The thematic interplay between poetic creation and loss, distance, or absence of the beloved is thus given a new twist: the rhetorical invocation refers quite literally to a female body, as though not only the poet's gift, but also the fading metaphor were to be reanimated. Yet in the course of this reconception several important changes occur. It is no longer the poet, daring to disacknowledge the Muse, who is punished for his audacity, but instead the woman chosen to be Muse. What she gives is not her song but rather her body and her life. And though it is her death which inspires the poet and takes possession of him, whether it provokes the experience of ecstasy or the production of narratives, the concept of possession has also taken on a duplicitous character. For while the original act of taking possession and giving birth to the poet is mimicked, the Romantic inversion is in fact an example of the poet's taking ultimate control over the departed woman.

The questions with which I want to confront several nineteenth-century texts involving the inspirational power of a dead beloved are thus aimed both at the function and at the reference or signifier of this image. Roland Barthes suggests that to stage absence in language is to 'remove the death of the other [. . .] to manipulate absence is to prolong the moment [. . .] where the other will move from absence to death'.[14] But when the object of this invocation is already dead, whose death is being deferred? Is the invocation of the dead beloved an attempt to preserve her artificially against death, or an attempt to eternalise the poet's skill? Whose triumph is it, when the poet reanimates and resurrects a dead beloved, and what desire is enacted when the artist defies the irrevocability of death? Above all, what is ultimately being signified by this dialogue? While on the one hand the addressee of this invocation is a beloved woman quite literally dead, she simultaneously serves a figurative function, namely as metonymy for death.

Once again the focus slips between her and where she leads. We thus have another duplicitous situation, for although she is being reanimated, she is likewise being effaced again when used as an emblem for something else, to which she is (in the end) incidental. Again one could say that this is involved in every form of translation, a process which, as J. Gerald Kennedy explains, 'entails duplication and effacement, a retracing which both mirrors the original and abolishes it in the sense that every translation sacrifices the letter of the original text to reconstitute its spirit in another language'.[15] In the invocation of the dead beloved, however, the original seems to be effaced more than once, literally by virtue of her death, and rhetorically not only because she is replaced by a text, but also because she serves an allegorical function amid this replacement. For, if the reference to the figure is the concrete death of a woman, it seems that more than just a rhetorical or textual convention is involved.

Novalis's first mention of Sophie von Kuehn's death is a stark entry in his diary on 19 March 1797 – 'This morning half past nine she died – 15 years and 2 days old.'[16] His reactions to her death, the satisfaction he obtains from his mourning are, however, minutely recorded in his journal over a period of three months, from 18 April through 6 July. As though to stage textually the intermediary position which a dialogue with the departed Sophie implies, everything appears twofold. He counts by two dates – the calendar day and the days since Sophie's death, thus emphasising that her death is both an end and a beginning. His ambivalent emotional reaction, a cross between sadness, psychic petrification and happiness, revivification, is duplicated by a style which is both pragmatically sober and enthusiastically idealising. One has the impression he is trying in an impartial and distanced voice to keep minutes of the changes in his emotional state as he records his acts of remembrance, while at the same time attempting to transmit the ecstatic revelation Sophie's death provokes. Conjuring up her image in his mind or visiting her grave becomes a means by which to keep her alive as addressee of their dialogue, making her present in absence. This dialogue, however, is two-way, for his invocation animates him as well – he is 'von ihrem Andenken belebt'.[17] It is meant to serve the purpose of being 'ganz bei ihr', in the sense of sharing the place in which she is now, i.e. to make her grave his own. Because, above all, the dead Sophie, semanticised as his soul, his inner or better life, his angel, serves as a kind of Doppelganger, signifier not only for a departed beloved but also for the part of the self lost at birth, from which he feels alienated during his conscious, earthly existence. At the same time, she also metonymically stands for death, so that his effort to reanimate her in order to be with her is the rhetorically displaced expression of his desire for the original state of identity and unity before the dynamic difference and opacity inherent to life; that is to say, his desire to be reunited with her also articulates his longing for reunion with a 'lost' self, for the anorganic peace of death.

The name he gives to Sophie in a short text written in 1796 – Klarisse – indicates that she never was a living body alterior to himself but rather always a mirror for self-reflection, clear, transparent and cold, in short an image of deathlike quality. Her death thus only finalises what she was all along: a figure (not a living woman) serving his narcissistic self-projections, whose signified belongs to the paradigm of death. Because he makes the dead Sophie the central axis of his life from which he can draw power, meaning as well as a new chronology ('she is the highest – the only being [. . .] everything must be brought in relation to her idea')[18] she inspires both an intensive self-absorption ('incessant thinking about myself and what I feel and do')[19] and the idea of suicide as liberation. This duplicitous desire recalls the image of the self-engrossed (and self-possessed) Narcissus wilfully pining away as he tries to become identical with his image projected on the water's surface.

Her loss translates into his gain because it opens a wound that is the prerequisite for any state of desiring – 'A lover must feel the gap eternally, the wound must always be kept open. Let God preserve forever [. . .] the wistful memory – this brave nostalgia – the male decision and the firm belief. Without my Sophie I am nothing – with her everything.'[20] As a perennial 'loss' she becomes the secure measure on which his interpretation of the world and his self-definition can be based, a void he can fill with explanations and poetic texts. At the same time her death endows his existence with a new meaning because it allows him quite explicitly to concentrate on where a reunion with her would lead. The wound her death inflicts is not to be filled, as Charlotte Stieglitz's mimicry had intended it to be, with narratives as an act of self-assertion in and for the world, but rather a security that he will imitate her act. His self-assertion is not defiance against but rather an embracing of death's triumph. To Schlegel he writes, 'Nevertheless, I experience a secret joy at being close to her grave. It draws me ever closer [. . .] it is very clear to me what celestial coincidence her death is – a key to everything, a wonderful adequate move.'[21] That is to say, by dying Sophie performs an exemplary act he can then emulate. As Muse she is not only meant to show him the way to his poetic voice but also to lead him in his flight from the world. Her death not only opens the wound that secures desire but also marks the promise that his longing will be quenched.

His descriptions of his sojourns at her grave suggest that he wishes to be possessed by her, made into her object, sucked out in order to eventually become identical with her (whereby, since she is his double, this is in fact a displaced form of self-absorption). In 'Hymnen an die Nacht', her duplicitous nature is explicitly understood as that of a bloodsucking *revenant*. He re-animates her so that she may de-animate him, a form of reversed birthgiving: 'tender beloved [. . .] you made me into a human – draw on my body with ghostly ardor so that I aerial may mingle with you more intensely and our wedding night last forever.'[22] In all of his invocations the beloved merges with the image of the mother, suggesting that a reunion would be the repetition of the symbiotic union with the maternal body, and death a second birth, so that the invoked Sophie recalls the semantic triad Graves assigns to the Muse: mother, seductress, and death. Although his dialogue with the dead Sophie is part of the cult of the distant and unattainable woman, its charm for him lies in the fact that it allows him to imagine a cancellation of the distance between him and the state for which the departed beloved stands: self-obliteration, eternal continuity, resolution of tension, movement, difference and desire.

Turning to Edgar Allan Poe's treatment of the dead beloved as Muse, we find an interesting shift in focus. As Marie Bonaparte suggests, his wife, Virginia Clemm, 'served as the unwitting Muse who first called Poe's genius as a writer of imaginative prose to life.'[23] The pale young woman dying of tuberculosis repeatedly functioned as model for his half-dead, prematurely buried, or (through metempsychosis) resurrected heroines Madeline, Morella, Berenice, and Ligeia. At the same time, Virginia's illness, which forbade any direct consummation of erotic desire, inspired those texts in which the fascination for a woman is dependent precisely on her unattainability – that is, her being physically absent while present when remembered or artistically recreated. In contrast to Novalis, who reanimates a dead beloved precisely because he wants to be made the object of death's desire, Poe's various speakers hold an intermediary position, balanced between an embrace of death and a successful denial or repression of it. The continued bond with a departed lover marks death not as the sought-for goal but rather allows the speaker to acknowledge both the mysterious way in which death penetrates the world of the living, while using his poetic inscriptions to fill the gap created by loss. Like her predecessors, Virginia, whether as model or as implicit addressee, serves as a signifier for the poet's own psychic states, with the focus again on where she leads. The important difference is, however, that her invocation now has, as reference, the ambivalent states of psychic petrification caused by an obsessional clinging to the dead and the hopeful defiance of or triumph over death by virtue of poetic inscription.

A comparison of the poems 'Ulalume' and 'Annabel Lee' will help illustrate these two variations. In the first poem,[24] the speaker describes his involuntary return to the vault of his beloved Ulalume. While he has repressed all memory of her death, signalled by his not recognising the path he is moving along, she is preserved in the form of an incorporation in his unconscious, poetically rendered as a name 'on the door of this legended tomb'. In what can be understood as a semantic reversal of Novalis's visits to Sophie's grave, the speaker depicts himself as unwittingly possessed by the dead, his return as an unconscious obsession. Ulalume's vampiristic hold, furthermore, stands in direct rivalry to Psyche, representing the soul's search for a new erotic attachment, so that her warning 'let us fly' remains unheeded. What Poe describes is thus a psychic impasse, for while the dead beloved draws the speaker to her tomb, binding him so that he is not free to find an alternative object of desire among the living, she does not lead him to death. While Poe leaves unexplained the kind of erotic satisfaction such an arrest of libidinal drives entails, he makes explicit that the speaker is in a duplicitous position, neither directed toward the living nor willing to give up life – that is, experiencing death by proxy, in the sense that his incorporation of the dead beloved turns his emotional state into a 'death-in-life'.

'Annabel Lee',[25] implicitly addressed to Virginia, can be read as the jubilant counterpart to the obsessive–compulsive form of memory. Although the speaker invokes his lost bride in order to idealise their love, this recollection ultimately serves to illustrate his imaginative and poetic powers, by virtue of which he places himself beyond the natural law of death. The rarity of their love – 'more than love' – consists for one thing in its exclusivity: 'she lived with no other thought than to love and be loved by me'. The measure of its value lies in the fact that it both attracted the coveting envy of the Seraphs and surpassed the result of their usurping desire. For while

Annabel's 'high kinsmen' bear her away and 'shut her up in a sepulchre' (a metaphor used to indicate her affinity to angels) his imaginative powers guarantee that nothing 'can ever dissever' their souls. For his response to the physical loss of his beloved is to endow his surroundings imaginatively with her ubiquitous presence and resurrect her in his poetic utterance. While he is drawn to the tomb of his beloved ('all the night-tide') this attraction to the site of death ultimately leads to its poetic rendition, a 'sepulchre' surpassing her tomb because it not only preserves but makes her 're-presented', present-in-absence.

While on a literal level the invocatory reanimation of Annabel serves to prove the inseparability of their souls, the displaced signified of this figure is the power of his poetic triumph over death. In contrast to Novalis, the focus in these depictions of the presence-in-absence of a dead beloved shifts to the question of what it means to maintain a 'fixed distance', regardless of whether this leads to compulsive repetition or to compensation and substitution of loss through poetic resurrection. Or, to put it another way, the emphasis shifts to an expression of the unfulfillability of desire.

III   INVERTING THE INVERSION TO EXPOSE THE TRADITION

What has been tacitly implied in these examples is admitted and explicitly thematised with astonishing candidness by Henry James – namely that the poet not only gains his artistic powers at the loss of a beloved but that he prefers his reanimated version of her to the real woman. Like Novalis, James recorded his reactions to the death of a woman – his New York cousin Minny Temple, who died of tuberculosis while he was visiting England. In several letters, James explains wherein the charm and satisfaction of privileging a supplement lies.[26] The most striking feature of his response is its ambivalence. He confesses to 'feeling a singular mixture of pleasure and pain', asks both his mother and his brother for details about her last hours, finding 'something so appealing in the pathos of her final weakness and decline' while expressing gratitude that he did not himself see her suffer and materially change. While he repeatedly asserts that 'it is too soon to talk of Minny's death or pretend to feel it', he expresses a certain satisfaction at having written more than twelve pages about her to his brother. This preference for the 'soft idea' over the 'hard fact' in respect to Minny's death signals the more global tendency to prefer a fixed distance, to privilege the mitigated and vicarious over the immediate. It seems that this distance allows the departed beloved to become an object entirely at his interpretative disposal and thus the central stake in his self-definition as an artist.

For Minny's death is not only the key to the past, inspiring a host of memories, but also the means by which he can take possession of this past and structure it as a meaningful whole. He reiterates that her death is a definite 'gain' – 'the happiest, fact, [sic] almost in her whole career'. While there may be a certain validity in this appraisal when one considers her illness, it seems that the gain is more his than hers. For as a dead body she becomes an 'unfaltering luminary in the mind', an image. As a living body she was a 'divinely restless spirit' – essentially one of the "irreconcilable" – 'flickering' in the sense that, like any living being, she was ambivalent and fickle enough to elude any attempt at fixing her meaning. As a dead body, however, she is translated from 'this changing realm of fact to the steady realm of thought'. As an image preserved in his mind she becomes a figure of whose stable meaning he cannot only be sure, but which he can also semantically designate at his will. She can thus stand for 'serenity and purity' as a 'sort of measure and standard of brightness and repose' or she can take on the function of representing aspects of his life. He thus sees their relation as an exchange of energies – she 'sinking out of brightness and youth into decline and death', while he 'crawls from weakness and inaction and suffering into strength and health and hope'.

By reducing her purpose in his life to 'the bright intensity of her example', the emphasis yet again is on where she leads. Her inspiration has a double goal, for she not only reanimates him by serving as the guiding example toward an embrace of life while herself yielding this intensity, thus standing as an emblem of his youth and the end of an episode in his development. As a dead beloved she also becomes a privileged object for memory – a 'pregnant reference in future years'. Embalmed in his mind, like Snow White 'locked away, incorruptibly, within the crystal walls of the past' and waiting to be reanimated, she becomes above all the measure for his skills at recollecting and creating. While her life was a 'question', disquieting because he could not offer 'the elements of an answer', her absence, it seems, could be met with such satisfaction because it both fixes her into a stable figure 'incorruptible' and opens the space for a plethora of poetic interpretations within which he could design, shape and recreate her (and their relationship) in infinite variations.

In his work, James repeatedly used the 'memory' of Minny as model for his heroines, notably Isabel Archer and Milly Theale (as well as in his autobiography, *Notes of a Son and Brother*). Yet he also wrote narratives which, doubling his own biography, can be read as a critical reflection on his relation to a dead Muse and the aesthetics inherent in this relation, above all from the point of view of mourning and erotic desire. In 'The Altar of the Dead',[27] the protagonist Stransom creates a shrine of remembrance for his 'religion of the Dead', as a means by which to stay 'in regular communion with these alternative associates', of whom Mary Antrim, who died after their wedding-day was fixed, is the central voice. He understands this dialogue as a 'connection more charming' than any possible in life ('Altar of the Dead', p. 87), and designates the effort of keeping the dead alive by force of his memory to be the central purpose of his life. What might on one level be seen as an attempt to possess the past, animating a departed lover in order to appropriate the shared experience she metonymically stands for, turns into Stransom's possession of the dead. As the central measure used to evaluate and interpret his world ('Altar of the Dead', p. 91), his dead also eclipse other emotional bonds. Because this form of 'communion' allows the absent woman to prove more powerful than her corporally present rival (signalled by the fact that the latter remains 'nameless'), it becomes for Stransom a way to shield himself from any direct erotic investment, thus becoming emotionally deathlike. That is to say, the exchange places both in an intermediary position: her presence-in-absence is reciprocated by his absence-in-presence, i.e. his inability to invest the living, immediate world with any form of desire. Ultimately she inspires the wish to share her position, to become the last candle on the altar, and thus fill the existent gap with his own body.

There is, however, another component to this exchange: while the nameless woman is rejected as a direct object of desire, it is for her benefit that he wishes to translate himself into the one last candle to fill and complete the altar, asking 'Isn't that what you wanted?' ('Altar of the Dead', p. 118). Their dispute had centred around the fact that she used his altar to worship the memory of the one friend he had rejected among his dead – Acton Hague. The knowledge he gains in the church when Mary's 'far-off face' smiles at him from the 'glory of heaven' is an insight not only into the rapture that his communion with Mary affords him, but also that this is marred by the fact that he refuses bliss to the other woman. Death suggests itself as the resolution of his ambivalent position between the two women and of his jealousy for the 'unnamed' woman's communion with Acton because it allows him to appropriate Acton's position and cast himself as the absent addressee of her worship. In what seems to be both paradoxical and repetitious, his conception of his own death entails both a unity with Mary and the opening of a new gap in respect to the 'unnamed' woman, thus leading not, as in the case of Novalis, to the cancellation of all differences, distances and barriers, but rather to the preservation of the intermediary position, which is informed by a tension between the living and dead. It translates into a glorification of loss and distance, not its effacement. His loss is also seen as his gain, because the distance of death is understood as the way to have a communion with the nameless woman that would not be possible in life. While Stransom recalls Charlotte Stieglitz's act, he inverts the Romantic version by imagining for himself the position of the Muse, who will inflict loss on a survivor as a way to procure his reanimation. What is striking is both the reversal of gender roles, making the man Muse to the woman, and the fact that this conception takes *ad absurdum* the traditional privileging of a 'fixed distance' over 'immediacy', the 'reanimation' over 'direct presence'. In so doing, the text brings into play an element of ironic distance between protagonist and implied reader, who, cast into the role of outside observer, is led to question and thus destabilise the primacy of mitigation and approximation. The narrative stance of James is thus in itself duplicitous, in that, without condemning or offering an alternative, it simply leaves the question of gain and loss open.

In 'Maud-Evelyn',[28] the reanimation of a departed lover helps the mourner to appropriate, or rather create, a past *post facto* and thus serves as a measure not only for his desire for vicarious, mitigated experiences but also his imaginative skills. Marmaduke decides to join the Dedricks in their religion of mourning, consecrated to their daughter Maud-Evelyn, who died when she was 15. As the narrative progresses it becomes clear that by dedicating himself to her memory, he can successfully keep his fiancé Lavinia at bay. The Dedricks' ritual, however, consists not only in cherishing preserved relics but also in the constant imaginative enlargement of the past, the growth of a legend, wherein real events are supplemented by 'figments and fictions, ingenious imaginary mementoes and tokens'

Dialogue with the Dead   255

('Maud-Evelyn', p. 344). In the course of their mourning, they invent whole experiences for her, which grow to include an engagement and marriage to Marmaduke, leaving him ultimately as her widower.

Graves suggests that when a Muse turns into a domestic woman she fades in her ability to inspire, and engenders the poet's demise. This leads one to speculate whether the Romantic fascination with the death of a young bride is not connected with a desire to prevent the Muse from turning domestic and thus ceasing to function as inspirational source.[29] What gives this instance its particular poignancy is, however, the fact that the reanimated woman Marmaduke privileges over Lavinia is a complete stranger to him and the past was not shared but invented. The satisfaction this vicarious loss offers seems to lie in the fact that the gap created by death can be inscribed with far less constraint than if the reference of the memory corresponded with some factually verifiable past experiences. Not only does the dead Maud-Evelyn lend herself to emblematisation in a way the living Lavinia never would, but the remembering Marmaduke has total freedom in respect to the content and semantisation of his reanimation.

And yet again the emphasis is on where the dead beloved leads, for what Marmaduke stresses is the heuristic quality of his cult of mourning: 'the more we live in the past the more things we find in it' ('Maud-Evelyn', p. 355). His act of memory lets him grow into 'a person with a position and a history', a growth whose charm lies in the fact that it is invented, the result of a change without the process of changing. That is to say, not only does his reanimation of Maud-Evelyn entail an invention of her experience but, since she is invoked always in her relation to him, it also lets him invent himself, endow himself with a past he never lived. As in the previous story, the narrative framing stabilises the privileging of the supplement, the vicarious over the immediate and direct, without offering a new hierarchy, letting a judgement of the case slip between 'self-deception' ('Maud-Evelyn', p. 348) and 'really beautiful' ('Maud-Evelyn', p. 352).

Yet this 'case' is the most extreme version of the effacement of the signified woman in the Muse–poet relations discussed in this paper, and could be read as an example of how the theme, by turning upon itself, exposes its own limitation. While in the previous examples the absence of the dead woman allows her to serve as a figure for signifying something else, in the sense that the literal signifier referring to a woman's death is displaced in favour of another that refers to the speaker's emotional and poetical state, in this story her absence is doubled. Maud-Evelyn is present-in-absence in an entirely rhetorical manner, a feminine name only, severed completely from any literal body and leading to a chain of supplementary signifiers which emanate from and reflect solely the speaker. That is to say, her invocation stages the absence not only of her body but of her signifier as well, the glorification of an empty, closed-circuit sign with no reference except to its own status as signifier. As such its function is to articulate the omnipotence of the speaker, who, denying the reality of any immediate world, disappears ever more into his museum and temple ('Maude-Evelyn', p. 358), which houses a fictional past, until he eventually wastes away 'with an excellent manner' ('Maude-Evelyn', p. 359). This 'case' shows the power of imagination and the desire for distance taken to such an extreme that it collapses the Muse–poet relation into a tautology, reducing the tension of a dialogue once again to a rhetorical convention, to a fictional figment.

What this comparative reading of several nineteenth century texts involving the poetic reanimation of a dead beloved reveals, then, is that one of the central motors of Western literary production is the force of effacement. The absence of a natural body as prerequisite for its symbolic representation, the privileging of the mitigated and vicarious over the direct and immediate, and the preference for the presentation of a rhetorical figure over the presence of a natural body, are persistent enough in our cultural discourses not to be limited to a discussion of the Muse–poet relation. My reading could thus lead one to reconsider the presuppositions underlying more general tendencies in nineteenth-century poetics. At the same time, because these chosen texts concerned with the Muse–poet relation both question and reinforce the gradual occultation of the signified woman, they expose (sometimes unwittingly) Woman's privileged function as figure for desires and meanings exterior to herself. The effectivity of these texts lies in their extremity, for they depict instances where poetic creation necessarily entails a woman's death, where the movement from literal body to figure is ultimately taken quite literally. As such, they point out the extent to which it now seems urgent to question the way nineteenth century society – and not only this period – has regarded Woman, in respect both to our culture's gaze and its esteem of her.

Notes

1. See Susanne Ledanff, *Charlotte Stieglitz. Geschichte eines Denkmals*, (Frankfurt/M: Ullstein, 1986) for a detailed discussion and documentation of this incident.
2. Ledanff points out that the confusion was shared by her contemporaries as well. Gutzkow calls her Caroline Stieglitz.
3. See Susanne Kappeler, *Writing and Reading in Henry James* (New York: Columbia University Press, 1980) chapter 7, 'A literary Taboo', pp. 75–82.
4. See Jacques Derrida, *Of Grammatology*, translated by Gayatri Chakravory Spivak (Baltimore: Johns Hopkins University Press, 1976) p. 159, and Barbara Johnson, 'Translator's Introduction' to Jacques Derrida, *Dissemination* (Chicago: Chicago University Press, 1981) pp. vii–xxxiii.
5. For a discussion of reanimation and its rhetorical function see Barbara Johnson, 'Apostrophe, Animation, and Abortion', in *A World of Difference* (Baltimore, Johns Hopkins University Press, 1987) pp. 184–99.
6. Plato, *The Collected Dialogues*, edited by Edith Hamilton and Huntington Cairns (Princeton: Princeton University Press) p. 492.
7. Homer, *The Iliad*, translated by Richard Lattimore (Chicago: University of Chicago Press, 1951) pp. 91–2 (lines 594–600).
8. See Sarah Kofman, *Melancolie de l'art* (Paris: Galilé, 1985).
9. Steele Commager, *The Odes of Horace. A Critical Study* (Bloomington: Indiana University Press, 1967) p. 9.
10. Ibid., p. 3.
11. Ibid., p. 8.
12. Ibid., p. 20 and p. 23.
13. Kaja Silverman, *The Subject of Semiotics* (Oxford: Oxford University Press, 1983) p. 279.
14. Roland Barthes, *Fragments d'un discours amoureux* (Paris: de Seuil, 1977) p. 22: 'la mise en scene langagière [de l'absence] éloigne la mort de l'autre [. . .] manipuler l'absence, c'est allonger ce moment [. . .] où l'autre pourrait basculer sèchement de l'absence dans la mort'. Barthes is referring to Chapter 2 of 'Beyond the Pleasure Principle', in which Freud describes a child's game with a spool and the articulation of the two words 'fort' (away) and 'da' (here) that significantly accompany this game: see 'Jenseits des Lustprinzips' (1920), in *Studienausgabe*, Band 3 (Frankfurt: Fisher, 1975) pp. 222–7. What has not sufficiently been appreciated to my knowledge by critics discussing this text is the way in which it is in part informed by the death of Freud's favourite daughter Sophie, who died of influenzal pneumonia on 25 January 1920, at the age of 26. Though most parts of the manuscript were written several months before Sophie's illness, it was completed between her death and her cremation. And while Freud negated his friends' challenge that his formulation of the concept of a 'death drive' was to be seen as a response to this personal loss, he did call this death a big, irreparable insult (*Kränkung*) to his

narcissism. Far more pertinent to my suggestion that Sophie Freud can be seen as a muse who, through her death inspires the grieving survivor, is the way Freud builds his daughter into his text on the death drive only to efface her. In two highly curious footnotes to this chapter, Freud explains that the child's fort-da game with the spool is not only a way of symbolising and thus controlling the absence of the mother but that this game changes into one which it plays with itself in front of a mirror, thus staging the possibility of a triumphant control over its own absence. In the second note Freud claims that this symbolisation of maternal loss was so successful that the child felt no serious grief when his mother really died some time later. What Freud significantly omits to say is that the 'lost mother' whose absence is staged long before any real absence occurs was in fact his daughter Sophie, and, if nothing else, the cryptic note pertaining to her death must have been added after the event of her death. Thus, since the woman, whose absence calls forth both Freud's and Ernest's symbolic representation is the same, a certain interconnection between the two acts suggests itself. Freud's own text seems to repeat his grandson's game with the spool and both can be seen as acts of making present while simultaneously effacing an absent woman. While Sophie's figurative death is understood at least by Freud, as the inspirational source for Ernest's important game, her literal death leads Freud not only to a theory about the relation between death and symbolisation but also to the imagery necessary for formulating it. See Jacques Derrida, 'Coming into One's Own', in *Pychoanalysis and the Question of the Text*, edited by Geoffrey H. Hartman (Johns Hopkins University Press: Baltimore, 1978).

15. J. Gerald Kennedy, *Poe, Death, and the Life of Writing* (Yale University Press: New Haven, 1987) p. 61.

16. Novalis, *Werke, Tagebuecher und Briefe Friedrich von Hardenbergs*, edited by Richard Samuel (Muenchen: Hanser, 1978) vol. 1, p. 456.

17. Novalis, p. 462.

18. Novalis, p. 465. 'Sie ist das Hoechste – das Einzige [. . .] Alles in Beziehung auf ihre Idee zu bringen.'

19. Novalis, p. 468: 'Unaufhoerliches Denken an mich selbst und das, was ich erfahre und thue.'

20. Novalis, p. 471: 'Der Liebende muss die Luecke ewig fuehlen, die Wunde stets offen erhalten. Gott erhalte mir immer [. . .] die wehmuethige Erinnerung – diese muthige Sehnsucht – den maennlichen Entschluss und den felsen festen Glauben. Ohne meine Sophie bin ich gar nichts – Mit Ihr Alles.'

21. Novalis, p. 633. 'Dennoch habe ich eine geheime Freude, so nah ihrem Grabe zu seyn. Es zieht mich immer naeher [. . .] es [ist] mir ganz klar [. . .] welcher himmlischer Zufall Ihr Tod gewesen ist – ein Schluesel zu allem, ein wunderbarschicklicher Schritt.'

22. Novalis, p. 151: 'zarte Geliebte [. . .] du hast [. . .] mich zum Menschen gemacht – zehre mit Geisterglut meinen Leib, dass ich luftig mit dir inniger mich mische und dann ewig die Brautnacht waehrt.'

23. Marie Bonaparte, *The Life and Works of Edgar Allan Poe. A Psycho-Analytic Interpretation* (London: Imago, 1949) p. 260.
24. Edgar Allan Poe, *Poetry and Tales* (New York: Library of America, 1984) pp. 89–91.
25. Edgar Allan Poe, *Poetry and Tales*, pp. 102–3.
26. See *Henry James Letters*, edited by Leon Edel, vol. 1, 1843–1875 (London: Macmillan, 1974), especially the letters to Mrs Henry James, Sr, William James, and Grace Norton, pp. 218–29.
27. Henry James, 'Altar of the Dead', in *Selected Tales* (London: Dent, 1982). Further references in the text are also taken from this edition.
28. Henry James, 'Maud-Evelyn', *14 Stories by Henry James* (London: Rupert Hart-Davis, 1947). Further references in the text are also from this edition.
29. Robert Graves, *The White Goddess. An historical grammar of poetic myth* (New York: Farrar, Straus and Giroux, 1983) p. 449.

Index

260